At the Fall of

SOMOZA

Lawrence Pezzullo and Ralph Pezzullo

UNIVERSITY OF PITTSBURGH PRESS

Pittsburgh and London

Published by the University of Pittsburgh Press, Pittsburgh, Pa., 15260
Copyright © 1993, University of Pittsburgh Press
All rights reserved
Manufactured in the United States of America
Printed on acid-free paper

Library of Congress Cataloging-in-Publication Data

Pezzullo, Lawrence.
    At the fall of Somoza / Lawrence Pezzullo and Ralph Pezzullo.
        p.   cm. — (Pitt Latin American series)
    Includes bibliographical references and index.
    ISBN 0-8229-3756-5
    1. Nicaragua—History—Revolution, 1979—Personal narratives,
American.   2. Somoza, Anastasio, 1920–1980.   3. United States—
Foreign relations—Nicaragua.   4. Nicaragua—Foreign relations—
United States.   5. Pezzullo, Lawrence.   I. Pezzullo, Ralph.
II. Title.   III. Series.
F1528.P49   1993
972.8505'3—dc20   93-1006
                                                                        CIP

A CIP catalogue record for this book is available from the British Library.
Eurospan, London

Ernesto Cardenal has graciously granted permission to reprint translations of his
poems, "Luces," "Los Muchachos," and "Ofensiva final," translated under the
titles "Lights," "Los Muchachos," and "Final Offensive." Poems by Juan Valázquez,
"León, June 2, 1979," and by Luis Vega, "Chronicle of La Barranca, I," are quoted
by permission from *Nicaragua in Reconstruction and at War,* edited and translated by
Marc Zimmerman.

Pitt Latin American Series

Anastasio Somoza of Nicaragua. Credit: Benoit Gysembergh Camera Press, London 30114-20 (97) Globe Photos, Inc. 1993

Dedicated to the
people of Nicaragua

---

*History doesn't come to an end
with the ringing of bells by the grave,
or with the rumbling of tanks
against a peaceful city.*

*History begins when it is firmly established
that an ideal lives in a people
though men die . . .*

—Pedro Joaquin Chamorro

Contents

List of Acronyms

ANC	Conservative National Action
ARA	American Republic Affairs
BANIN	Independent Banking Group
BECAT	Batallón Especial Contra Ataques Terroristas
CEPA	Ecclesiastic Committee for Agrarian Progress
CEPAD	Evangelical Committee for Development Assistance
CGT-I	Confederación General de Trabajo–Independiente, a pro-Soviet trade federation
CTN	Central de Trabajadores de Nicaragua, the country's second largest trade union federation
CONDECA	Central American Defense Council
COSIP	Superior Council of Private Initiative, a private-sector business group; changed to COSEP (Superior Council of Private Enterprise) in 1978
CUS	Labor Union Federation
CUUN	National University student government
DN or FSLN-DN	National Directorate of the Sandinista National Liberation Front; its present nine-person body dates from March 1979
EEBI	Basic Infantry Training School
FAO	Broad Opposition Front (Frente Amplio Opositora)
FAR	Fuerzas Armadas Revolucionarios, Guatemala
FER	Frente de Estudiantes Revolucionario (Revolutionary Student Front)
FNCF	Carlos Fonseca Northern Front
FORH	Eastern Front

FORL	Western Front
FRS	Sandino Revolutionary Front
FSBZ	FSLN Southern Front
FSLN	Sandinista National Liberation Front
FSLN-DN	see DN
GN	Guardia Nacional (National Guard)
GPP	prolonged popular war strategy
IAF	Inter-American Foundation
IMF	International Monetary Fund
INDE	Nicaraguan Development Institute
INR	Intelligence and Research, U.S. State Department
JGRN	Government of National Reconstruction
JPN	Nicaraguan Patriotic Youth
MCR	Movimiento Cristiano Revolucionario (Revolutionary Christian Movement)
MPU	Movimiento del Pueblo Unido (United People's Movement)
NSC	U.S. National Security Council
OAS	Organization of American States
PLN	Partido Liberal Nacional (Liberal party)
PCN	Partido Conservador de Nicaragua (Conservative party)
PCdeN	Partido Communista de Nicaragua (Communist party)
PCT	Traditional Conservative party
PSN	Partido Socialista de Nicaragua (Socialist party)
SCC	Special Coordinating Committee of the National Security Council
TI	Tercerista or insurrectional tendency (Third Way)
TP	Tendencia Proletaria; concentrated on organizing urban workers and farm laborers in the western lowlands along orthodox Marxist lines
UDEL	Democratic Union of Liberation, founded by Pedro J. Chamorro
UNAN	National University of Nicaragua
UNO	National Opposition Union

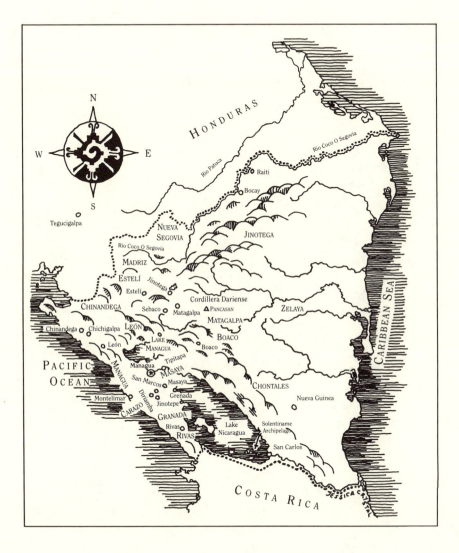

✳

Preface

For several weeks during the summer of 1979, the small Central American republic of Nicaragua galvanized the world's attention. Some cheered; others watched in horror as the Somoza dictatorship was overrun. On the humble stage of Nicaragua, different ways of life and beliefs had been drawn into inevitable conflict. The United States, as a longtime patron of the Somozas and the Guardia Nacional, played an important role. Given our close, paternalistic relationship with Nicaragua, we couldn't turn away. Given our ideological revulsion toward communism and our fear of a second Cuba on the American mainland, we were afraid to step aside and let the Nicaraguan people decide their own fate.

This is the story of the last weeks of the Nicaraguan Revolution and the United States' participation. Centering on my negotiations with the exhausted, desperate, and grotesquely human Somoza, it attempts to weave a vivid tapestry of the final days of the forty-year-old Somoza regime. Rather than a traditional ambassador's memoir, my son and I have introduced the voices of people on all sides of the conflict. To this end we have interviewed Sandinista *comandantes*, middle-class Nicaraguans, U.S. foreign policy makers, observers, diplomats, journalists, and priests in Nicaragua, Miami, Virginia, Maryland, and New York. In some cases their names have been changed. We have also drawn from the many journals—published in Central and South America—of people who were participants in or witnesses to the civil strife in Nicaragua.

The valuable National Security Archive, and particularly Peter Kornbluth, helped us find the secret cables relayed back and forth between Managua, Washington, and San Jose in June and July 1979. Pete Vaky, Robert McCloskey, Tom O'Donnell, and David Pezzullo gave important advice on the shape and tone of the final manuscript. Additional thanks go to Sally Vasek, Mike Sydorowitz, Jessica Crystal, and Jane Flanders and Catherine Marshall of the University of Pittsburgh Press. Finally, we owe a great debt to the New York Public Library, the Columbia University Library, and the Library of Congress. May these great institutions continue to provide the material for the free pursuit of understanding and truth.

At the Fall of
SOMOZA

1

When once the people have taken arms against you, there will never be lacking foreigners to assist them. —Machiavelli, *The Prince*

It was brilliantly clear. From overhead, the greens, the sand, and the blues of the ocean stood in sharp contrast. We had followed the white beach up the Pacific coast of Costa Rica into Nicaragua. Suddenly the twin-engine U.S. Army Beechcraft dipped its right wing, bringing us in line with an asphalt airstrip that ran like a scar across the verdant bluff. More than ninety minutes after taking to the air in Panama, we touched ground.

We raced down the runway past two American sedans and a National Guard weapons carrier featuring a .50-caliber machine gun. The pilot taxied to the waiting sedans and, without cutting the engines, let me off. He then moved to the end of the runway and returned to the serene sky. It was the morning of June 27, 1979. We had landed at General Anastasio (Tachito) Somoza's 25,000-acre sugar plantation on the Pacific coast of Nicaragua, named "Montelimar."

The day before, Ambassador William Bowdler and I had been quickly dispatched from Andrews Air Force Base, outside Washington, D.C., on an air force jet to Panama. This morning, over breakfast, we discussed with our ambassador to Panama, Ambler Moss, the attitudes of Panamanian strongman, General Omar Torrijos, toward the civil strife raging in Nicaragua. It was no secret that General Torrijos was supplying the Sandinistas, who opposed the Somozas' forty-year domination of Nicaragua, with important counsel and materiel. Torrijos knew that Ambassador Bowdler and I had come to Central America to attempt to bring the violent struggle for control of Nicaragua's future to a peaceful resolution. Today Bowdler was meeting for the first time with representatives of the Sandinista Junta of National Reconstruction in Panama. Their talks would continue over the following weeks in San José, Costa Rica.

I looked out at the shimmering fields of young sugarcane as we began our journey to Managua. Because the area we were passing through had been the scene of recent fighting, the embassy's security officer Frank Juni and the U.S. Marine gunnery sergeant guided the way at breakneck speed in the lead car. I followed in an armored sedan with the chargé d'affaires, Frank Tucker, driving and filling me in on recent developments.

I had landed at "Montelimar" because the Sandinista "final offensive," launched on May 29, had spread as far as the northeastern barrios of Managua. For two weeks Managua's Las Mercedes International Airport had been cut off from the city. All commercial airlines were overflying Managua.

Coincidentally, the evacuation of nearly one thousand U.S. embassy dependents and nonessential personnel, Americans living in Managua, and third-country diplomats and their families had taken place from "Montelimar." Also, many families closely associated with the Somoza dynasty had hastily locked up their homes and escaped to Honduras, Guatemala, and Miami.

Nicaragua was in the throes of civil war. People were quickly being overtaken by events. Within four weeks the Sandinista insurgents had seized control of most of Nicaragua north of its capital, Managua, and the majority of towns and cities in the northwest highlands. With pride they would reel off the list of liberated towns and cities: Masaya, Matagalpa, Estelí, Chichigalpa, and so on.

As we approached the capital city of Managua, the physical devastation of the civil war became more apparent. The occasional small car, or light pickup, we passed on the highway flew a white banner from its antenna. Frank Tucker explained that this was a purely cosmetic symbol of neutrality to preserve life and limb. Few in this country of two and half million were less than passionately involved. Hatred for Somoza and his regime ran deep. The barricades of the *muchachos*—the thousands of teenage boys and girls who spontaneously took to the streets to take on the Guardia Nacional (National Guard)—had been pushed aside by government bulldozers. The concrete paving blocks produced at the Somoza-owned cement plant had served the *muchachos* as convenient barricade builders.

Nicaragua was filled with strange twists and tragic ironies. Dramas were being played out in the streets, priests were wielding guns, daughters from good families had become Sandinista *comandantes*, an alcoholic dictator was awaiting salvation. Destiny had brought me here to play a role in the final act of the Somoza dynasty. It was fair to ask why the United States government felt compelled to urge the president of Nicaragua, Anastasio (Tachito) Somoza Debayle, a devoted friend of our country, to resign. One might also wonder why a superpower was so deeply involved in the internal affairs of a country of two and a half million people.

As we drove, I asked myself: "How did the seventh child of Italian immigrants, who was raised in the Bronx, end up here?" Twenty-two years earlier, married with three children, I had decided to enter the foreign service at the maximum age of thirty-one. That decision would have been inconceivable for someone from my background had it not been for World War II. Like millions of other young Americans, I had been jolted by the war out of the provincialism that marked prewar U.S. society. And the G.I. Bill opened the door to opportunities.

Once I entered the foreign service, challenging assignments followed: visa and consular work on the Mexican border; a two- year stint in the nerve center of the State Department, the Secretariat; and an administrative assignment in Vietnam (1962–64), where I had my first brush with terrorism and witnessed the fall of the Nho Dinh Diem regime and the buildup of U.S. forces. After Vietnam, I returned to Latin America and a succession of assignments as a political officer in Bolivia, Colombia, and Guatemala.

All three countries were wrestling with the social, political, and economic inequities endemic to underdevelopment. And in all three, Marxist guerrillas, following Fidel Castro's example, struggled to build a base among the disenfranchised. Shortly after I left Bolivia in 1967, Castro's comrade-in-arms, Che Guevara, was captured and executed in the southern mountains. Three years later, while serving as head of the Political Section in our embassy in Guatemala City, my labor attaché was kidnapped by guerrillas of the Fuerzas Armadas Revolucionarios (FAR) and held for ransom. After two harrowing days, he was released.

Returning to Washington in 1971, I spent a year at the National War College, then a two-year stint in the office of Central American Affairs. I was now in my mid-forties and beginning to feel lost in the State Department's bureaucratic maze. I probably would have languished there and retired at age fifty if it hadn't been for Ambassador-at-Large Robert McCloskey. McCloskey had recently been recalled from his post as ambassador to Cyprus by Secretary of State Henry Kissinger to oversee the Office of Public Affairs. Since McCloskey wasn't thrilled by the prospect of returning to an office he had directed during the darkest days of Vietnam, he was named ambassador-at-large and given the added responsibility of renegotiating our base agreements with Spain and the Azores.

When McCloskey appointed me his chief of staff in the base negotiations, a world opened that I had been shut off from—the fascinating play between policy makers and the media and the exhilaration of seventh floor politics. The seventh floor of the State Department housed the offices of the secretary of state and his principal advisers, and it was here that U.S. foreign policy was directed and framed.

Midway through the Spanish base negotiations, Secretary of State Kissinger asked McCloskey to take on the duties of the Congressional Relations Office. I followed as deputy assistant secretary for congressional affairs. Together we reorganized what had become a moribund office to represent more accurately the interests of the geographic and functional offices of the department and to sensitize those offices to the needs and interests of the Hill.

I was quickly promoted during my four years with McCloskey. After he was appointed ambassador to the Netherlands during the last months of the Ford administration, I began to be considered for an ambassadorship of my own. That opportunity came with the Carter administration, which named me ambassador to Uruguay in August 1977. In Uruguay I faced the challenge of persuading a military dictatorship to heed the evolving human rights concerns of the new administration in Washington.

It was early April 1979 when a call came to my office in Montevideo, Uruguay, from the director general of the foreign service, Harry Barnes. He informed me that he had just come from a meeting with Secretary of State Cyrus Vance, Deputy Secretary Warren Christopher, and Assistant Secretary of State for American Republic Affairs Viron (Pete) Vaky. "It was our unanimous view," said Barnes, "that you are the best man for the job that needs doing in Nicaragua." Before I could respond, he made it clear that they were hardly asking for my concurrence. He asked for an immediate reply. I said I would get back to him after I had spoken to my wife, Josephine. Her reaction was prescient: "It's a no-win situation." I called Barnes the next morning to inform him that I would accept the challenge.

That challenge was literally around the corner. We were entering Managua. Makeshift markets had sprung up at major intersections. Fresh produce was in short supply. Many of the established markets and supermarkets had been looted and closed. Merchants improvised, selling whatever foodstuffs they could get their hands on. The sight of people bargaining for tortillas, eggs, and pineapples was oddly reassuring. Despite the continuing peril, people had to eat.

We had driven nearly forty minutes when we turned into the Chancery compound situated on the South Highway, which is part of the Pan-American Highway that winds from the Texas border to Panama. The building was an unimpressive and flimsy prefab erected after the Chancery collapsed, with the rest of downtown Managua, in the earthquake of December 1972. A skeleton staff of fewer than fifty huddled inside. Soon I would ask for their appraisals of the situation that pressed in on them. First, a call was put through to the fortresslike bunker to set up a meeting with President Somoza. He would see me in two hours.

The staff of the United States Embassy had been caught in a peculiar bureaucratic limbo. In early spring Ambassador Mauricio Solaun, a political science professor appointed by the Carter administration, quickly left the post because of concerns for his personal safety. Threats had been made against his life. Without an ambassador, and facing increasingly volatile and complicated political conditions—a situation that required leadership and good analysis—the embassy staff had pulled back. Their reporting diminished to a trickle. The dominant political dynasty in Central America was coming apart, and our embassy had little to say.

Washington wasn't happy. In such circumstances, an alert foreign service officer could stake a reputation. Not only could an officer be certain that his or her reports were being read by the State

Department desk officer and regional director, but also there was a good chance they would receive the attentions of the secretary of state, the national security adviser, even the president. No one at our embassy in Managua had risen to the occasion. Contact between our embassy, the Somoza government, and opposition groups was close to nonexistent.

This is one of the reasons Somoza had dispatched his cousin and congressional leader, Luis Pallais, to Washington in early June. At the time, I was awaiting Senate confirmation. I joined Assistant Secretary of State for American Republic Affairs Pete Vaky, Director of the Office of Intelligence and Research Bill Bowdler, Secretary of State Cyrus Vance, Deputy Secretary Warren Christopher, members of the National Security Council, and others in studying and agonizing over possible U.S. responses to the Nicaraguan crisis.

In this environment, Vaky, Bowdler, and I were asked to initiate a series of talks with Somoza's cousin, Luis Pallais, and Guillermo Sevilla-Sacasa, Nicaragua's ambassador to the United States—not to mention ambassador to the Organization of American States, dean of the Washington diplomatic corps, ever present lion of Washington's cocktail party circuit, and Somoza's brother-in-law. Later Foreign Minister Julio Quintana—an earlier political rival of Somoza's who had once been expelled from Nicaragua—joined the discussions. Through these talks we communicated what had emerged as the administration's position:

1. There is no way the situation can be resolved, peace restored, and extremism avoided unless General Somoza steps down and he and his family leave the country.
2. We fully understand the need to avoid a collapse in the period immediately following General Somoza's departure, and we will use our best efforts to that end.
3. We will negotiate with the Sandinista junta in San José to preserve an environment that will allow the freest expression of political forces in a post-Somoza Nicaragua.
4. The United States will receive General Somoza and his family if they wish to come to this country. This option becomes improbable, however, if he is forced out of power and leaves behind a hostile successor government.
5. We see this as the only workable formula. If it is not accepted, we see no way to prevent further bloodshed and disaster.
6. Action must be taken quickly.

Luis Pallais conveyed our position to Somoza, flying back to Managua on a Somoza jet and returning with queries from his leader. Both sides were interested in a transfer scheme that would keep some people and institutions in place. We realized that the only way to have Somoza pull out and at the same time avoid chaos, reprisals, and even arbitrary attacks on innocent people was to plan for a transfer of power that offered security to all parties. Since Somoza adamantly refused to talk to the FSLN (Frente Sandinista de Liberación Nacional), which had to figure prominently in post-Somoza Nicaragua, it was left to the United States to devise an acceptable scenario. At one meeting Foreign Minister Julio Quintana suggested that the Nicaraguan constitution provided a possible solution: The president could resign and turn over power to a member of Congress who would act as interim head of state until a new government was formed. This was to become a central feature of the plan.

Because these discussions had been conducted under a veil of highest confidentiality, our embassy in Managua had been deliberately kept in the dark. Now, anticipating my meeting with Somoza, I quickly filled them in. They in turn briefed me on the conditions, moods, and attitudes in the country.

In late May the Sandinistas had launched their "final offensive" with a series of raids against Guardia Nacional outposts in towns and cities across Nicaragua. This new offensive started to take shape much as the Sandinista offensive had in September 1978, when some major cities—including Estelí in northeastern Nicaragua—actually fell into insurgent hands, only to be retaken later, brutally, by Somoza's Guardia Nacional. At first it wasn't clear how strong, or sustained, the new attacks would be. Gangs of teenage boys and others, armed and directed by the Sandinistas, converged on Guardia outposts in various towns and cities. This tactic put an immediate strain on the Guardia's abilities to communicate with, reinforce, and resupply their forces.

By early June 1979, as garrisons across the country were increasingly hemmed in, it became clear the Guardia was facing a popular insurrection of unprecedented magnitude. It was unable to cope. One by one the outposts fell. Towns and cities celebrated their liberation from the oppressive arm of Somoza. The red and black flag of the FSLN became the symbol of liberation.

The Guardia was on the defensive with little capacity to counterattack. The Sandinistas grew so bold as to strike the poor northeast barrios of Managua itself. Now, on June 27, the situation on the ground for Somoza's Guardia was, to most observers, irreversible. Still Somoza clung to the hope that at the eleventh hour the United States would bail him out—a fantasy probably reinforced by his contacts in Washington. The Guardia Nacional was not likely to collapse. Concentrated in defensive positions from Managua south to the country's third largest city, Granada, and on to Rivas near the Costa Rican border, it was capable of inflicting great damage. The South Highway afforded them clear lines of communication, redeployment, and resupply. Well disciplined, U.S.-trained and U.S.-supplied, the Guardias were fighting for their lives. There was little wavering in their loyalty to Somoza.

When his turn came to speak, Lieutenant Colonel James McCoy, the U.S. military attaché, offered the Guardia point of view: "The United States is abandoning us in our hour of need." Indeed, the Carter administration, with the cooperation of Congress, had cut off military sales to the Somoza government in mid-1978 after reports of large-scale human rights abuses in Nicaragua. The tone of the attaché's remarks bothered me. "We're not going to feel guilty," I said. "Somoza brought this on himself. Let's keep that straight. Our role is to find a solution that's as painless as possible for all concerned, especially the Nicaraguan people."

It was time to leave. I had been accompanied to Managua by Malcolm Barnebey, a veteran of the State Department's Latin American Bureau, but decided to go to my first meeting with Somoza alone to permit him, if he chose, to conduct our sessions one-on-one.

The drive to Somoza's headquarters was short. The city of Managua lies on a crescent of flat land that encloses the southern shore of Lake Managua. The city was built on a large structural fracture—running down western Nicaragua from the Gulf of Fonseca to Lake Nicaragua—indicated by a string of young volcanoes, many of them active. As one travels from the center of Managua toward the south, southeast, and southwest, the terrain gradually rises into the crests and foothills of the Diriambi Highlands. These outlying suburbs survived the devastating earthquake of 1972.

Just beyond what was once downtown Managua stand two promontories. On the western promontory called Tiscapa, near the pyramid-shaped Intercontinental Hotel, was Somoza's headquarters. The eastern promontory accommodated the United States ambassador's residence. To anyone looking south from downtown Managua, this striking visual representation of the two powers presiding over Nicaraguan political life was unmistakable.

As the security car and my armored car—a well-designed and unobtrusive Ford Grenada—wound up the road, we passed a Staghound armored car and then Somoza's military headquarters, an authentic bunker cut into the volcanic rock. We were on our way to "La Curvita," Somoza's California-style residence built along the curved summit of the promontory.

Unlike the bunker one hundred and fifty yards below it, "La Curvita" could have fit inconspicuously into most U.S. upper middle-class suburbs. A nonuniformed guard greeted me at the door. He led me into a beige-toned living room. It gave off an unlived-in feeling. Those residing here had either recently arrived or were getting ready to leave.

I was kept waiting the proper length of time befitting a foreign emissary calling on a chief of state—the customary twenty minutes. Then Somoza strode in.

His appearance had changed dramatically since the last time I had seen him, six years before. He had suffered a serious heart attack in the interim, but, even so, I was taken aback. The Somoza I had met back then was a big, flabby man, six foot two or three. He wore the khaki summer uniform of the Guardia Nacional. The man who had just walked in was at least fifty pounds thinner, almost emaciated, and dressed in a dark three-piece business suit. Take away the mustache and he could pass for a Wall Street banker. He seemed fragile and frightened. This was not the vigorous, self-confident man I remembered.

Behind Somoza were Foreign Minister Julio Quintana and United States Congressman John Murphy, Democrat from Staten Island. Murphy, I knew, was a longtime friend of Somoza's, but even so, I was astonished. What the hell was he doing here?

Somoza and I exchanged greetings. He said, "You're alone," clearly puzzled that I had come without aides.[1] He seemed to be expecting someone else. He led the way to an L-shaped couch in a corner of the large living room. I sat on the couch, with Somoza directly across from me in an armchair, Murphy and Quintana to his left and right. The space between was filled by a large coffee table.

Somoza spoke first. "I welcome you to Nicaragua, Mr. Ambassador. I realize we meet under unusual circumstances."[2] He spoke fluent English with only a hint of an accent. After thanking him for his words of welcome, I read from the talking points that had been presented to Luis Pallais and Foreign Minister Quintana in Washington.

Somoza looked on sullenly. I told him the United States saw no way out of the current crisis short of his relinquishing the presidency and leaving the country. We were prepared to facilitate his entry into the United States. I came to the end of my presentation. Somoza said, "I would like to give my point of view, if that's possible." "That's what I'm here for, Mr. President," I replied, feeling rather foolish. Then, dramatically rising to his feet, he said, "I'd like to confer with my associates," and, turning, he marched out of the room with Quintana and Murphy in tow.[3]

I sat alone, waiting. To my left, beyond the entry foyer was a hallway that led to the room where Somoza, Quintana, and Murphy had gone to deliberate. At the beginning of the hallway, several large paintings had been taken down and were leaning against the wall.

In front of me were wall-to-wall beige curtains. Behind them was a glass door leading to a patio and swimming pool. The setting had a relaxed, country club atmosphere, very much at odds with the strained cordiality of our proceedings. I had the eerie feeling I was in a surrealist play or a story by Jonathan Swift. Wasn't it Swift who said, "I never wonder to see men wicked, but often wonder not to see them ashamed"?

I keep wondering how Congressman Murphy felt being called an "associate" by Somoza. Being close to Somoza was one thing, but actually being on his side of the table in a negotiation with an ambassador from his country on the other was unconscionable. Clearly his being there was no accident. Just how deep was their association? Murphy and I had met for the first time only two weeks earlier in his Capitol Hill office. It was a courtesy call, customary for a new ambassador to make to a congressman with a strong interest in the country of posting. Murphy, along with Rep. Charles Wilson (D-Tex.), Rep. George Hansen (R-Idaho), and Rep. Larry McDonald (D-Ga.) were known as the Somoza lobby on Capitol Hill. Murphy's ties to Somoza were the deepest, going all the way back to their days as classmates at the La Salle Military Academy in Oaksdale, Long Island.

What I remembered most about the meeting with Murphy was the cold look in his eyes. He told me the Carter administration was making a serious mistake in not supporting his friend Somoza.

Communists would take over Nicaragua, he warned. I pointed out that Somoza had brought on the crisis himself by turning the country against him. I asked if he thought the United States could ignore that reality. He didn't answer or argue. He just looked at me with disdain.

Somoza and his associates were still conferring. Twenty minutes had gone by. I considered leaving. "This is ridiculous," I thought. "They know our position. Are we going to play games while the country bleeds?" Suddenly, I heard Murphy's voice coming from the hallway, saying something about Korea. That's the only time I heard him speak.

Once seated, Somoza launched into a long speech. He was prepared to step aside if that would serve his country. But what a strange thing this was for the United States to demand: "You're asking a constitutionally elected president to resign!" Didn't we realize what a great friend he was to the United States? He practically grew up in New York, having lived there since the age of ten. "I'm a Latin from Manhattan, like you, Mr. Ambassador."[4] And he had graduated from the West Point Military Academy, class of 1946. His wife, Hope, was an American. He loved the United States and probably knew parts of it better than I did.

I gave him that. But he wasn't finished. He had modeled his country after the United States. Why? Why were we doing this to him? What reasons did we have for stabbing a good friend in the back? He excused me personally. He understood—I was just doing my job. "Let's not bullshit ourselves, Mr. Ambassador. I know I'm talking to a professional. You have your dirty work to do, and I have mine."[5]

I let him ramble on. I figured this was strictly for the record or, more precisely, for the tape. He had better say these things so he could defend himself later. You don't dominate a country like Nicaragua single-handedly. He was going to have many distressed followers to answer to. (Later, in 1980, Somoza would publish his side of the story and a self-serving version of our conversations in *Nicaragua Betrayed*.)

Before leaving Washington I had been warned that Somoza would probably be taping our conversations. This brought to mind a story I had heard about a meeting between Robert Kennedy and President Lyndon Johnson after Bobby had left the Johnson administration and both men were vying for power within the Democratic party. According to the story, Kennedy knew going into the meeting that LBJ would record it, so he wore on his person a mechanical device that made taping impossible. He got a big kick out of leaving the president with a tape filled with nothing but buzz.

The idea appealed to me, so I had asked the director of security in the State Department if he could supply such a device when I met with Somoza. He assured me any apparatus would either be so big or so noisy as to seem ludicrous. So much for the Bobby Kennedy story.

With the tape recorder running, Somoza continued. Now he was playing the victim: the Carter administration was out to get him. He couldn't understand why, but the signals were clear. Wasn't the Carter administration's refusal to sell arms to the Guardia Nacional a green light to the Sandinistas to organize the revolution? Why, in their fight for democracy, and against communism, were his Guardias being called violators of human rights? After all, they were fighting communism as the United States had taught them to in Fort Gulick, Fort Benning, and Fort Leavenworth.

I broke in: "You're misreading history, Mr. President. The concern in the United States regarding support for governments that abuse their peoples became an issue in Congress before the Carter administration. I have just come from Uruguay. Congress cut all military sales to their government in 1976, before Carter was elected."

As deputy assistant secretary of state for congressional affairs from 1974 to 1977, I was very familiar with debates within Congress and the hearings before the House Subcommittee on International Affairs, chaired by Congressman Donald Frazier. "In fact, the Frazier Subcommittee had heard charges from the Catholic church that your Guardia Nacional had been mistreating campesinos in the northern highlands. Didn't you later issue new instructions to Guardia field commanders, at our suggestion, to avoid further abuses? Surely, Congressman Murphy here knows that history better than anyone." Murphy said nothing. I continued, "And, besides, Mr. President, if anything, you had stronger advocates in Congress than any leader in Latin America."[6]

Somoza changed the subject: He would not turn Nicaragua over to communists. He had a war to fight, and the people of his country were counting on him to do that. The easiest thing for him to do would be to walk out. But he wasn't a quitter. He wasn't a man to turn his back on responsibilities. He was a patriot, a man who loved his country and his people. The United States was asking him to do something unconscionable.

I responded: "You're missing the point, Mr. President. Nicaragua is in the midst of civil war. The Carter administration didn't bring this about. These are forces within your own country. Your staying on is impossible. You have lost the capacity to govern. The United States is offering a way out of the suffering. If you accept, you'll go down in history as a man who was big enough to have ended a senseless slaughter of your own people. You have to face it, you have become the core of the problem."[7]

Somoza cut in. "They have a saying in my country, 'Muerto el perro se acaba la rabia.' Kill the dog and you'll get rid of the rabies. Maybe I should remove myself and the rabies will go away."[8]

I sat up with surprise. This is not what I had anticipated. Consultations in Washington had conditioned me to expect an obdurate leader who would give up power only after being pushed up against a wall. Taking advantage of his opening, I asked, "Can I tell Washington you're prepared to leave?"

"Only if certain conditions are met, including guarantees to protect my Liberal party and the National Guard."

"We can't offer guarantees, Mr. President. But we're willing to talk. We would like to see the institutions worth preserving, preserved. We would like to see a security force of some sort that can prevent chaos and senseless bloodshed. Let's do this with grace."[9]

Somoza didn't answer. His mind was elsewhere. Agreements would have to be hammered out in detail in the days ahead. Our meeting had gone on for nearly two hours. Night had fallen, along with the five o'clock curfew. Somoza and I agreed to meet the next day. A Guardia Nacional patrol car with a blue flashing light escorted us from "La Curvita" down to the city, and then up again to the U.S. ambassador's residence.

With the patter of gunfire in the distance, I drafted my first message to Washington. "Although Somoza promised to plan his final days, his character and past performance leaves much doubt. At least he got the message that there are no easy ways out. He clearly wants safe haven in the United States. He roared with laughter when he learned that his priority status for an immigrant visa derives from his relationship to his U.S. citizen estranged wife, Hope."[10]

I imagined Washington would be pleased that Somoza was at least talking about leaving. I learned later that it provoked serious concern.

Between sips of scotch and soda, I reviewed the events of the afternoon. Clearly, Somoza had run out of options. The Somoza family's system of dominating Nicaragua (known as *Somozismo*) was coming to an end. Maybe I had been blunt in telling him so. But there was no time for diplomatic niceties. I'd heard that envoys before me had to look over their shoulders when dealing with Somoza. Tacho had friends in high places, real and feigned. He was not above telling an American ambassador how well wired he was, or threatening to use his influence in Washington. No doubt that was the symbolic message of Murphy's presence.

The end game had begun. The time when problems could be talked away was past. I was confident that the United States' position was in everybody's interest, even Somoza's. I was, as they say in Washington, comfortable with my brief. My own doubts centered on Somoza's possible refusal to leave, which would prolong a senseless conflict. His regime was over. He couldn't govern anymore. We were offering him as graceful and safe an exit as was possible under the circumstances.

I heard later that people around Somoza were impressed by my self-assurance. They said no one had ever spoken to him the way I had. I was selected for the mission because my superiors in the State Department were confident that I wouldn't blink when negotiating face-to-face with Somoza. I didn't, but I did misjudge his emotional state. It proved to be a critical miscalculation.

2

History is philosophy teaching by example.
—Dionysus of Halicarnassus

Anastasio Somoza Debayle (Tachito) lived in the long shadow of his father, Anastasio Somoza García (Tacho), the flamboyant founder of the Somoza dynasty, who often complained that neither of his sons had his brains or cunning. "My daughter Lilian is more like me than either of them,"[1] said the old man. Tachito did inherit many of his father's tough-guy mannerisms and love of the United States.

"Except for the first four years," the younger Somoza wrote, "all my education was received in the U.S.A. I took my high school course at La Salle Military Academy in New York. Later, I passed the examinations for the United States Military Academy at West Point, and graduated from that outstanding military institution in 1946."[2] It's been said that Tachito is the only West Pointer in history to have received an army as a graduation present.

Like his father, Tachito relied on the National Guard to guarantee his domination of Nicaraguan political and economic life. Coincidentally, it was the United States that created the National Guard and installed his father at its helm.

Since 1821 when the captain-generalship of Guatemala, as Central America was called, gained its independence from Spain,

Nicaragua had suffered cycle after cycle of political unrest. In the early years, the primary source of conflict was the rivalry between its two main cities—Granada on the shores of Lake Nicaragua and León seventy-five miles northwest. The great landed families of Granada, with their enduring attachment to Spain, considered themselves aristocrats. They imagined a semifeudal system informed by their faith in the Roman Catholic church. Their Conservative beliefs are still reflected in the serene colonial architecture of the city.

The Liberals, to the northwest, dominated the thriving commercial center of León. Here the Masonic principles of free trade and the French and American revolutions were more in vogue. Where Granada was inventive and luxurious, León was industrious and pragmatic.

Between 1825 and 1842 alone, differences between Liberals and Conservatives accounted for seventeen major battles and the accession of eighteen new heads of state. As time went on, another factor aggravated Nicaraguan political life—the imperial and commercial ambitions of foreigners. For the San Juan River and Lake Nicaragua almost add up to a natural interoceanic canal.

When gold was discovered in California in 1849, the lure of easy passage between the Caribbean and Pacific led to periods of foreign intervention and civil wars. That year robber baron Cornelius Vanderbilt, together with several other New York investors, created the Accessory Transit Company to ferry passengers and goods bound for the California goldfields across Nicaragua. Vanderbilt's steamers would ply the San Juan River all the way to the western shore of Lake Nicaragua. From there, mule trains would complete the journey to San Juan del Sur on the Pacific coast. When Great Britain, which claimed a protectorate over Nicaragua's north coast, tried to take over Vanderbilt's terminal at San Juan del Sur, a diplomatic crisis ensued. The crisis was resolved in 1850 with the Clayton-Bulwer Treaty, which provided that all water and rail crossings of Nicaragua would be jointly controlled by Great Britain and the United States. Typically, Nicaragua was excluded.

Meanwhile, Liberals and Conservatives continued to fight. In 1851 a Conservative dictator, Laureano Pineda, tried to mediate the crisis by moving the capital to the small city of Managua, roughly midway between León and Granada. It didn't work.

By 1855, with another Conservative leader, Fruto Chamorro, in the presidency, Liberals started looking for outside help in their struggle to unseat their rivals. William Walker, a journalist and adventurer from Tennessee who a year earlier had tried to carve out a piece of Mexico for himself, answered the call. Leading an army of fifty-eight well-armed soldiers of fortune and several hundred Liberal troops, Walker overwhelmed Granada and seized Vanderbilt's lake steamer. Within a year he had himself proclaimed president, instituted slavery, and declared English the official language. This being the heyday of the Monroe Doctrine, the United States quickly recognized him.

Still, Walker's ambitions weren't satisfied. A southerner and ardent supporter of slavery, he dreamed of creating a Central American empire. His flag bore the motto *Five or None!* Financed by the British and by Cornelius Vanderbilt, El Salvador, Guatemala, Costa Rica, and Honduras raised an army of 18,000 troops to oppose Walker. They scored their first victory in May 1857 at the port of Rivas. Walker made his last stand at Granada, raising a flag that read *Aquí Fue Granada* (Here Was Granada) before attempting to set the old city afire. Fortunately, his flame didn't take.

His back against the lake, Walker took shelter on a U.S. Navy ship and received a hero's welcome back home in New Orleans. Four years later he was captured by the British in Honduras after seizing the town of Trujillos. This time, however, Walker was turned over to Honduran authorities and shot.

Compromised by their support of Walker, the Liberals endured thirty years of Conservative presidents. It was during this period that the demand for coffee swept Nicaragua into the world capitalist market. Inspired by the "green gold" rush, the conservative aristocracy created a number of legal recourses for expropriating land and providing cheap farm labor.

In 1893 Liberal General José Santos Zelaya came to power with a program to modernize the country. Backed by the rising middle class that had expanded during the coffee boom, Zelaya accelerated the pace of liberal reforms, beginning with a new constitution. He encouraged foreign investment, established a system of public primary education, speeded up infrastructure development, heavily encouraged export commodity production, and instituted a national labor draft. An authoritarian nationalist, he also tamed the recalcitrant cities of Granada and León, reduced the economic power of the church and of certain Conservatives, built a professional army to replace the militias led by caudillos, and expanded communication networks, education spending, and the number of registered voters.

Things went wrong after 1902 when the United States chose to build a canal across Panama rather than Nicaragua. General Zelaya, who had lavished favors on U.S. interests in the hope of winning the canal, was incensed. In retaliation he not only opened negotiations with the Japanese about constructing his own canal, but secured a French loan for the construction of a railway to the Caribbean. At a time when the United States was particularly sensitive about European influence in the area, Zelaya could not have been more tactless. Not only that, he stepped on the toes of the Fletcher mining and lumbering interests of Pittsburgh, who were closely associated with Secretary of State Philander Knox.

Repressive and increasingly unpopular, especially among the landholding Conservatives, Zelaya made many enemies. With money and arms, the United States was able to foment a revolt against him in 1909. When government troops caught and executed two American filibusters—military adventurers—laying mines in the San Juan River, Secretary Knox declared Zelaya "outside the law of nations" and U.S. Marines were landed at the Caribbean port of Bluefields.

Zelaya relinquished power. But the United States refused to recognize the new Liberal government. With a coalition government installed, the Marines withdrew on December 31, 1910. After more intrigue, Conservative Adolfo Díaz, former bookkeeper of the Fletcher mines, emerged as president.

Without supporters of his own, Díaz was virtually a figurehead for the United States. When an army revolt was launched against Díaz in 1912, U.S. Marines were sent to quell the rebellion. In return for the favor, Díaz accepted the Byran-Chamorro Treaty giving the United States exclusive canal rights, rent of the Corn Islands off the Atlantic coast, and permitting the establishment of a U.S. naval base in the Gulf of Fonseca.

In 1916 Emiliano Chamorro succeeded Díaz with the active goodwill of the U.S. delegation. A U.S. customs collectorship was instituted at the behest of President Taft to ensure the payment of U.S. debts. Four years later, when Chamorro made way for his uncle, a journalist remarked, "The Conservative Party, resting on U.S. bayonets, has become a machine for turning out Chamorro presidents."[3]

These were the days of dollar diplomacy. General Smedley D. Butler, who headed many of the U.S. interventions in Latin America, gave this account toward the end of his life:

I spent thirty-three years and four months in service as a member of our country's most agile military force—the Marine Corps. . . . And during that period I spent most of my time being a high-class muscle man for Big Business, for Wall Street and the bankers. In short, I was a racketeer for capitalism. . . . I helped purify Nicaragua for the international banking house of Brown Brothers 1909–12. I brought light to the Dominican Republic for American sugar interests in 1916. I helped make Honduras "right" for American fruit companies.[4]

The cozy relationship between the United States and the Chamorros ended in 1924 when dissident Conservatives formed an alliance with the Liberals and elected a weak Conservative president and a Liberal U.S.-trained doctor, Juan Batista Sacasa, as vice president. Emiliano Chamorro raised an army and went to war. When General José María Moncada called the Liberals to arms to oppose Chamorro, twenty-eight-year-old Anastasio Somoza García joined the rebels.

Having failed at several businesses, this was an opportunity the young Somoza had been waiting for. Born to a modest coffee-growing family from San Marcos in 1896, Tacho had been sent by a cousin to bookkeeping school in Philadelphia after fathering a child with the family maid. Not a studious type, he passed his time gambling and selling cars. His charm and grace on the dance floor made a favorable impression on a young Nicaraguan woman from an excellent family, Salvadora Debayle, who happened to be studying in Philadelphia at the time. Soon he was meeting her every afternoon with flowers under Wanamaker's clock.

Salvadora, whom many considered the more politically astute of the two, convinced Tacho to return to Nicaragua, where they were married despite her family's strong objections to his questionable character and Liberal background. Even though Somoza's father had served eight years as a Conservative senator, Tacho was already calling himself a "Liberal of four ribs."

The most colorful of these ribs came from his great-uncle Bernabé Somoza, one of Nicaragua's most notorious bandits and leader of one of the many Liberal uprisings against Granada. Known in folklore as Siete Pañuelos (seven handkerchiefs) for all the blood he had to wipe off his hands, Bernabé is reputed to have seduced the wives of his foes to provide intelligence and once to have killed twenty men with a machete over a cockfight. As Tacho told it, "He was so handsome that when he played guitar women shivered and swooned. He could put himself in a yoke and pull like an ox."[5] Bernabé ended up hanging from a lamppost in Rivas in 1948, compliments of his Conservative rival Fruto Chamorro.

Determined not to end up like his great-uncle, Somoza tried his hand at legitimate business. When a general store he owned went bankrupt because of his gambling debts, he opened a Lexington motorcars agency. It was a time when Nicaragua had few roads.

For a while, Tacho inspected latrines for the Rockefeller Foundation's Sanitation Mission, checking to see whether citizens had poured kerosene into their outhouses to keep the mosquitoes down. Because he carried a long batonlike flashlight, his friends dubbed him El Mariscal (the field marshal).

Later he eked out a living in León installing electric fixtures and reading meters for the power company. In 1921 and growing impatient, Tacho and a boyhood friend, Camilo González, (later his chief of staff) were caught in Mexico with molds for counterfeiting gold coins. It took the influence of the Debayle family to have proceedings dropped. Amid these and other activities, Tacho sought distraction by umpiring baseball games.

In 1926, now the father of three—Luis (born in 1923), Lilian (1924), and Anastasio (Tachito, 1925)—Somoza turned to political warfare as a means to better himself. When General Moncada began seizing territory for the Liberal party, Tacho raised a small force of peasants and invaded his hometown of San Marcos. Quickly defeated when government troops arrived, he fled into hiding, only to emerge a few days later calling himself "General." He accepted a pardon in return for his promise "not to join any other subversive uprising."

On August 27, 1926, United States Marines landed once again, ostensibly to "protect American lives and property." Their real interest was to maintain U.S. supremacy in the region, which Secretary of State Frank B. Kellogg claimed was threatened by "Mexican fostered Bolshevik hegemony between the United States and the Panama Canal."[6] Revolutionary Mexico had the temerity to side with General Moncada and the Liberals.

After installing U.S. favorite Adolfo Díaz in the presidency, the marines left, but returned again in January 1927 at the outbreak of a new Liberal uprising. This time President Coolidge dispatched Henry L. Stimson, former secretary of war, to Nicaragua to resolve the crisis. Tacho, who attached himself to General Moncada's staff, was interviewed by Stimson. Stimson recorded these impressions in his diary: "Somoza is a very frank, friendly, likeable young Liberal and his attitude impresses me more favorably than almost any other."[7]

Stimson asked Somoza to serve as his interpreter for subsequent meetings. It wouldn't be the first time that Tacho's command of English and ability to ingratiate himself with influential Americans would serve him well. Before long, the ambitious young Nicaraguan was so closely identified with U.S. interests that people called him El Yanqui.

According to the terms of the Peace of Tipitapa (1927) negotiated by Stimson and agreed to by Liberals and Conservatives, Liberal soldiers would lay down their arms and receive ten dollars for every rifle surrendered. They would also relinquish control of the six provinces they had seized and take part in United States–supervised elections to be held in 1928. To ensure against further civil conflict, the U.S. would organize and train a nonpolitical National Guard.

After several days of consideration, all but one of Moncada's generals signed a telegram of acceptance. The holdout was Augusto C. Sandino, a magnetic wisp of a man who objected to the fact that Conservative Adolfo Díaz would remain in the presidency until the 1928 elections. Calling Moncada a traitor, he led his troops into the northern mountains around Nueva Segovia, Jinotega, and Matagalpa. His opponents this time were not the Liberals, but the U.S. Marines and the nascent National Guard.

Sandino himself was virtually unknown in Nicaragua up to that point. Born in 1895 a few miles from Somoza's hometown of San Marcos, Augusto C. Sandino was the illegitimate son of a local landowner and a young Indian girl who soon after her son's birth sank into prostitution. Sandino later became obsessed with the parallel between his country's plight and his mother turning to streetwalking in her misfortune.

In 1920, following a violent argument over a card game in which he wounded a man, Sandino fled to Mexico where he worked in the oil fields, became a Freemason, and was inspired by the nationalism of the Mexican revolution—especially its exaltation of that nation's Indian heritage. A fervent believer in Liberal ideals, he returned to Nicaragua in 1926, just before the Liberal revolt against Chamorro.

Sandino's cause, which initially had nothing to do with anti-Americanism, soon became an explicit rejection of U.S. imperialism and, as such, a model for guerrilla struggles in Latin America for the next sixty-some years. His battle cry, "Patria libre o morir," would reverberate through fifty years of Nicaraguan history to haunt the Somozas and the United States.

Back in 1927, U.S. Marines characterized Sandino as a bandit, to which Sandino replied: "We are no more bandits than was Washington."[8] His political goals were simple. When interviewed by Carleton Beals of the *Nation,* he gave three conditions for disbanding his army: one, the U.S. Marines must leave; two, an interim civilian president must be appointed; three, elections must be held under the supervision of other Latin American countries.

When asked whether he would run for the presidency, Sandino professed no political ambitions. "We have taken up arms for the love of country because all of our leaders have betrayed it and have sold themselves out to the foreigner or have bent the neck in cowardice."[9] A visionary to his followers, Sandino had a way of incorporating Vishnu and Christ into his military commands and claimed to be guided in battle by the voice of Simón Bolívar.

With no outside assistance, fighting with guns mainly ripped from the enemy and hand grenades fashioned from sardine cans filled with gunpowder and stones, he and his rag-tag army were able to resist the marines and the Guardia Nacional for five and a half years.

The conflict began on July 16, 1927, when Sandino attacked the Guardia garrison at Ocotal, which also housed eleven U.S. Marines. First, Sandino offered terms of surrender to the marine commander Captain Hatfield and signed it, "Your most obedient servant who ardently desires to put you in a handsome tomb with beautiful bouquets of flowers."[10] When Hatfield turned down his offer, Sandino and several hundred men charged the city hall and Guardia barracks, only to be repulsed by machine gun fire. Then they were surprised by strafing attacks by five U.S. DeHaviland bombers, which drove Sandino and his men back into the mountains.

The marines claimed 300 rebel dead. Sandino learned from his mistake. Hereafter, he adopted a guerrilla strategy of ambushes and surprise hit-and-run raids against the enemy.

Although he never fought his way out of the thinly populated north-central mountains, Sandino developed a loyal base of support among the peasants who felt dispossessed after years of exploitation and land expropriations. In a "war that we are bound to lose," he prevailed.[11] Along the way, he amassed an international following of Latin American nationalists and avant-garde social activists in the United States and Europe.

Back in Managua, Tacho's good luck hadn't run out. His political mentor General Moncada won the 1928 elections. Because of Somoza's ability with Americans, he was appointed subsecretary of foreign affairs. This gave Tacho an opportunity to turn his charm on U.S. Minister Matthew Hanna and his wife, whose relationship to Somoza has been the subject of much speculation. That Somoza completely won over Hanna and his wife is undoubtedly true.

Amid these developments, a great earthquake demolished Managua on March 31, 1931. Hundreds died immediately, and great fires swept through the ruins and threatened to consume the remaining outskirts of the city. The fledgling Guardia National and the U.S. Marines had to use dynamite to keep the blaze from spreading.

Many considered Managua doomed. Conservative Granada and Liberal León started raising armies to fight. This time the U.S. Marines kept them apart. For reasons of political expediency rather than geologic stability, Managua held on as the capital.

Somoza prevailed again in 1932 when his wife's uncle, Juan Batista Sacasa of the Liberal party, was elected president. At the urging of U.S. Minister Hanna, outgoing President Moncada and Sacasa agreed that Tacho should be groomed for the *jefe director* of the Guardia Nacional when time came to replace the U.S. commander with a Nicaraguan.

With order fully restored, the last marines sailed from Nicaragua on January 2, 1933, leaving behind a fully equipped and trained National Guard and their hand-picked man, Anastasio Somoza García, "the last marine" to lead it.

Arthur Bliss Lane, who succeeded Hanna as U.S. minister in 1934, was not the first to see the dangerous legacy created by the United States. "Did it ever occur to the eminent statesmen who created the National Guard that personal ambition lurks in the human breast, even in Nicaragua? In my opinion, it is one of the sorriest examples on our part, of our inability to understand that we should not meddle in other people's affairs."[12]

With the marines gone, time had come to make peace with Sandino. After President Sacasa appointed Sandino's cousin Sofonias

Salvatierra as minister of agriculture and labor, the rebel leader was persuaded to leave the mountains and talk. He agreed to terms disbanding his army in return for an armed guard of a hundred men, promises of public works projects in Nueva Segovia, Jinotega, and Matagalpa, and an allotment of land along the Rio Coco for his men.

Amid much public celebration, Somoza and Sandino embraced, and the country was at peace. But Somoza wasn't satisfied. As he later explained: "We Nicaraguans are a Spanish and Indian mixture, and that's dynamite. Give us a finger and we take a hand. Give us a hand and we take an arm."[13]

So Somoza conspired. First, he proposed an alliance to one of Sandino's lieutenants against President Sacasa, stating: "The old imbecile is ruining the country. Together we could force a new cabinet on him with Sandino as war minister."[14] When Sandino refused the offer, Somoza filled Sacasa's ears with stories of Sandino's plots.

Relations between Sandino and Somoza deteriorated rapidly after August 20, when the Guardia opened fire on a group of Sandino's men who were driving cattle near Yali. Five were killed and one guardsman wounded. Somoza admitted the incident was a mistake, but insisted that Sandino's men disarm. Sandino called instead for the disbanding of the Guardia, which he said had been created "by an act of foreign intervention."

Both Somoza and Sandino appealed to President Sacasa, who stayed in his palace surrounded by the presidential guard. He couldn't decide which man to fear most. With tensions mounting, the president invited Sandino to Managua to try to resolve the crisis.

Sandino was welcomed warmly by Somoza when he arrived on February 16, 1934. Five nights later, after days spent discussing the crisis with government officials, Sandino and several of his aides attended a dinner given in their honor by President Sacasa. As they drove from the presidential palace to downtown Managua, a truck blocked their way. Guardia soldiers ordered Sandino, his father, Don Gregorio, Minister Salvatierra, and generals Juan Pablo Umanzar and Francisco Estrada out of the car and into El Hormiguero prison nearby.

Somoza, who had not attended the dinner, was across the street in the Campo de Marte at a poetry reading. When fellow Freemason Sandino issued a distress call by telephone, Tacho refused to take it.

Along with his two generals, Sandino was taken by truck to a nearby airfield where they faced a firing squad. When asked why he was crying, Sandino reportedly said it was not because he was afraid, but because he had been betrayed. From the prison Don Gregorio and Salvatierra heard the shots. That same evening the Guardia Nacional surrounded Sandino's camp at Wiwili and machine-gunned over three hundred men, women, and children. Within weeks, Somoza ruthlessly destroyed Sandino's movement and its followers.

President Sacasa didn't protest. Nor did the upper classes, who were happy to be rid of the man who "had fired the imagination of the humble people of Nicaragua."

With the Guardia Nacional increasingly loyal only to himself and with no other effective force to oppose him, Somoza forced Sacasa from the presidency in May 1936. After ruling behind a succession of interim presidents, Tacho made himself a candidate and assumed the presidency on January 1, 1937. Washington's recognition soon followed.

Two years later, Tacho and Salvadora made a historic visit to Washington at the invitation of Franklin Roosevelt, who, legend has it, remarked to an aide, "He's a son-of-a-bitch, but he's ours."[15] The Somozas were received with such pomp and circumstance that journalists dubbed their triumphant tour a dress rehearsal for the imminent visit of Britain's King George VI and Queen Elizabeth. Tacho shot back: "Dress rehearsal, my eye. We'll see if the king does as well."[16]

Tacho's visit was a landmark in Nicaraguan history and cemented his personal affection for and admiration of the United States. In keeping with his good neighbor policy, FDR bestowed on Nicaragua $2 million in credit.

Feeling on top of things, Somoza shared his views with reporters: "I want to treat everybody good. I told FDR about democracy in Central America. Democracy down there is like a baby—and nobody gives a baby everything to eat right away. I'm giving 'em liberty—but in my style. If you give a baby a hot tamale, you'll kill him."[17]

Friend and foe had to admit that Anastasio Somoza García had style. He assumed the roles of president and proprietor of Nicaragua as though he were born to them. Through a series of smart business deals, he grabbed for himself more than fifty of Nicaragua's best cattle ranches, forty-five of the best coffee *fincas*, interests in lumber, mining, electric power, salt, and a percentage of all

President Franklin Roosevelt welcomes General Anastasio Somoza García to Washington, May 5, 1939. Behind them are Eleanor Roosevelt and Salvadora Somoza Debayle. Credit: Globe Photos, Inc. 1993

new businesses. In 1948 he put the number of his enterprises at 117 and reasoned: "You would do the same thing for yourself if you were in my place."[18]

One of his more devious schemes involved cornering the meat market. In order to ensure that only his cattle were sold, Tacho issued a decree requiring a permit to move cattle. A rancher bringing his cattle to Managua, for example, would be asked to show a permit. He would wire Managua for it and wait. In the meantime, he would have to pay for grazing land or his cattle would grow thin. When the rancher grew desperate, a certain Ponciano Muñoz would show up and offer the rancher a ridiculously low price for his herd. With no permit in sight, the rancher would be forced to sell. Then, mysteriously, the permit would arrive and Muñoz would move the cattle to market. Ponciano Muñoz was Somoza's number one cowhand.

Wherever Nicaraguans turned, they saw Somoza or his Guardia Nacional, which doubled as both army and police force. When he boasted, "I know every man in Nicaragua and what he represents,"[19] he probably wasn't far wrong.

Even when he was repressive, Tacho maintained his bizarre sense of humor. He claimed to kill opponents only as a last resort. When a few days in jail didn't bring an enemy around, he used a little electric device known as *la maquinita*. A wire was wrapped around the prisoner's testicles and the current turned on. When critics protested, Somoza retorted: "Hell, that damned thing isn't so bad. I've tried it myself—on my hand."[20]

Once a Conservative who had been placed under house arrest charged up to Somoza at a party and roared: "I want to know why you ordered my arrest!" Replied Tacho with a grin: "I did it to please your wife. She told me she couldn't keep you at home nights."[21]

When his gargantuan appetite for power roused the opposition against him, Tacho squashed their plans with characteristic flair. Once, in 1944, an old Liberal ally General Pasos felt that Nicaragua could use a little more democracy. He reached an agreement to form a united opposition with exiled Conservative chieftain Emiliano Chamorro. For the Liberal convention, Pasos prepared a speech cataloguing Somoza's personal business deals. A couple of Liberal delegates went to Tacho to get his views.

"Tell Pasos that I know that twice last night at the home of Castro Wassmer he read the speech that he has prepared, and if he insists on reading it at the convention, let him not forget to come armed. I am certainly not a man to let myself be overthrown by speeches. There'll certainly be some gunplay there."[22]

Pasos did not make the speech. Instead he went to jail for three weeks. His textile mill and other businesses weren't touched.

Although severely undertrained and overstuffed, the middle-aged dictator was still boasting in 1948 about his physical strength, his horsemanship, his shooting, his card playing. "It's the fantastic luck I have. It's that way with anything I want to try—I'm the champ. I'm the champ shot of the Guardia Nacional, did you know that? Pistol or rifle. Jeez, I never seem to miss."[23]

At fifty, Tacho was still the life of the party and could shake a light foot in the rumba, tango, bolero, or samba. If he felt so inclined, he would dance the whole night at his palace at "La Curva," then adjourn to one of his ranches for another six to eight hours.

Panamanian calypso king Rupert (Kontiki) Allen even honored him with a song:

> A guy asked de dictator if he 'ad any farms
> 'E said 'e 'ah on'y one—
> It was Nicaragua."[24]

Visitors to Somoza's office were regaled with off-color jokes and his collection of naughty pictures. When the spirit moved him, Tacho would take his cabinet and visiting VIPs to his ranch to watch bulls servicing his cows. His office was littered with sports trophies, jukeboxes, bronze models of horses and elephants, and hangers-on. No fewer than four photos of FDR were displayed prominently on the walls. If Tacho agreed to a proposal and gave an order then and there, the order was carried out. If he said he'd think it over, he would forget about it.

Time magazine correspondent William Krehm described the scene in 1944—"Behind it all in a khaki shirt open at the collar, a rock-sized diamond on his pudgy finger, a sagging paunch, an effusive manner and thinning hair sat Tacho. His English was fantastically incorrect and fluent—akin to that of an Italian-American mobster. 'Goddammits' interrupted his speech when he was making an effort at persuasiveness."[25]

As years passed, Tacho laid plans to turn his dictatorship into a dynasty. When his daughter Lilian was married in 1943, her husband, the debonair Guillermo Sevilla-Sacasa was awarded the ambassador's post in Washington as a wedding present. Sons Luis and Tachito were dispatched to La Salle Military Academy in New York for training. Luis went on to Louisiana State University for a degree in agronomy and as a graduation present received a captaincy in the Guardia. After Tachito graduated from West Point in 1946, he returned to Managua and several key Guardia commands.

As the two boys matured, they seemed to take on opposite sides of their father's personality. Luis, urbane and personable, chose to stay away from the dirty side of the dictatorship. He preferred the life of gentleman farmer. Realizing that Luis's easygoing manner was perfect for the gamesmanship of congressional politics, his father named him to lead Congress and his National Liberal party.

Tachito, who worshipped his more politically astute brother, had returned from West Point with democratic ideas. After his father quickly disabused him of such nonsense, Tachito took to the barracks life and progressively became more abusive. In 1951, after marrying his first cousin Hope Portocarrero (a U.S. citizen), Tachito was named chief of staff of the Guardia Nacional. The elder Somoza felt that the extremely well-groomed attractive brunette would make a perfect wife for Tachito. "She's got class," he explained.[26] It soon became apparent, however, that Tachito preferred drinks, brawls, and the company of soldiers and prostitutes to Hope's refinements.

On September 21, 1956, Tacho and Salvadora were taking part in a whirlwind of fiestas celebrating Tacho's nomination by his National Liberal party for the February 1957 elections. The sixty-year-old Somoza was in high spirits—merry, solicitous, and always the patron. Between cha-chas with Salvadora and a local beauty pageant winner, Tacho stopped to glance at a newspaper article. Suddenly, a young man with a pencil-thin mustache pointed a snub-nosed .38 at the 220-pound dictator and fired four times. Somoza dropped the paper, fell backward, and gasped, "Aye mi Dios!"[27]

The assassin, a twenty-seven-year-old poet and printshop worker was shot thirty-five times, kicked, and spat upon. His body was thrown out onto the sidewalk and then disappeared.

U.S. Ambassador Thomas Whelan rushed to Tacho's side. Somoza muttered, "I'm a goner," in the colloquial English that had served him so well, and lost consciousness.[28] A U.S. helicopter rushed Tacho to the Canal Zone at the behest of President Eisenhower. There he was operated on by the commander of Walter Reed Army Hospital. A poisoned bullet had lodged at the base of his spine. He died seven days later without ever regaining consciousness. Salvadora was at his side.

Tacho's assassin, Rigoberto López Pérez, left behind a "Last Will and Testament" dated September 4, 1956, addressed to his mother:

My beloved mother:

Although you never knew it, I have always taken part in all the attacks on the deadly regime of our country and, since all our efforts have been useless in attempting to see that Nicaragua become once again (or for the first time) a free country without insults and manipulations, I have decided, although my comrades were not in agreement, to be the one who initiates the beginning of the end of that tyranny. If God wills that I perish in my purpose I want absolutely no one to be blamed since it has been my decision. . . . I hope that you will take these things calmly and you will think of what I have done as a duty that any Nicaraguan who truly loves his country should have accomplished long ago.

Your son, who has always loved you so much

3

The most gifted members of the human species are at their more creative when they cannot have their way. —Eric Hoffer

The lights in the baroque Pan American Union Building on Constitution Avenue across from the White House dimmed behind us. A light drizzle softened the sultry evening as Assistant Secretary of State for American Republic Affairs Viron (Pete) Vaky, Special Ambassador William (Bill) Bowdler and I walked down the marble stairs. Tonight Washington was very much the tropical capital that European diplomats complained about.

It was Saturday, June 23, 1979, four days before my first session with Somoza in his bunker. The Seventeenth Meeting of the Consultation of Ministers of Foreign Affairs of the Organization of American States (OAS) had ended an hour earlier. The other delegations and permanent staff had already left.

It had been a bruising session for Pete Vaky, especially since he had engineered the call for the special session to provide an OAS mandate to end the crisis in Nicaragua. As we turned west toward the State Department, Robert Pastor, the energetic head of Latin American Affairs at the National Security Council materialized out of the twilight mist. He was rumpled and winded from his brisk walk down Seventeenth Street from the Executive Office Building.

Pastor greeted us and asked Pete Vaky about the wording of the final OAS resolution. Vaky replied that it wasn't what Secretary of State Cyrus Vance had proposed—an OAS-supervised cease-fire and the creation of a transition government. But the resolution did "permit constructive actions by member countries."[1] It would allow us to negotiate a peaceful transition to the Nicaraguan crisis.

Pastor was disappointed. He said National Security Adviser Zbigniew Brzezinski would be upset. Vaky, uncharacteristically, snapped back. It was too late in the game to expect the United States to command much support in the OAS on the Nicaraguan issue. He knew the Latins blamed us for not delivering during the OAS mediation of 1978. And he felt that they were justified in doing so. "Where was the toughness in the White House nine months ago when we needed it to force Somoza to step down?" Vaky asked.[2] Pastor, looking flustered, answered that he had never seen any evidence that Somoza was about to step down. He turned to Bowdler for support. Bowdler responded morosely: "It was always a long shot, at best."[3]

Bullshit was the word that came to mind.

When I recalled this episode to Vaky recently, he remembered it only vaguely, though his memory sharpened when I relived the exchange with Bob Pastor. Shaking his head sadly, he observed that the episode was emblematic of U.S. policy during the Nicaraguan crisis. "We were always behind the curve."[4] As Vaky and I continued to discuss the U.S. response to the political turmoil convulsing Nicaragua in the late seventies, this became a familiar refrain: "We were always behind the curve."

The Nicaraguan crisis grabbed Washington's attention on January 10, 1978. Before then it appeared to many that the Somoza dynasty could go on forever. On that morning, Pedro Joaquín Chamorro, the stately and robust editor of *La Prensa,* followed the route he traveled every day. He paused at a neighborhood Catholic church before driving through earthquake-scarred downtown Managua for a meeting with his editorial staff.

Death and torture seemed to have shadowed him all his life. But his international renown as the most outspoken and eloquent opponent to Somoza, appeared to protect the fifty-three-year-old editor. Unless Somoza wanted to create a powerful martyr, he wouldn't touch a hair on Chamorro's head.

As Chamorro approached busy Avenida Kennedy, a man driving a Chevy rammed his Saab from behind. Their bumpers locked and Chamorro screeched to a stop. As he hit the curb, a green Toyota pickup pulled alongside on Chamorro's left. Three men jumped out and fired shotguns point blank. Chamorro slumped over the steering wheel with twenty-six pieces of buckshot in his body.

He was rushed to Hospital Oriental, but it was too late. Radio bulletins flashed the news. By the time Chamorro's son, Pedro Joaquín, Jr., arrived at the hospital, a crowd of 40,000 people had gathered. It took five hours for the car bearing Chamorro's body to reach his home in the suburb of Las Palmas.

Somoza was distressed. He praised Chamorro as "a man faithful to his principles" and called his assassination "a tragedy for Nicaragua."[5]

Still, people everywhere blamed the dictator for Chamorro's death. "Whether Chamorro was shot to death by supporters of the Somoza dictatorship or by extremists who wanted it to look that way," said the *Mexico City News*, "the tragic result is the same, and the cause is the same—the venomous asphyxiating atmosphere of a dictatorship in which the exercise of freedom is almost tantamount to suicide."[6]

Only two days earlier Pedro Joaquín had received a written threat at *La Prensa*. Perhaps it was a response to a series of articles Chamorro had run about Industrial de Hemoterapia, known as Centro Plasmaferesis—a blood plasma exporting center jointly owned by an exiled Cuban, Dr. Pedro Ramos, and Somoza. Donors at the center were reputedly paid between five and ten dollars for a unit of plasma. The plasma was sold in the United States at a 300 percent markup. Dr. Ramos and Somoza took home a yearly profit of $12 million.

After being exposed in *La Prensa*, Dr. Ramos had sued Chamorro for libel. Only a week before Chamorro was murdered, Ramos lost his suit and moved to Miami. When the assassins were captured days after their heinous act, one confessed that Dr. Ramos had paid him $15,000 to organize the hit.

Chamorro had relished his role as Somoza's chief critic. In an interview published shortly after his death he was prophetic:

> I am very optimistic. I see the end of the Somoza dynasty. The majority of people are against Somoza, except for the government workers. Somoza's regime is near the end because he lost support of the U.S. administration and public opinion in America and Europe. The newspaper now gives the truth about Somoza. He is a thief. He doesn't distinguish between his own interests and the interest of the State.[7]

Chamorro's death sparked a popular insurrection. When Chamorro was buried two days later, a crowd of 50,000 enraged mourners followed his casket. A group split off and surrounded Centro Plasmapheresis. Chanting "Casa de vampiros!" and other anti-Somoza epithets, they battered down the doors and set it on fire. Venting their anger on cars and stores along the route, the mob also destroyed a Somoza-owned textile mill called El Porvenir.

"When Somoza murdered Pedro Joaquín," said Chamorro's friend, the poet Pablo Antonio Cuadra, "the people forgot their fear of death. We saw that we had to do something if we didn't want to end up like him."[8] Certainly the assassination convinced many, especially those who had been reluctant to declare publicly against Somoza, to join the opposition.

Chamorro had won in death a seemingly impossible objective— the unification of the opposition. His political alliance (UDEL), now led by Rafael Cordova Rivas, joined the private-sector business group (COSEP), the Conservative party (PCN), the Nicaraguan Socialist party (PSN), the Independent Banking Group (BANIN), and two trade union associations (CGT-1 and CTN) and called a general strike to demand an investigation of the murder and later Somoza's resignation. On the first day of the strike, January 24, 1978, 80 percent of stores and businesses were closed in León, Granada, Chinandega, Estelí, Masaya, Rivas, and other towns across the nation, and 50 percent closed in Managua. It was the beginning of what Somoza called "the most serious crisis of [his] political career."[9]

The Carter administration, which had been critical of the regime's human rights abuses, backed away further. A planned visit to Managua by Assistant Secretary of State Terence Todman was quickly canceled, and on January 30 the State Department announced that because of continuing human right violations Nicaragua's 1979 military assistance program was being suspended.

Somoza tried to play it cool. As the strike began, he was quoted by the government-controlled newspaper *Novedades:* "As my father said, I will not go, neither will they force me to go."[10] By the second week of February, when the strike was petering out, he sounded more confident. "If I was a merchant and was asked to join in a show of a demand for justice, I probably would. But I'd think again about wanting to upset the whole applecart."[11]

A new, more volatile form of anti-Somoza resistance showed its face on February 20, 1978, when Monimbo, an Indian enclave in

In Managua, passengers flee a bus that has been tear-gassed by the National Guard. *Credit:* Benoit Gysembergh Camera Press, London 24584-6 (87) Globe Photos, Inc. 1993

the city of Masaya, rose in revolt after the Guardia Nacional tried to disperse the crowd at a memorial mass for Pedro Joaquín Chamorro. The heavy-handed methods of the Guardia had gone too far. "A government helicopter started dropping tear gas," remembered housewife María Chavarría. "They didn't care that the people were being asphyxiated. It was horrible!"[12]

The proud residents of Monimbo fought back with sticks, knives, homemade contact bombs, hunting rifles, and pistols. "I remember my son came back in the house looking for one of the masks that belonged to my father that we wore for the fiesta of Tata Chombito," said María Chavarría. "He put the mask on and said: 'Now we'll show the Guardia who's got balls, and this time they won't be up against some assholes.' "[13]

María Chavarría continued: "That day the red and black handkerchiefs came out. We all started to join the fighting. We all put up barricades to stop the Guard. The problem was we only had a few pistols, but that didn't matter. We said: 'Either we win, or we all die.' "[14]

By the second day, fires burned throughout Monimbo as the Guardia fought back. It took a week of tough fighting and 600 troops with air and armored support to retake the barrio. The Red Cross estimated that 200 civilians died in the fighting.

Monimbo became a rallying cry for other towns and barrios across the country. Within days there were uprisings in Diriamba, Jinotepe, and the Subtiava Indian barrio of León. Suddenly, the political climate had shifted against Somoza in a dramatic way. People were taking action. Every week brought news of another student strike, Sandinista action, or campesino land seizure.

By the end of June, Somoza was getting nervous. In a nod to public opinion in the United States and the hemisphere, the dictator invited the Inter-American Human Rights Commission to visit Nicaragua and allowed Los Doce (the Twelve)—a political front organization created by the Tercerista faction of the Sandinistas—to return to Nicaragua.[15] Many of Somoza's advisers considered the second move a mistake. When Los Doce arrived at Managua's airport, a crowd of 30,000 gathered to cheer them on. Their first stop as they toured the country was Monimbo, where they vowed to work within the newly formed Broad Opposition Front (FAO) to pressure Somoza to resign.

In the meantime, the Sandinistas were planning a dramatic strike of their own—Operación Chanceria (Operation Pigsty). It was the brainchild of longtime guerrilla Edén Pastora. "I'm not sure if it was in '70 or '71," said Pastora,

> but I remember it was at the time when the Frente had such limited resources that we had spent three days almost not eating. We fed ourselves with turtles we'd caught fishing and iguanas. . . . It was one of those nights when we had nothing for supper, and so we went to bed with a glass of thick coffee. I tell you sometimes hunger does wonders. Maybe it was combination of black coffee on an empty stomach that didn't let me sleep all night. I was just thinking about where to get money to eat, when the idea of taking over the Palace came to me. During that night I planned how it could be done.[16]

While Los Doce were triumphantly touring the country and Somoza's Guardia was putting down the resulting riots, a group of Sandinistas disguised as divinity students were busy training at a farm on the outskirts of Managua. Twenty-nine-year-old Walter Ferrety was one of the leaders. "In all we had twenty-five soldiers

divided into two groups. One was under the command of Dora
María Tellez (Comandante Dos) and Edén Pastora (Cero) and the
other was under the command of Hugo Torres (Uno) and myself
(Tres)."[17]

The operation was so clandestine that Dora María Tellez was informed only two days before it was to happen. Arriving at the
farm, she quickly assessed the preparedness of the group:

> I thought the training by Hugo and Edén was a little superficial.
> So in those two days we trained them to arm and disarm, reload,
> etcetera. . . . The most important thing we taught them was the-
> ater. Edén has great capacity for that. He has a great dramatic
> talent and the *compañeros* had to learn their parts.[18]

The plan called for twenty-five commandos to enter the palace
disguised as members of the Guardia. Trucks were found and
arms and uniforms smuggled to the farm in vats used by a candy
factory. Walter Ferrety remembers spending hours cleaning cara-
mel off the uniforms and rifles:

> We wanted the trucks painted olive green, but the compañero
> who painted them used a brilliant green color, which didn't look
> like any military color at all. We took turns giving each other
> haircuts to look like the Guardia. Then we dressed and armed
> ourselves and drove to the Palace, in the very center of Managua,
> in two trucks. It was 12:30 in the afternoon, August 22, 1978.[19]

Luis Pallais Debayle, Somoza's cousin, was sitting as acting
president of the Chamber of Deputies. He remembers being concerned that only four or five guards were on duty. The government had received information that the palace might be attacked.
Pallais called the bunker. For some reason, the sixty-man Guardia
special detail had not arrived.

Arriving instead through the main and side entrances were the
twenty-five Sandinistas in disguise. The palace guards suspected
nothing. When one asked what was happening, Pastora snapped
back: "Keep quiet, the *jefe* is coming."[20]

Pastora climbed the marble stairs to the Chamber of Deputies.
At the ornate emerald green doors, two guards waited with their
weapons ready. The Sandinistas quickly killed one and disarmed

the other. As they burst through the Chamber door, Pastora fired in the air. "The Guardia. Everyone to the floor!"[21] Pallais and the other fifty-eight deputies obeyed.

Walter Ferrety (Tres) was given the special assignment of capturing José Mora, the minister of interior, who controlled the police and prisons where many of the Sandinistas had been tortured. "Once inside the Palace we ran upstairs and banged on every door, looking for Mora's office," Ferrety said. "And when we found the door was locked, we had to kick a hole in it. We ordered those inside to come out through the hole. And this fat Minster Mora said to me, 'How can I pass through that?' And I told him, 'Pass through or die,' and he crawled through on his hands and knees."[22]

After months of planning, the Sandinistas had seized the national palace. Twenty-five commandos were holding fifty-nine deputies and some 1,200 to 2,000 other office workers and visitors. When Somoza's helicopters strafed the building, the Sandinistas "gathered the most prized Somocista prisoners and placed them in front of the windows," according to Pastora.[23]

Somoza was not amused. "When I think of their barbaric behavior, it reminds me of the horrible stories of the Middle Ages," he recalled.[24]

"They were trembling with fear and believed that the Guardia was going to kill them without further thought," Pastora remembered. "It was at this moment that Luis Pallais telephoned Somoza and asked him not to leave them to die."[25]

"Luis told me that, as he talked, a gun was being held to his head," wrote Somoza. "I remember very well hearing the voice of Edén Pastora, known as Comandante Cero screaming out orders. . . . I also remember the voice of Dora María Tellez, the only woman in that room, telling Pastora to calm down."[26]

At the commandos' direction, Archbishop Obando y Bravo, delivered their demands—the release of fifty-nine political prisoners, publication of a series of FSLN communiques, and $10 million in cash. According to Luis Pallais, Somoza was more concerned about reducing the money demand than the other two.

Forty-eight tense hours later, a deal was struck. Somoza agreed to release about fifty political prisoners (including Tomás Borge and René Nuñez), pay half a million dollars in cash, and publish a six-page Sandinista communique. The governments of Panama and Venezuela dispatched planes to pick up the freed prisoners and commandos. As they rode in a convoy to the airport, thousands of Nicaraguans lined the route to the airport, chanting, "Down with Somoza!" and "Somoza to the gallows!" Pastora, with his G-3 rifle held high and a grenade hanging from his shirt, was the hero of the day.

Walter Ferrety was overwhelmed. "In that moment the people lost their fear of the Guardia and they clapped and cheered as we drove by," he recalled. "The airport was packed with more people. Emotions were very high and it was like a great celebration of the entire people."[27]

Inspired by this outpouring of anti-Somoza feeling, the FAO called another general strike. Two days later, armed *muchachos* took over the streets of Matagalpa in the north. It took a week of skirmishing, aerial bombardment, and armored assault by elite EEBI (Basic Infantry Training School) units of the Guard to crush about 400 ill-equipped teenagers. On the ninth of September the Tercerista faction of the FSLN launched coordinated attacks on Managua, Masaya, León, Chinandega, and Estelí. Once again, the cities were retaken only after aerial bombing and high civilian casualties.

The United States and its OAS partners realized that something had to be done. At the request of Venezuela, the Sixteenth Meeting of Consultation of Ministers of Foreign Affairs was convened on September 21, 1978. The result was a convoluted resolution stating that the OAS hoped Nicaragua would be willing "in principle, to accept the friendly cooperation and conciliatory efforts that several member states of the Organization may offer toward establishing the condition necessary for a peaceful settlement."[28]

The United States had lobbied for the inclusion of this language so that the OAS could authorize sending a team to Nicaragua to mediate a settlement. When Somoza voiced resistance, our ambassador to Panama, William Jorden, was dispatched to meet with Somoza on September 23 and inform him that Nicaragua's relations with the United States would be negatively affected if Somoza did not accept an OAS-sponsored mediation. Two days later Somoza agreed, but vowed to serve out the rest of his term until March 1981.

William D. Rogers, a distinguished Washington lawyer who served in the Ford administration under Secretary of State Henry Kissinger as assistant secretary for American republic affairs (ARA) and later replaced William Casey as undersecretary for

Assistant Secretary Vaky, Director General of the Foreign Service Harry Barnes, and Ambassador William Bowdler in 1979. *Credit:* Department of State Visual Services Division

economic affairs, had already been approached by the Carter administration to represent the United States on an OAS mediation team. Rogers indicated a willingness to serve on two conditions: One, that he have a face-to-face meeting with President Carter to ensure that he had his full support; and, two, that he be given assurances that the administration was prepared to "go all the way." According to Vaky, Deputy Secretary Warren Christopher tentatively agreed to the conditions. The matter became moot when Somoza refused to accept Rogers.

"He has biased opinions about the Somoza family," the dictator said to Ambassador Jorden.[29] Somoza recalled that it was during Rogers's tenure as assistant secretary that the level of U.S. support he had become accustomed to had begun to slip away.

Significantly, Rogers saw at the outset that the bottom line in an OAS mediation would come down to the issue of Somoza's departure from office. Short of Somoza's stepping down, it was clear to Rogers and certainly to Vaky, there was no other viable, peaceful solution to the Nicaraguan crisis.

Others in the administration did not see it that way. The State Department's Director of Policy Planning Anthony Lake and Robert Pastor of the National Security Council argued against "interventionism." According to Pastor, "our current problems in the region stemmed in part from the history of U.S. interventionism, which although almost always undertaken with good intentions, frequently had adverse effects on U.S. interests and outweighed any shorter-term benefits."[30]

While one could admire the purity of the principle, especially in view of our past interventions, it didn't make sense when dealing with a regime as brutal as Somoza's. Nor was the principle honest in the context of the OAS mediation. For OAS members understood that the United States was the only country that could exert enough pressure on Somoza to step down. In fact, they expected us, at the critical moment, to do just that. Anyone who knew Somoza accepted the fact that if there was a way to wiggle free and retain power, he would.

William Bowdler, who had been ambassador to El Salvador, Guatemala, and South Africa, as well as deputy assistant secretary of American republic affairs and assistant secretary for intelligence and research, was selected to represent the United States on the OAS mediation team. Hurriedly signing on two experienced career officers—Malcolm Barnebey and James Cheek—Bowdler met in Guatemala City with his OAS counterparts—Alfredo Obiols, former Guatemalan vice foreign minister, and Adm. Ramón Emilio Jiménez of the Dominican Republic—in early October 1978. They saw their task as threefold: to achieve an environment conducive to negotiations; to evaluate the situation and promote direct talks between the government of Nicaragua and the opposition; and ultimately to bring about an agreement leading to a democratic, peaceful, and lasting solution.

The opposition forces, the Frente Amplio Opositora (FAO), spanned the political spectrum from the Partido Communista de Nicaragua (the Communist party) to the Partido Conservador de Nicaragua (the Conservatives), and included the private sector, Los Doce (and unofficially the Tercerista faction of the Sandinistas in the person of Sergio Ramírez), labor, and the Catholic church. Very quickly, and to no one's surprise, the OAS mediators found consensus on one point—the departure of Somoza was seen as a sine qua non for a peaceful resolution to the crisis in Nicaragua.

Bowdler was well aware that FAO members took it as an article of faith that the United States would remove Somoza. He was concerned that this single-mindedness was impeding the FAO from addressing critical issues, such as the type of government that would succeed Somoza and the constitutional process to be followed.

Assistant Secretary Viron (Pete) Vaky with Secretary of State Cyrus Vance *Credit:* Department of State Visual Services Division

The FAO was reluctant to address these issues at first. But, once convinced that the OAS mediators would not move forward without such a comprehensive plan, they proceeded with alacrity and in short order produced a thoughtful and comprehensive transitional framework.

At this point, Los Doce and the Tercerista faction of the Sandinistas grew nervous and pulled out of the negotiations. Los Doce spokesman Father Miguel d'Escoto claimed, "We have realized that the mediation commission did not really want to extract the cancer from our society."[31] The Sandinistas wanted a complete break with the past, one that would require not only Somoza's ouster, but also the disbanding of the Guardia Nacional and expropriation of Somoza's business empire.

The FAO continued without them. The next obstacle, and the one that would ultimately abort the mediation, was the "plebiscite issue." It arose undramatically as one item among several presented to the OAS mediators by the Somoza-controlled Liberal party (PLN). As proposed by the PLN, the plebiscite was not to be a referendum on whether or not Somoza retained the support of the Nicaraguan voters, but rather a measure of the relative popular strength of the PLN and the political parties that made up the FAO. When presented with the idea, the FAO reacted negatively to what they perceived as a stalling tactic.

The OAS mediators met with Somoza on November 7 before returning to their respective capitals. It occurred to them that the plebiscite could be turned into a referendum of Somoza's support. With this in mind, they asked Somoza for the first time if he would consider resigning to facilitate a solution to the crisis. Somoza said he would not, asserting that a plebiscite would demonstrate his wide popular support.

Back in Washington at a Policy Review Committee (PRC) meeting chaired by Secretary of State Cyrus Vance on November 13, Bowdler and Vaky argued against the plebiscite. Bowdler saw it as a blatant stalling tactic. Vaky stated of Somoza, "He's throwing sand in our faces."[32] From the PRC discussion, three options emerged: (1) transform the plebiscite into a vote on Somoza's staying power and negotiate terms that would ensure a free election; (2) dismiss the plebiscite and pressure Somoza to negotiate his departure in accordance with the FAO plan; (3) discontinue the mediation and walk away. The PRC recommended option 1 (with Vance, Christopher, Pastor, and Brzezinski in support); Bowdler and Vaky voted for option 2. Bowdler stated at the time that in his judgment there was a fifty-fifty chance that Somoza would leave if we applied the sanctions proposed in option 2. Option 1 was approved.

The way Robert Pastor saw it, "The career officials—Vaky and Bowdler—were more attuned to the debate in Managua and more disposed to make the opposition's case for pushing Somoza out, whereas the President's appointees were more sensitive to developing a policy that was defensible in the United States and more inclined to advocate a North American approach to solving the problem—elections."[33]

On his return to Nicaragua, Bowdler first had to convince his mediation partners to go along with the U.S. position. The atmosphere in Managua was further heightened by the release of the Inter-American Human Rights Commission's report. The eighty-one-page report was the most critical ever issued by the commission and called upon member nations to impose sanctions against the Somoza regime "for the horrendous crimes committed" and urged them to take "immediate action to prevent a repetition of these acts of genocide."[34]

Having agreed on pursuing the plebiscite, the mediators then had to convince the FAO and Somoza's Liberal party to go along. The FAO was skeptical that a free election could be held in Nicaragua, even with international supervision. The Liberal party argued that the plebiscite as revised violated the Constitution. Despite the reluctance of both parties, the OAS mediators pressed forward and by November 21 were able to elicit terms and conditions for direct talks.

The Somoza government demonstrated its earnestness at this point by declaring a general amnesty for political prisoners and lifting the state of siege. By so doing, it was responding to the FAO's insistence on the creation of a "propitious climate" for negotiations. With the *Washington Post* warning that "all guns are on a hair trigger," discussions resumed December 16.[35] A four-part agenda was accepted by the FAO and Somoza's Liberal party: to be discussed about the plebiscite were its (1) purpose, (2) consequences, (3) conditions, and (4) mechanics.

Both parties agreed on the first point. The purpose of the plebiscite would be to allow the Nicaraguan people to express whether or not they felt Somoza should continue in office. Disagreement surfaced on the second. The FAO took the position that if Somoza was favored, they would remain a peaceful opposition movement but would not participate in the government. If the vote went against Somoza, the FAO demanded that Somoza resign and leave the country with his family. Following a transition of power in keeping with the constitution, a government of national reconciliation would be installed to implement a program designed by the FAO. The constitution would then be reformed as well.

Ironically, Somoza's Liberal party objected strongly to the FAO's unwillingness to join the process of political reconciliation headed by Somoza, should he win. Holding firm to this position, they refused to consider any other agenda items until this issue was resolved.

After careful deliberation, the mediators presented the two parties with a compromise proposal on December 20, 1978. They decided it was useless to try to force the FAO to join a new Somoza government. As a concession to the other side, the new proposal permitted Somoza to stay in Nicaragua during the plebiscite campaign, although his son and half brother would have to leave. The FAO, acting in good faith, accepted the compromise proposal.

Everyone was waiting for Somoza's answer. On December 21, Gen. Dennis McAuliffe, commander of the U.S. Southern Command in Panama, flew in to see Somoza. He was accompanied by Bowdler. General McAuliffe told Somoza that because of the continued political instability and violence, the Joint Chiefs of Staff supported the plebiscite idea. He said the U.S. military leaders did not feel Somoza was cooperating with the mediation. "Speaking very frankly, Mr. President," the general said, "it is our view that peace will not come to Nicaragua until you have removed yourself from the presidency and the scene."[36]

Somoza, the West Pointer, responded: "General, we are fighting people who are not anti-Somoza, but people who have a different ideology than yours or mine. It seems impossible for me to get this point across to the United States."[37]

If Somoza followed the mediator's plan, McAuliffe said, "The leftists and communists will not take over and we will have a moderate government. What I'm saying, Mr. President, is that we will have a moderate government that does not have the name Somoza."[38]

"If the plebiscite is organized along traditional lines," retorted Somoza, "which the people of Nicaragua understand, there will be no problem."[39] Naturally, the opposition disagreed. The FAO was trying to guard against just such a "traditional" election, namely, one in which Somoza committed massive fraud.

A day or two later, Somoza's cousin Luis Pallais recalls, he was summoned into a Cabinet meeting to discuss the December 20 proposal. Uncharacteristically, Somoza didn't say a word. After some debate, the Cabinet voted no. "All Somoza had to do was say yes and the vote would have changed," Pallais recalled. But a number of advisers led by Foreign Minister Julio Quintana "had persuaded Somoza that he would lose a free election and he wanted to stay in power."[40]

Instead of rejecting the compromise proposal outright, Somoza and his Liberal party decided to quibble over its constitutionality, maintaining that the proposed international safeguards over the balloting were unconstitutional. Somoza's political instincts told him that any arguments based on his constitutional position would carry weight in the Carter White House. He was right.

President Carter found Somoza's objection to an international authority over the plebiscite to have merit. Maybe the FAO would go halfway. Could a national authority be established, supervised by an international authority? The FAO was getting nervous. Domestic critics charged that they were being duped by Somoza. Still, President Carter's idea was worth a try.

In early January 1979, Bowdler was prevailed upon once more to return to Managua to try to convince the OAS mediators and the FAO to keep the negotiations alive. He assured them that if the FAO accepted the new compromise and Somoza rejected it, the United States would impose sanctions. Assistant Secretary Vaky asked Pastor and Brzezinski: "Are you people prepared to cross the Rubicon?" They answered yes.[41]

When the OAS mediators delivered their final proposal to Somoza on January 12, 1979, they found no give. In private, Somoza belligerently told Bowdler, "you have been threatening me since January, 1977."[42]

The next week the FAO issued a statement condemning the "brutal intransigence of the dictator" and declaring the mediation closed. The January 19, 1979, headline of *La Prensa* read: "Somoza Buries Mediation." On February first, President Carter signed a memo confirming that the mediation was over and that, because of Somoza's unwillingness to compromise, the United States would impose sanctions against his government. On February 8 the State Department announced the following steps: (1) military assistance to Nicaragua was being terminated and the Military Assistance Group was being withdrawn; (2) current assistance loans were being frozen and no new lending would be approved; (3) the Peace Corps was being recalled; and (4) the embassy staff was being reduced from eighty-two to thirty-seven.

For those who had been watching in Nicaragua and Latin America, the sanctions were too few and too late. Although the onus of the failure of the OAS mediation had been placed squarely on Somoza's shoulders, it was the moderate opposition in Nicaragua (namely, the FAO) who were the big losers. FAO leader Alfonso Robelo expressed the frustrations of the group.

> When the United States put it to Somoza that they wanted him out, they didn't expect him to say no. But what pressure did they use? They used no pressure. If, at that moment, in October, November, December of 1978 they had been ready to put pressures on Somoza, like saying, 'Okay, forget it, you're not going to have a sanctuary in the States' . . . things of this nature or other things they can do, Somoza would have stepped down. . . . We lost the opportunity we had at that time. . . . After that the FAO was left with nothing and the only people who had initiative were those in the violent mode, the FSLN.[43]

Furthermore, FAO members found there was a price to pay for having come forward courageously and having taken a public stand against Somoza's authoritarian regime. That message came through loud and clear when labor leader and FAO member Luis Medrano Flores was gunned down in the streets of Managua on January 9, 1979.

Somoza was through negotiating. In interviews he sounded defiant. "How about those jerks," he told Voice of America correspondent Jack Curtiss. "First they send me this," he said, tossing him a letter from President Carter praising the suspension of the state of siege in 1977, "and then they send an ambassador down here to tell me I have to resign."[44] To Karen DeYoung of the *Washington Post* he lamented the decline of U.S. influence. "They've lost it," he said. "They've spent two years harassing my government. If they remove the military and lower representation, materially I will not lose anything but a few nice gentlemen who are living in Nicaragua."[45]

Somoza assured his cousin Luis Pallais that he would "ride the waves" of U.S. policy. He had used the relative calm of the mediation to beef up his defenses. A major recruiting drive in November and December had increased the size of the Guard from 8,000 to 11,000. He also stockpiled arms. With U.S. arms supplies cut off, Somoza found Israel more than willing to sell him Galil automatic rifles, ammunition, and light trucks. When the United States pressured Israel to stop arm shipments in April, the dictator bought on the black market through South Africa, Argentina, Guatemala, and the Bahamas.

The Sandinistas were also using this time to put their house in order. According to Humberto Ortega: "With the breakdown of the U.S.-sponsored mediation process, the Terceristas abandoned their relative tolerance of negotiations and began to move closer to the positions of their comrades in the other Sandinista tendencies."[46] Leaders of the three tendencies—*Prolonged War,* advocated the slow accumulation of forces in the countryside; the *Proletarians* favored a more strictly Marxist-Leninist approach, building bases of support among union members and barrio dwellers; the *Terceristas* believed in creating alliances with non-Marxist groups and nationalist elements to foment popular insurrection—had been summoned to Havana in December.[47] Fidel Castro made them an offer—stop bickering and cooperate with each other and Cuba will supply arms, ammunition, and logistical support.

On December 9 a joint communique was issued in Havana. The Terceristas agreed to terminate their dialogue with political moderates in return for the Prolonged War group's and the Proletarians' acceptance of their insurrectional strategy. Humberto Ortega would act as de facto commander in chief. "If division provided a broad field of opportunities for the enemy to fight us, unity means restricting the enemy's field of activity," explained FSLN founder Tomás Borge.[48] Three months later, a nine-man combined National Directorate was named, with three men from each tendency. Henceforth, all military units and strategy would be integrated. But true unification was still hampered by lingering personal animosities.

Shortly thereafter, major quantities of supplies began to flow to the Sandinistas via airstrips in Liberia, Costa Rica. There were M-14 and FAL assault weapons from Venezuela, .50- caliber machine guns from Cuba, and uniforms, boots, and mortars from Panama. A great deal of this materiel was smuggled into Nicaragua hidden in cars and trucks in preparation for the final offensive.

Mario Rapaccolli, a successful businessman who sold insecticides, fertilizers, and small farm machinery, told me years later that he was not alone in allowing his warehouses to be used to receive, assemble, and store arms. "Boxes were being trucked in from Costa Rica to my warehouse in Chinandega marked agricultural equipment," he reported. "Each box contained only one part of an automatic weapon to ensure that the Guardia could not make use of them if a shipment was intercepted. The parts were assembled and stored there by my cousin Fernando (Negro) Chamorro, who later fought with Edén Pastora on the Southern Front."[49]

Some ten miles into Costa Rica, Alejandro Murguia, a Chicano from East Los Angeles, was training in a Sandinista camp. One morning he was awakened before dawn and ordered to drive a truck to the Liberia airport. "A DC-8 4-prop cargo plane, all silver streamlined without marking touched down with a thump," he wrote. "The trucks lined up at the two port entrances and the cargo doors swung open. An assembly line was formed for each truck; two *compas* on the plane, two between the plane and the truck ramp, and two more *compas* under the canvas top. The belly of the plane was loaded with heavy wooden crates stamped Fabriqué d'Armes Leger-Belgique."[50]

They discovered fourteen FAL automatic rifles to a crate and plenty of crates full of 7.62 NATO-type ammunition. After loading about seventy-five crates, they were stopped by a Costa Rican Civil Guard at the exit gate. After making a cursory inspection of their truck, he waved them through with, "Good luck, *muchachos.*"[51]

The presidents of Costa Rica and Venezuela, Rodrigo Carazo Odio and Carlos Andrés Pérez, and Panamanian strongman Omar Torrijos had been extremely interested in the outcome of the mediation. All three were convinced that Somoza had to go. Back in September 1978, Torrijos had characterized the Nicaraguan crisis for President Carter—"It's a simple problem. A mentally deranged man with an army of criminals is attacking a defenseless population."[52]

When Vice President Walter Mondale had breakfast with outgoing President Pérez in March 1979, Pérez asked how the United States would get rid of Somoza. Mondale replied that although the United States shared Pérez's distaste for the Somoza regime, it did not intend to depose him. According to Pete Vaky, Pérez, a man who usually didn't show his feelings, was visibly upset. "In that case, blood will flow," he warned.[53]

When the mediation failed, all three threw their full support to the Sandinistas. Costa Rica became, in the words of Humberto Ortega, "an excellent rearguard network that made it possible to . . . end the war quickly."[54] According to a 1981 report issued by a special commission of the Costa Rican Congress, "approximately one million pounds of arms and munitions entered that country between December 1978 and July 1979."[55]

Inexplicably, our intelligence services were unaware of the widespread clandestine supply network. In the dark and without a position, Washington was ineffective. Robert Pastor concluded, "It would have been logical to review the differences in the positions between the FAO and Somoza on the plebiscite more closely, because a plebiscite remained the only apparent method of moving Somoza out."[56] Brzezinski, the National Security Council, and others in the administration turned their attention away from Nicaragua and focused on Iran, China, and the SALT talks in Geneva. They hoped the crisis in Nicaragua would go away.

Vaky left the OAS mediation exhausted and admitted he "didn't know what to do." "Sound options had disappeared," he lamented. "The bureaucracy was numb."[57] This should have been a clear sign that something was wrong. If any foreign service officer who specialized in Latin America deserved being considered the "best and the brightest," it was Pete Vaky. Admired by his peers, subordinates, and supervisors because of his exceptional intellectual and diplomatic skills and ethical standards, Pete had moved up through the ranks of the foreign service from 1949 until 1972 when he was selected for the ambassadorship to Costa Rica at the relatively young age of forty-seven.

As in all his previous assignments, he stood out among his colleagues in the Latin American region—as he dealt, for example, with the nettlesome case of stock manipulator and Nixon campaign financier Robert Vesco, who had fled to evade charges of fraud. From Costa Rica, Pete went on to become ambassador to Colombia and, then, to Venezuela. By mid-1978, when he was summoned to Washington to head the ARA Bureau, which had fallen into another of its characteristic troughs, Vaky's knowledge of and experience in Latin America were exceptional.

I was serving as ambassador to Uruguay at the time of Vaky's appointment as assistant secretary, and I recall my delight and that of my colleagues on hearing the news. In our view, that amorphous, depersonalized, and seemingly mindless entity that we called "the system" had sputtered and shaken and had actually made an intelligent decision for a change. You could almost hear the collective sigh of relief in embassies throughout the hemisphere.

Among the crises Vaky inherited, none was more pressing than the upheaval in Nicaragua. And he plunged in with his characteristic single-mindedness. It was almost as if destiny had selected him to fill this key position at a critical moment in history. There was no one more suited to the challenge.

To my mind, the rarest of all individuals is the natural, or instinctual leader. Vaky didn't need exhaustive briefings or reams of analytical reports to reach the judgment early on that Nicaragua would continue in turmoil until it was rid of Somoza. He recognized at the outset that the quicker this was accomplished, the greater the likelihood that moderate elements in Nicaraguan society would play an important role in the post-Somoza government. The longer it took, accompanied by continuing and escalating violence, the more the political center of gravity would shift to violent extremists.

Vaky knew that Somoza had to be induced to step down. He also understood that it would be up to the United States, alone or in concert with other Latin countries, to pressure Somoza. The OAS mediation, in Vaky's view, offered a viable means of achieving this objective. The FAO felt that way, as did presidents Carlos Andrés Pérez and Rodrigo Carazo Odio, and General Omar Torrijos. Even Somoza, according to his cousin Luis Pallais, saw the handwriting on the wall and was expecting the Carter administration to deliver the coup de grace. Had President Carter at the end of 1978 summoned Somoza to the White House and urged him to resign, Pallais is convinced that Somoza would have complied.[58]

When the proverbial window of opportunity afforded by the OAS mediation was closed, despite all of his efforts to move the administration, Pete Vaky suffered a letdown that was palpable to those who knew him best. When the United States could have done the right thing and spared tremendous suffering and bloodshed, we failed.

At the end of 1979, still a relatively young man and at the top of his career, Pete Vaky surprised a lot of his colleagues by retiring.

4

If you plan on eating the chicken, you have to hide the feathers.
—Anastasio (Tacho) Somoza García

The United States ambassador's residence, an ungainly structure, faintly reminiscent of an antebellum Mississippi River plantation manor, was built after World War II on land overlooking the city of Managua given to us by Anastasio Somoza García. Over the intervening thirty some years, it had been subjected to the whimsical decorating tastes of various ambassadors' wives. Even the greatest of architectural masterpieces would be hard-pressed to withstand such a fate. The house had been added to, its numerous porches and porticos enclosed, and it had been secured against surprise attack.

The master bedroom, at the instigation of my predecessor, had been attack-proofed by the addition of metal shutters and armored plating. The door had been made grenade-resistant. Standing in the middle of the room was an elaborate console, complete with video monitors, which allowed the occupant to shoot tear gas at unwelcome visitors. Imagine all this to inspire sound ambassadorial slumber. The trouble was, you couldn't breathe in the damned place.

The last time I had been in Managua, a few months after the 1972 earthquake, the embassy staff—many of them homeless after the disaster—operated out of tents pitched on the residence grounds. The ambassador's wife, Mrs. Turner Shelton, had gained notoriety for putting concern for her rose beds over the comfort of embassy personnel. She adamantly refused to allow them the privilege of using the residence's bathroom facilities. Latrines were dug at a proper protocolary distance. At least one Nicaraguan female employee found the experience degrading enough to quit.

The situation now, in late June 1979, was severely different. Most of the embassy staff was living in the residence, camped four or five to a room. Their families had already been evacuated. Parts of the city were under attack. Other areas were not considered safe, and we never knew when we might have to clear out—fast. There was an advantage in keeping most of the staff in one place. For one, we could provide them with the little security we could depend on. Our old protectors from the Guardia were turning more sullen and edgy. Americans hadn't been singled out as targets, but in a situation this confusing and volatile, no one felt like taking chances.

Only a week earlier, on June 20, ABC News correspondent Bill Stewart, while covering the fighting in Managua's northeastern slums, had been ordered to lie down in the street and was shot in the head by a Guardia sergeant. His murder was videotaped and broadcast on the evening news in the United States. Even Somoza's friends were outraged. A group of U.S. congressmen and senators issued a declaration calling him "the Idi Amin of Latin America."[1]

From the high vantage point of the residence, we could watch the battle for Managua as it raged through the night. Observing this terrifyingly beautiful display of tracer bullets and exploding gasoline bombs, I felt a strange sense of déjà vu. Somehow my darkest premonitions and those of many of my American and Nicaraguan friends had come to pass.

Six and half years earlier, two days before Christmas 1972, downtown Managua was leveled by two devastating seismic shocks. Electricity, water, and telephone service was cut off immediately. Within hours 10,000 people perished. Of some 75,000 homes, 90 percent were destroyed. The devastation was so complete that the downtown was never rebuilt. It remains a desolate grid of broken, potholed streets and patches of overgrown rubble.

According to an eyewitness: "Downtown Managua became a scene out of Dante. Near the Lake Managua shorefront, the earth opened to swallow buildings, jeeps, everything. All stores, restaurants, offices, and homes within a two-mile radius of Avenida Central were destroyed. Masonry structures collapsed on their occupants; wooden ones, tender after a long drought, burst into flames."[2] At the modern Intercontinental Hotel, the ninth floor restaurant bounced four feet into the air and came crashing down, sending hotel guests, including the reclusive billionaire Howard Hughes, running for safety. The next morning the city was under a pall of smoke and red dust.

"The spectacle was horrible," recalled a Nicaraguan who arrived in Managua two days after the quake. "You could see that the whole city was in flames. . . . It made quite an impression seeing whole families sitting on the ground at the edge of what had been their homes, on the sidewalks, some with dead bodies beside them, and apparently totally indifferent. It was as if they were dead."[3]

Anarchy prevailed for three days as Guardia soldiers left their posts to search for their loved ones or to pillage. The spectacle of the Guardia virtually decomposing during a major crisis left an indelible mark on all Nicaraguans. Businessmen and merchants, who expected Guardia soldiers to protect them, watched as they joined in the looting of their homes and stores.

Tachito Somoza, shaken but not hurt, was afraid to leave his 100-acre suburban estate, "El Retiro." Feeling dangerously exposed, he appealed to U.S. Ambassador Turner B. Shelton, who called the U.S. Southern Command in Panama. Five hundred U.S. troops were dispatched immediately. They bivouacked in the garden of "El Retiro" until order was restored.

When the earthquake struck, Anastasio (Tachito) Somoza Debayle was commander of the Guardia Nacional. Although his term as president had expired in May 1972, there was no doubt in anyone's mind who wielded power. To preserve the veneer of legality behind which the Somoza dynasty flourished, Tachito had made a deal with the leader of the opposition Conservative party, Fernando Aguero. Under the Nicaraguan constitution, a president could not succeed himself. So Somoza relinquished executive authority to a three-man transitional government—Aguero, a retired general, and a member of his National Liberal party—until a new constitution could be written and elections held. Of course, Tachito retained his position as commander of the Guardia Nacional.

Astute observers saw this Somoza ploy for what it was—legal hocus-pocus to perpetuate his political control, which would result in his predictable reelection, with the Guardia as campaign enforcers. Aguero's gullibility in agreeing to Tachito's "pact" split the Conservative party and marked the decline of Aguero as a viable and respected opposition figure.

When the earthquake hit, Somoza immediately seized control. The triumvirate was pushed aside and ignored. Aguero accused Somoza of usurping authority and, tucking his tail between his legs, retreated to his home in Masaya to lick his wounds. Hardly anyone outside Nicaragua took notice.

Naturally, the focus of attention was the horrifying death and destruction caused by the earthquake. There was an urgent need for competent authority to address the emergency. Victims needed to be attended to, rubble had to be cleared, food and medicines had to be distributed, and, ultimately, the arduous task of reconstruction begun.

Somoza gave the impression of a leader superbly suited to the job. Drawing on his military training at West Point, he organized the emergency effort along the lines of a military campaign. He formed a National Reconstruction Committee headed by you-know-who, which was divided into subcommittees dealing with food distribution, planning, rubble removal, and so forth. In practice, however, Tachito directed everything down to the smallest detail. To hear him tell it, this was necessary because, as he claimed paternally, "I know my people . . . and what they are capable of."[4]

Somoza's actions hardly masked his interest in retaining power and taking advantage of the generous humanitarian assistance that began pouring into Nicaragua from the international community and development banks to further enrich himself and his circle of cronies. What he failed to see was how isolated he had become from the realities of Nicaraguan society. His blindness would cost him dearly.

At the time, I was deputy director of the Office of Central American Affairs in the State Department. Earlier in the year I had visited Nicaragua and met Somoza. He was always solicitous of visiting Washington officials, even someone of my modest rank. Tachito had learned from his father that the political fortunes of their dynasty depended in large measure on maintaining close, friendly ties with the United States. He used this friendship, especially his purported access to officials in high places, to intimidate the national opposition and enhance his prestige among the parochial military leaders of Central America. Having deftly cultivated his West Point classmates over the years, Tachito was able to trade heavily on his "friends" in the U.S. Congress and the Department of Defense. Despite his claims, however, the Somoza dynasty was merely tolerated by most U.S. administrations. However, on occasion, such as when Tachito's brother Luis allowed Nicaraguan territory to serve as a training and staging area for the Bay of Pigs invasion, the Somozas were convenient allies.

The Nixon White House was an exception. Tachito was *simpatico* with confidantes of President Nixon, including his close friend Bebe Reboso. When Nixon dispatched Turner B. Shelton as ambassador to Nicaragua in 1970, Shelton had instructions to promote neighborly relations. Shelton went even further than instructed. He was completely won over by Tachito.

When I visited Managua in 1972, Ambassador Shelton and I had a short meeting with Somoza in which Tachito spent most of his time trying to convince me that he was the United States' best friend in Latin America. Throughout the session Ambassador Shelton kept referring to Somoza as "Mr. President." He wasn't the president anymore. I reminded our ambassador of this in the car as we drove away. He dismissed it as "a habit."

When a new twenty cordoba note was minted in 1974, Ambassador Shelton was pictured on the face of the bill with his head bowed to Somoza. It quickly became know as a *sapo*. In Nicaraguan slang a *sapo* is a toady.

But embassy officers who maintained ties with key figures in the Catholic church, the university, opposition parties, the private sector, and the press—especially Pedro Joaquín Chamorro, the charismatic editor of *La Prensa*—recognized Somoza's weaknesses. Their reporting pulled no punches. Certainly, embassy officials concluded, we shouldn't let Tachito use us to back up his domination of Nicaragua.

The United States' response to natural disasters does us proud as a nation. We react with generosity and efficiency. Nicaragua is a case in point. Hours after the earthquake, a U.S. military survey team from Panama was in Managua assessing the extent of the destruction and priority needs. The embassy staff, supplemented by technical advisers from Washington and Panama, quickly developed an assistance strategy. It was two-phased: first, emergency humanitarian relief to treat the wounded, prevent the outbreak of epidemics, provide emergency food supplies and housing, and clear the rubble; second, a reconstruction effort to get the capital back on its feet.

Problems of personnel and administration at the embassy, resulting for the most part from Ambassador Shelton's hapless leadership, stimulated a series of exploratory visits to Managua by Washington-based officers. My turn came in February 1973.

Soon after I arrived, Ambassador Shelton informed me that Somoza had requested a meeting. (I suspected that Shelton had suggested it to Somoza rather than the other way around.) Nevertheless, the meeting was routine. Tachito played the role of self-sacrificing, indispensable leader.

On the second day of my visit, the embassy's economic and commercial officer, Tom O'Donnell, recommended a get-together with business leaders. The Nicaraguan private sector had the usual chambers—commerce, industry, professionals—organized under an umbrella organization called COSIP (Consejo Superior de la Initiativa Privada). O'Donnell warmed me to expect COSIP leaders to be critical of Somoza's handling of the humanitarian relief and reconstruction effort. Even so, I was not fully prepared.

We met in shirtsleeves in a private house on the outskirts of the inner-city devastation. Those who attended were remarkably young, the oldest in his forties. They all spoke English, and most were graduates of U.S. universities. I was struck by the incongruity of this high-quality human talent in such a severely underdeveloped country.

The president of COSIP, Alfonso Robelo Callejas, a merchant who had made millions in cooking oil and cotton, spoke for the group. He wasted no time in articulating the private sector's concerns, which went something like this:

> As businessmen operating in Nicaragua, we have become conditioned to working with Somoza and his corrupt crowd. Business has been relatively good. We have accepted ineffective government and have been conditioned to pay graft to Somoza and his associates to be allowed to survive. We had no other choice. But the earthquake has changed the situation drastically. We face a national disaster. For the first time in our lives, we need a government that functions. There is no question that we have within the private sector the best technical expertise that exists in Nicaragua. We're willing to work without compensation to help plan

and implement a national reconstruction program. Every member of the private sector has been affected. Some businesses have been completely destroyed. We have personal, nationalistic, and business interests in helping to bring about a speedy recovery. But Somoza has frozen us out because he and his cronies see a golden opportunity to enrich themselves. We are witnessing the rape of our country at a time of desperate need. We no longer trust our government. If Somoza refuses to change, the national tragedy will be compounded.[5]

The conversation went on for several hours. At one point, I suggested that COSIP petition Somoza publicly. "It was pointless," they answered. "We've made every effort to cooperate, but at every overture, we've been turned away."[6]

I urged them to continue their efforts. I would explore ways in which the United States might help. After all, the United States had mounted an enormous assistance program and had an interest—indeed, a responsibility—to ensure that its aid contributed to the national recovery and was not being used to enrich certain individuals, especially those associated with the Somoza government.

Somoza asked to see me again before I left Nicaragua. Following the sessions with COSIP, I raised the private sector's complaints with Ambassador Shelton. He jumped to Somoza's defense—Somoza was sensitive to the needs of the country and was sacrificing himself, even at the risk of his own health. According to Ambassador Shelton, the private-sector leaders I had talked to were only interested in "lining their own pockets."

But, I asked myself, shouldn't a government facing a national emergency make maximum use of its resources? If it didn't, one had to ask why not? There was much more at play than personalities. This was a time to see beyond petty concerns. Anything that enhanced the recovery effort had to be viewed as a plus. As things stood, Somoza was refusing help from an important sector of society which had outstanding talent to offer and a vital interest in quick recovery. Why would any leader want to put himself in so vulnerable a position?

We met for breakfast at Somoza's suburban estate and office, "El Retiro," the morning of my departure. He wasted no time with formalities. He knew whom I had spoken to and probably what we had discussed. He asked if I had gained any insights from my visit that he might find helpful.

I told him I had little respect for instant experts who think they know it all after a short visit to a country. But I would venture one observation. Even a cursory study of the revolutionary movements that had displaced the established orders in the American colonies, France, Russia, China, Vietnam, and Cuba revealed that they were not led by the urban or rural poor. Their leaders came from the urban middle class—intellectuals, businessmen, professionals, and students. Revolutions were made by individuals aware of and reacting violently to conditions that they considered unacceptable, not by those overwhelmed by the exigencies of life. If that applied to Nicaragua, Somoza had the portents of a major problem. I quickly reviewed the grievances of the private sector and recommended he demonstrate his leadership by channeling these frustrations into constructive programs.

Somoza put down his cigar and shook his head sadly. "You've been talking to the cry-babies." The problem, he explained, was not as simple as the COSIP leaders thought. "They see it only from the perspective of their private business interests, whereas I have to consider the national needs."[7] Once again, I challenged him to invite the private sector to contribute, thus ensuring that all available resources were being used to the fullest extent possible. Somoza was clearly bored. He thanked me and, excusing himself, left to attend to the real problems at hand.

Returning to Washington, I reported my concerns. Further efforts were made to move Somoza toward accepting broader participation in the reconstruction effort. For the benefit of his Washington audience, Somoza went through the motions of involving the private sector, but never got to the heart of the matter.

It required no prescience to recognize that the seeds of discontent were being gratuitously sown. Many of my colleagues in the State Department and our embassy in Managua continued to remind Ambassador Shelton and the White House of the mistakes being made and the need to pressure Somoza. Warnings were also offered by journalists like Bernard Diederich of *Time* and Jerry O'Leary of the *Washington Star*.

While most Nicaraguans were trying to put together the shards of their broken lives, Somoza saw another opportunity to solidify his political control and enrich himself. AID funds from the United States and other donor countries were not crudely skimmed off. Somoza was too shrewd to be caught with his hand in the cookie jar. Instead, financial aid that was meant for reconstruction was channeled through Tachito's banks; materials for reconstruction were manufactured by his businesses. Those parts of Managua that were rebuilt were built on Somoza's land or on that of his cronies. He made a huge profit, for instance, on one parcel of land that was sold as a site for refugee housing.

La Prensa editor Chamorro was enraged: "Is it possible that while hundreds of children die from dysentery, from the squalor that the earthquake produced, that our society continues to indulge in these archaic, grandiose business arrangements made at the official level, at the expense of social needs? They can say that the transactions are legal. They can also justify the price of a square yard and provide dates of acquisition before the earthquake, but they can never explain the fundamental question: Is it not incredible that after a tragedy like the one of December 23rd there can be such commerce, such trade, with the lives of the homeless and their children?"[8]

Even Tachito's oldest son, Anastasio (El Chiguín), a recent graduate of Harvard Business School, got in on the action. Like a good Somoza, the twenty-two-year-old donned a uniform and started barking orders at the airport, directing relief supplies into Somoza warehouses. When Spain offered Nicaragua an $80 million line of credit for the purchase of jeeps, tractors, and parts of Spanish make, "Captain Earthquake" (as he was known) became the representative.

To large numbers of Nicaraguans in the private sector, in the news media, universities, and political opposition, the 1972 earthquake revealed Somoza for what he was—a greedy, self-serving despot who stood in the way of political, economic, and social development in Nicaragua.

His self-hatred was often barely disguised. "You are just human beings like I am—you're a bunch of shits," he confided to a group of foreign journalists one drunken afternoon.[9] And his contempt for his own people informed many of his decisions. "All right, what the fuck is good for this goddamn underdeveloped country?" he asked the same gathering.[10]

Had Anastasio Somoza Debayle not been so blindly self-serving, corrupt, and insensitive, the Somoza regime theoretically could have faded into the background and permitted a more democratic system to take its place. His brother, Luis, who preceded him in the presidency following the assassination of their father, talked openly of wanting to move in that direction. Tachito wasn't convinced.

When his father was gunned down in León in 1956, Anastasio Somoza Debayle was visiting New York City with his wife, Hope. She had been trying to convince her husband to run the family's shipping business from Manhattan. Shocked by the tragic news, Tachito immediately flew back to Managua, declared his father the victim of a communist conspiracy, and began arresting thousands of Nicaraguans. Even by Nicaraguan standards, the repression was extreme.

Pedro Joaquín Chamorro Cardenal, editor of the Conservative opposition daily *La Prensa* was one of the first to be detained. For months, his whereabouts unknown to his family, Chamorro was subjected to a series of questioning-torture sessions in the sewing room of the presidential palace. Tachito, as head of the Guardia, frequently took part in the interrogations.

"They stripped me completely," Chamorro recalled in his book *Estirpe Sangrienta: Los Somoza* (Bloody Stock: The Somozas): "made me squat with a lighted cigarette in my mouth, until I finished it, until I chewed it up and burned my mouth, squatting until I felt intense pain in my knees and fell for the first time. Then I received a hail of blows from fists and booted feet. . . . I especially remember those below the belt."[11]

Fortunately, Chamorro escaped the more diabolical tortures suffered by his companions—repeated near drownings, being lifted and dragged by a cord tied around the genitals, or time spent in the Somoza's private zoo, where prisoners were kept in cages with lions and panthers in the palace garden.

Chamorro remembered: "In front of these animal cages strolled the current president of the dynasty, Luis Somoza, and his brother Anastasio, with their wives, relatives, and children. From the end of the garden where I was being held . . . several times I saw their innocent children, carrying their dolls and toys, pass before the cages where men lived together with the beasts. More than once I saw children of the palace servants pass before them, their young faces revealing a mixture of pain and astonishment caused by this spectacle."[12]

While Tachito was eliciting confessions, Luis, who had been elected by acclamation of Congress, was gaining a reputation for openness and was stirring hopes for liberalization. Compared to his brother Anastasio, "Luis decidedly deserved to be called 'Luis the Courteous,' " wrote Chamorro. "His brother killed and Luis made excuses. Anastasio witnessed the terrible drama of torture and death, while Luis gave the courteous explanations to the families of the dead and tortured."[13]

Luis, the more politically sophisticated of the two, was convinced that he should extricate the family from direct control of the country. He understood that the Somoza name had already become anathema to the opposition. He sent members of the Somozas' National Liberal party to Mexico to study the workings of the Partido Revolucionario Independiente (PRI), which had dominated Mexican politics since 1929. Why not rule through the National Liberal party, "changing the monkey" (or puppet president), as he called it, every five years?

In April 1958, Luis Somoza even introduced a constitutional amendment barring him, or anyone related to him by blood "up to the fourth degree," from succeeding himself as president. He declared: "It is my intention to retire at the end of my elected term and to deliver my robe of office to the man who wins the majority of votes in the election of 1963."[14]

Tachito had other ideas. Like his father, he believed that the Somozas' only reliable guarantee of power was the Guardia Nacional. But he lacked his father's political finesse. Leopoldo Salazar, who had been an aide to the elder Somoza, explained:

> The difference with the Somozas is, I believe, if I'm not mistaken, as follows—Tacho, the old man, Tacho Somoza García, he was a remarkable, charming fellow . . . nice-looking and he was more liked than disliked; Luis, he was a goody-goody and very moderate and everybody liked him; but Tachito, he was more aggressive. I knew him as a kid, and later on he was accused of being even blood-thirsty. Nobody liked the young Anastasio Somoza Debayle. Hardly anybody liked him. He was too arrogant.[15]

In 1961, President Kennedy, recognizing the need for change in Latin America, launched the Alliance for Progress, an ambitious economic and military assistance program. Fearing the onslaught of other political movements like the one that brought Fidel Castro to power in 1960, he warned: "Those who make peaceful revolution impossible will make violent revolution inevitable."[16] He challenged Latin American dictators to reform.

Tachito and Luis clashed over how to handle their Yanqui patrons. Luis insisted that Washington's current mood ruled out any return to old Tacho's style of government. Tachito felt that Washington would overlook the dynasty's authoritarian approach if it proved a reliable anticommunist ally. Both approaches had validity.

As a sideline of the cold war, the Central Intelligence Agency (CIA) had already enlisted Nicaragua as a staging area for their overthrow of the socialist regime of Jacobo Arbenz in Guatemala in 1956. In January 1961, when Tachito traveled to Washington to attend Kennedy's inauguration, he claimed it was a cover for his meeting with CIA director Allen Dulles. The Somozas had already been asked to provide training bases for anti-Castro rebels who were planning an invasion of Cuba. Dulles wanted to know: "Now, General, what is it that you want out of this?"[17]

As Tachito told it, "Dulles pulled on his pipe and let out a cloud of tobacco smoke when I told him, 'Nothing, Mr. Dulles, not a damned thing.' He was very cordial and assured me that the project would continue. Reassuring him, I said, 'We are brother officers.' Then because of the enormous pull Dulles had with the new administration I did say: 'Mr. Dulles, you could do one thing. You can tell those Liberals [in Washington] to get off my back and get off the back of Luis Somoza's government.' "[18]

Luis Somoza's efforts to liberalize behind puppet President René Schick pleased Washington, and Alliance for Progress funds flowed. The economic effect was dramatic. During the first half of the 1960s, Nicaragua's gross national product increased by 40 percent, the highest rate of growth in Central America. Thirty million dollars was spent on the construction of 350 miles of roads to facilitate dairy and beef production and reduce the country's dependence on cotton. The Somozas were not as heavily invested in cotton as they were in cattle. The middle-entrepreneur class grew and benefited from the economic integration that resulted from the establishment of the Central American Common Market in the early sixties.

In addition to economic aid, U.S. military assistance to the Guardia Nacional increased sevenfold. Aid included substantially improved equipment (helicopters, fighters, cargo planes, trucks, and communications gear) and personnel training (for jungle warfare, counterinsurgency, and police action). As a safeguard against the spread of communism, the U.S. tried to integrate the Nicaraguan armed forces into a hemispheric defense plan. In 1961 Nicaragua joined the Central American Defense Council (CONDECA), which included all the Central American nations with the exception of Costa Rica. CONDECA, a unified Central American regional command equipped and trained to coordinate with the U.S. Army's Panama-based Southern Command, was designed to protect against a possible Cuban invasion, to secure regional supply and communication routes, and to conduct anticommunist counterinsurgency and "civic action."

With improved training, transport, and communication, Tachito was able to easily squash two rebel incursions. The first crossed the Honduran border in 1958, lead by Ramón Raudales, a sixty-two-year-old lieutenant of Sandino's. Raudales was dead within a month, of a bullet to the head. The second, an airborne invasion, was launched in 1961 by Pedro Joaquín Chamorro and gynecologist Enrique Lacayo Farfan. Surrounded by the Guardia and unable to enlist peasant support in the southwestern province of Chontales, they surrendered after fifteen days.

Meanwhile, Tachito's appetite for power grew. When President Schick's term expired in 1967, Tachito prevailed upon his brother Luis to let him receive the National Liberal party nomination, even though it meant he had to give up his title as head of the Guardia. Many of those close to the Somozas thought this was a mistake. Luis Somoza, who ran his brother's campaign, told his cousin Luis Pallais: "It will be easier getting Tachito in than it will be to get him out."[19] Still, Tachito's election wasn't realized without widespread electoral fraud. Ballots were counted in Guardia barracks, the opposition was harassed, and voters were intimidated at the polls.

Luis, overweight and unhappy, suffered a major coronary a month before Tachito was inaugurated and died at the age of forty-four. Without Luis's restraining hand and political savvy to guide him, Tachito, in violation of the constitution, took back his title of head of the Guardia and gave himself a new rank: *jefe supremo*, commander in chief of Nicaragua's armed forces.

As with the protagonist of a Greek tragedy, but with none of the grandeur or heroic character, a self-destructive tendency in Tachito drove him irrevocably toward policies and actions that would destroy the Guardia Nacional and himself.

By 1973 Tachito was by far the largest landowner and entrepreneur in Nicaragua. His holdings included one-fifth of the cultivated land and an unending list of companies he owned or held share in. Among the largest were Lanica (the national airline), a merchant marine fleet, a Mercedes Benz franchise (hence, most government vehicles were Mercedes, including many Guardia trucks), the cement company, which had a monopoly on the concrete blocks used almost exclusively for new construction and the paving of roads, a textile mill, at least one construction company, and so forth. Private-sector growth that had taken place under his brother Luis came to a standstill. It seemed that every cordoba was somehow filtered through one of Tachito's businesses.

Somoza's gross appetite became legendary. In 1975 and again in 1976, columnist Jack Anderson dubbed him "the world's greediest dictator." He elaborated: "Anastasio Somoza runs Nicaragua as if it were his private estate. . . . His enormous wealth has been squeezed out of his impoverished subjects. . . . They lie in shacks and teeming slums and eke out a living as best they can while the Big Banana stashes millions in foreign banks."[20]

As the years passed, Tachito's regime developed into an odd mixture of arbitrariness, cruelty, and corruption. It wasn't the impersonal totalitarian state described by George Orwell in *1984*, but rather a personal, inefficient, gangsterlike regime in which family, friends, and those who cooperated and kept quiet got along just fine.

His brand of authoritarian rule and profit taking required an ever increasing circle of partners, associates, and managers who had a strong interest in perpetuating his regime. These included close friends in the U.S. Congress and top officials in the Guardia Nacional, the government, and the Somozas' National Liberal party. Sycophants, principally interested in enriching themselves, fed Tachito's ego the flattery it required.

Furthermore, his paranoia restricted the advancement of anyone with more than mediocre talents (with the exception of those who advised him strictly on banking and financial matters), so that by the end he was surrounded by toadies who served him badly. Aides of quality, like Foreign Minister Julio Quintana, were called upon too late.

Those who opposed him developed a strange, fatalistic sense of humor that was distinctly Nicaraguan. This ad, for example, ran in *La Prensa* in August '73:[21]

Señor GENERAL ANASTASIO SOMOZA DEBAYLE
CHIEF OF THE NATIONAL GUARD
SUPREME COMMANDER OF THE ARMED FORCES
PRESIDENT OF THE NATIONAL EMERGENCY
COMMITTEE
PRESIDENT OF THE AGRICULTURAL COMMITTEE
LEADER OF THE NATIONAL LIBERAL PARTY
HEAD OF THE FOREIGN FINANCE COMMITTEE
CANDIDATE FOR THE PRESIDENCY OF THE REPUBLIC
EX-PRESIDENT OF THE REPUBLIC
GRAND MASTER OF THE ORDER OF "RUBEN DARIO"
SENATOR FOR LIFE
PROMOTER OF RURAL ELECTRIFICATION
PROMOTER OF AGRO-INDUSTRY
PRESIDENT OF LANICA AIRLINES
PRESIDENT OF THE MAMENIC SHIPPING LINE
CHAIRMAN OF THE NATIONAL CEMENT PLANT
CHIEF EXECUTIVE OF "EL PORVENIR" PLANTATION
CHIEF EXECUTIVE OF CENTRAL DE INGENIOS
REFINERIES
LEADER, FLAGBEARER, OUTSTANDING ONE, GUIDE,
INSPIRED AND ILLUSTRIOUS ONE, GLORIOUS ONE,
TALENTED ONE, MAN OF DESTINY, COUNSELOR, ILLU-
MINATOR, WISE, VIRTUOUS, UPSTANDING, INSPIRING,
INTELLIGENT, REGAL, SERENE, PRUDENT, BUILDER,
CREATOR, HURRICANE OF PEACE, NEGOTIATOR, FU-
TURE PRESIDENT, REFEREE, ARBITER OF JUSTICE,
SUPREME COMMANDER, GENERAL IN CHIEF, FAMOUS
ONE, MAGNANIMOUS AND GENEROUS ONE, HIS
EXCELLENCY, MOST EXCELLENT ONE, JUDGE, PREDES-
TINED, DISTINGUISHED, RENOWNED, CHOSEN, VICTO-
RIOUS, BRILLIANT, STRONG PERSONALITY, CLEVER,
FABULOUS, MAGNETIC, WEST POINTER, STRATEGIST,
ORGANIZER, PROTECTOR, STATESMAN, COMFORTER
OF THE AFFLICTED, STATISTICIAN, WINNER, SWORD,
PACIFIER, POLAR STAR, MORNING STAR, GENIUS, RE-
STORER, EMANCIPATOR, LIBERATOR, IDEALIST, LIB-
ERAL, PLANNER, SOLID ACADEMIC BACKGROUND,
MAN OF SCIENCE, ENGINEER, HELMSMAN, PILOT,
CAPTAIN, DIRECTOR OF INDUSTRY, BASTION, BUL-
WARK, FORTRESS, BEACON, THE MAN, PALADIN, PA-
TRIOT, DEMOCRAT, SAVIOR OF THE REPUBLIC, GIANT,
FIRST TAXI DRIVER (AND ALL "FIRSTS" EVER KNOWN
OR IMAGINABLE), SACRIFICED TO HIS PEOPLE, ALTRU-

ISTIC, DOCTOR HONORIS CAUSA, BACHELOR AD HOROEM, CHIEF OF CHIEFS, INDISPUTABLE CHIEF, SUSTENANCE OF DEMOCRACY, SUPPORTER OF LATIN AMERICA AND GREAT FRIEND OF NIXON

SEÑOR GENERAL:
WE READ ALL THESE DESCRIPTIONS OF YOU IN YOUR NEWSPAPER *NOVEDADES,* AND WE HAVE UNDERLINED THEM DAILY TILL LAST MONDAY, AUGUST 12.
IN THE NAME OF ANY OF THESE OFFICES OR QUALITIES, WE WOULD LIKE TO ASK YOU TO DO SOMETHING TO STOP THE PRICE OF CONSUMER GOODS FROM RISING AND TO MAKE THE RAIN FALL.
YOUR HUMBLE SERVANTS, WORKERS OF THE CITY
OF MANAGUA,

ANTONIO GARCIA, F. CRUZ, H. MARTINEZ

When Tachito ran for reelection in 1974 against his hand-picked opponent Edmundo Paguaga Irias, *La Prensa* editor Pedro Joaquín Chamorro ran the headline "Candidates Who Won Tomorrow's Election" a day before the vote. As predicted, Somoza won. *Time* correspondent Bernard Diederich analyzed the results: "Although forty percent of the electorate did abstain, Tachito's vote counters declared that he had received 748,985 of the 815,758 votes cast. There was no secret ballot. It was imperative for almost everyone to be recorded as having voted 'National Liberal' because only those who voted for Somoza were given the ID card called a *magnifia,* required for all government employees."[22]

As the Somoza regime ran its course—a course that made evolutionary change impossible—armed overthrow of his regime became the only option open to the increasing number of Nicaraguans who opposed his continuance in power. As President Roosevelt said in 1937: "The ultimate failures of dictatorship cost humanity far more than the temporary failures of democracy."

Nicaragua in June 1979 was tragically bearing that out.

5

I honestly believe it iz better to know nothing than tew know what aint so. —Josh Billings, *Encyclopedia of Proverbial Philosophy*

The day after I told Harry Barnes I would accept the ambassadorship to Nicaragua, Pete Vaky called to invite me to a major review of Central American policy scheduled to be held in San José, Costa Rica.

The Conference of Chiefs of Missions ran from May 16 to 18, 1979. It was held at the U.S. Embassy Chancery in San José and was the most widely attended conference I have ever been to in the field. Diplomatic concern for every country in Central America was represented by either a U.S. ambassador or chargé d'affaires. Pete Vaky came from Washington with Luigi Einaudi from the Latin American Office of Policy Planning; in addition, there were Wade Matthews, the country director of Central America and the head of the OAS Economic Policy Office; Bob Pastor from the National Security Council; an admiral from Defense; and Sapia Bosch from the CIA's analytical branch. Ambassador to Costa Rica Marvin Weissman and his deputy chief of mission acted as hosts. It was quite a gathering.

Here we were less than two weeks before the final FSLN offensive began in Nicaragua, and six and a half weeks before Somoza fled the country and the Sandinista Junta of National Reconstruction took over. The central topic of discussion was Nicaragua and *whether or not Somoza could be convinced to step down when he finished his term in 1981.* That's how out of it we were.

The consensus was that the FSLN, with less than 2,000 trained combatants, could be handled easily by the Guardia Nacional. The FAO and political opposition were described as fragmented and disheartened. When I asked at one point whether we had any contacts within the FSLN, the Defense Department admiral found my question inadmissible. In effect, he wondered why we should be speaking to our enemies. I told him that I found it inconceivable that we chose to remain uninformed about such an important opposition group. Shortly after the conference, the CIA did meet for the first time with Edén Pastora—arranged, I assume, through General Torrijos or, his right-hand man, Manuel Noriega.

Our chargé d'affaires in Nicaragua described a political situation that, in hindsight, bore no resemblance to reality. Apparently, the officers in our embassy in Managua were sitting on a volcano without the vaguest idea of what was building up under them. No one at the meeting took exception to the analysis given, or offered a different scenario, or raised the specter of imminent hostilities. No one!

There were almost two years remaining in Somoza's term as president. So there was plenty of time to put together a strategy. I left San José on the nineteenth to return to Montevideo to pack up my effects and bid my farewells. Based on what I had heard at the conference, or what Vaky or anyone else had told me in private, I felt no sense of urgency.

Nor did other attendees at the conference. When Robert Pastor traveled to Panama in early June, he was surprised by General Torrijos's first remark. "It's too bad the United States is always so slow to recognize new realities," said the general, "and that you didn't have the foresight to buy a share of Sandinista stock when I was first offering it."[1] Although the Sandinista "final offensive" had begun a few days earlier, Pastor was confident that Somoza would snuff it out.

By the time I arrived in Washington on June 7, 1979, the fighting had spread. On my first morning at the State Department,

Vaky invited me to sit in on an INR (Intelligence and Research) briefing by James Buchanan, a man I had known previously as an Argentine expert. Using a stiff-backed map, he pointed out areas of fighting, supply routes, and the early battle lines that were forming along the Southern Front, with Edén Pastora and his forces pitched against the elite Guardia units of Major Emilio Salazar (alias Comandante Bravo).

Buchanan described a consistent pattern. The people in a given area would rise up in arms, seemingly spontaneously, throw up barricades, burn tires and vehicles, and slowly drive the town's Guardia back into their *cuartel* (fortified barracks or command post). The central Guardia command in Managua would attempt to either resupply or reinforce the defenders. In most cases, access by road was too dangerous and resupply by air was futile. One by one, towns had fallen, followed by small cities. When asked how many Sandinista cadres were involved and where they were coming from, Buchanan was stumped. He suggested that the townspeople seemed to be the principal combatants and that practically every family abetted the attacks on the Guardia. There were also reports that the FSLN were resupplying their fighters from small planes. The markings on Buchanan's map were vivid testimony to the extent and intensity of the insurrection.

This eruption of violence shook Washington out of its stupor. The idea that Somoza would serve out his term was put to rest. Vaky gave Bowdler the assignment of drafting policy scenarios. As a newcomer, I had little to offer. Each scenario began with the assumption that Somoza would step down. How that was to be accomplished and who and what would succeed Somoza became the focal points of discussion.

As a start, Bowdler borrowed from the transitional plans drafted by the FAO during the OAS mediation. What emerged was the concept of a transitional government, composed of an executive committee and constituent assembly, that would draft a new constitution, enact electoral law, and serve as a legislative body until elections were held. The executive committee would be composed of prestigious individuals ("wise men") who had a reputation for even-handedness and sober judgment. By Nicaraguan standards, they could be called middle-of-the road democrats. Among those mentioned were Ismael Reyes, president of Nicaraguan Red Cross; Emilio Alvarez Montalban, an ophthalmologist widely respected for his political sagacity; Mariano Fiallos, rector of the León

Junta members Violeta Chamorro (center), Sergio Ramírez, and Alfonso Robello (with arms folded) and Foreign Minister Miguel D'Escoto meet the press under a portrait of Sandino. Credit: Agencia de Comunicación Internacional, Managua

branch of the National University; Adolfo Calero, a Conservative party leader and manager of the local Coca-Cola bottling plant; Felipe Manteca, owner of a food store chain and member of Los Doce; and Rafael Cordova Rivas, a longtime Conservative politician and leader of the FAO.

The various scenarios were amended daily as the situation in Nicaragua deteriorated. Then on June 16 the FSLN announced the creation of a Government of National Reconstruction based in San José, Costa Rica. Its executive junta included Tercerista commander Daniel Ortega Saavedra; Sergio Ramírez, a novelist and Los Doce member; Moises Hassan Morales, the relatively unknown leader of the United Peoples Movement (MPU), with a Ph.D. from North Carolina State University; Violeta Barrios de Chamorro, widow of the slain *La Prensa* editor; and Alfonso Robelo, a successful businessman and leader of the FAO. Suddenly, the United States was forced to deal with a serious new actor.

Three days later, the junta broadcast its Plan de Gobierno. Strongly resembling the FAO's program, it promised socioecomonic reconstruction, a nonaligned foreign policy, and the confiscation of Somoza property. The junta said it would honor

Nicaragua's foreign debt obligations and would form a new army. Soldiers who immediately abandoned the Guardia Nacional would be invited to join. Sergio Ramírez, speaking for the group, promised the new government would "take the route of representative democracy based on periodic elections, but with universal participation . . . within a multiparty system, of course."[2]

As the fighting escalated and town after town fell to the rebels, it became apparent that the Somoza regime would not survive. Somoza would either succumb militarily, to be replaced by a seemingly extreme leftist guerrilla group, or the United States could remove him and preserve some political space for the moderates, whom we felt deserved a role. The reasons for pursuing the second course were found to be compelling. Not only did Washington fear a communist or communist-leaning government in Central America, but also it sought to stem the loss of life, destruction of property, reprisals, and anarchy that a protracted civil war could produce.

The Legal Adviser's Office of the State Department was asked to draft a position paper that could be used to broach the legal issues with Somoza. We knew from questions raised during the OAS mediation that Somoza was interested in safe haven in the United States. Back in November 1978, Somoza, through his cousin Luis Pallais, had raised the issue of diplomatic immunity. Our legal advisers informed them that immunity could be conferred only on diplomats and visiting dignitaries. It could not be offered to a former president.

On the question of extradition or the possibility of Somoza's having to go back to Nicaragua to face charges, our advisers determined that no special protection could be offered to him beyond recourse to normal legal proceedings. They pointed out that Somoza's chances of being extradited depended on the political climate in Nicaragua. As a footnote, they noted that he would enjoy privileged status under U.S. immigration law, since his wife, Hope, was a U.S. citizen.

Once spurred into action, the Carter administration was able to cobble together a general policy. If we could prevail upon Somoza to step down and end the bloody civil war, the political capital earned could be used to: (1) limit reprisals; (2) preserve the portion of the Guardia that was relatively unspoiled by Somoza and use it to balance the strength of FSLN forces; (3) invite hemispheric oversight to guarantee political space for independent parties; and (4) hold the junta to its published promise to preserve a mixed economy and a pluralistic political process.

We then invited Somoza to send an emissary to Washington. He responded quickly. On June 18, Bowdler and I met with Somoza's cousin Luis Pallais, president of Congress, and Sevilla-Sacasa, Nicaragua's ambassador and Somoza's brother-in-law, at the Guest Quarters Hotel on Pennsylvania Avenue. Bowdler and I went down the list of talking points, beginning with our assessment that conditions had deteriorated to the point where Somoza could rule but not govern. His continuation in power would only prolong the bloodshed. The United States was prepared to offer Somoza, his family, and close associates asylum in the United States. As expected, Pallais asked about immunity. He also raised the issue of extradition. We answered, drawing from the guidelines provided by the State Department's legal advisers.

Pallais, always the gentleman, said he would return to Managua immediately to report the substance of our talks. Ambassador Sevilla-Sacasa had nothing to say, except to express chagrin at one point that the United States was considering deposing a constitutionally elected president. Pallais returned to Managua and met through the night with Somoza, his son El Chiguín, General José Somoza, the dictator's half brother, the cabinet, and Liberal party leaders. At two in the morning, Somoza said he had made up his mind and dictated the following remarks to Pallais: (1) he resented the ultimatum; (2) if circumstances were created for an orderly transition under OAS auspices, he would resign; (3) he demanded protection from extradition from the United States for himself and his family; (4) he demanded exile visas for himself and his family while living in the United States.

With Somoza's reply in hand, we felt it was essential to enlist the support of our hemispheric neighbors. In close consultation with other Latin American countries, especially the Andean Group (Venezuela, Colombia, Ecuador, Peru, and Bolivia), Assistant Secretary Vaky arranged for a meeting of the Consultation of Ministers of Foreign Affairs of the OAS to take place on June 21. The day before the delegates met in Washington, ABC reporter Bill Stewart was filmed by his camera crew as he was ordered by a Guardia soldier to lie face down on a Managua street and then was shot dead in cold blood. The dramatic footage, which ran repeatedly on U.S. television newscasts, was shown at the OAS session at the suggestion of the Panamanian delegation. It lent even more drama to what was to become a tension-packed session.

The Seventeenth Meeting of the Consultation of Ministers of Foreign Affairs will be remembered because of a diplomatic blunder of considerable proportions committed by the United States. It turned a meeting that we had called to force the resignation of Somoza and to moderate the ensuing transition into a fiery anti-American cabal that nearly handed us a diplomatic drubbing. The State Department had prepared a comprehensive speech for Secretary Vance. Vaky, aware that Vance's address would be a keynote of the session, took pains to include not only a realistic appraisal of the situation in Nicaragua, but what we saw as a possible solution.

On the afternoon of June 21, 1979, Secretary Vance came right to the point. "Solution [to the Nicaraguan crisis] must begin with the replacement of the present government with a transitional government of national reconciliation, which would be a clear break with the past." To a packed chamber, he urged the OAS to "immediately send a special delegation to Nicaragua . . . to facilitate the formation by Nicaraguans of a transitional government." To spare further bloodshed, he suggested the OAS "consider on an urgent basis the need for a peace-keeping force to restore order" and warned, "we must not leave a vacuum."[3]

A pall fell over the assembly at the mention of a peace-keeping force. Jerry O'Leary, who covered Latin America for the *Washington Star,* pulled me aside as the session broke for recess. "You don't have to tell me who inserted that goddamned stupid phrase," he snorted. "It came from the NSC."[4] Before I could feign ignorance, he went on to ask rhetorically how any U.S. official could be so "ignorant of the negative reaction this would provoke."

Indeed, Vaky had said just that when the damning phrase was written into the speech at the White House. He had argued strongly that it should be removed. Secretary Vance had agreed and tried to persuade the president. The day before the speech was delivered, Vaky asked Secretary Vance to make another attempt to get the White House to relent. In Vaky's words, "[Secretary Vance] listened in his gentlemanly way, picked up the phone and presented my arguments to Zbig Brzezinski. I assume it was Zbig. Then Secretary Vance turned back to me and in a calm, resigned fashion said that the President insists that the peacekeeping force proposal remain in the speech."[5]

The reason for the heated Latin American reaction goes back to the crisis in the Dominican Republic in 1965, following the assassination of dictator Rafael Trujillo. Given the resulting vacuum of power and lack of institutional mechanisms for a peaceful transition, there was a mad scramble for power. Concern in Washington was fanned to panic proportions by reports that grossly exaggerated the strength and intentions of "communist elements" in the country. Lyndon B. Johnson, not one to ponder when action seemed appropriate, forced a resolution through the OAS authorizing the dispatch of a "Pan-American Peace Force" to end sectarian violence and bring the parties to a peaceful resolution of the crisis. The ink was hardly dry before U.S. troops went ashore. Although there was token military representation by Brazil and other OAS members, it was seen as a U.S. show. The OAS was left with a black eye for serving as a tool of U.S. policy.

Why did the NSC insist on the inclusion of that highly inflammatory phrase? As astounding as it may seem, the White House clearly did not understand how deeply the Dominican peace-keeping effort had offended Latin American sensibilities. According to Robert Pastor, "Although Brzezinski viewed the 1965 intervention in the Dominican Republic by the inter-American peace force positively, I tried to explain that this was not the way many Latin American leaders remembered it."[6]

More intriguing is what gave birth to the concept. At one of the earliest meetings at which the policy papers prepared by Bowdler, myself, and others at the State Department were debated, concern was raised by Brzezinski and his subordinates over the "vacuum" that Somoza would leave in his wake. I was struck by the way this obsession worked its way into every discussion. On one occasion, I recall David Aaron of the NSC went so far as to suggest that we might consider using U.S. troops if an intervention to preserve order became necessary. Vance retorted heatedly that he wanted that idea buried and for good.

Apparently, Vance didn't get his wish. Robert Pastor, in *Condemned to Repetition: The United States and Nicaragua*, reports that Brzezinski used a breakfast meeting on June 22—the day after Vance's speech—with Secretary of Defense Harold Brown, Hamilton Jordan, Vice President Walter Mondale, President Carter, and Secretary Vance to make the case for unilateral U.S. military intervention. Pastor writes, quoting from Brzezinski's own notes, that the national security adviser spoke "about the major domestic and international implications" of a Castroite takeover in Nicaragua. The United States would be considered "incapable of dealing with problems in our own backyard and impotent in the face of Cuban intervention. This will have devastating domestic implication, including for SALT," Brzezinski said.[7] President Carter made it clear that he had no intention of intervening unilaterally.

Although it was discussed in private meetings with the president, the Pan American peace force proposal was never on the Policy Review Committee agenda. We did discuss OAS involvement, but always in a diplomatic context. Vaky suggested that the foreign ministers of neighboring countries might be present during the interregnum to guarantee a peaceful and orderly transition. At one point, it was even suggested that the ministers could be encouraged to take along military aides to add a token military presence. All this was a far cry from the eleventh-hour inclusion of the peace force concept in Vance's speech. It was more than a small blunder. It undercut U.S. credibility at a time when we needed hemispheric support and reinforced the stereotype of the United States as an insensitive giant that used, but rarely heeded, its hemispheric neighbors.

Vaky and Deputy Secretary of State Warren Christopher were left to literally clean up the mess at the meeting. Father Miguel d'Escoto, representing the FSLN junta, flung mud in our faces, alleging: "The United States is not as concerned with what is happening in Nicaragua as it is afraid that it will lose control of what will happen in the future. The United States is afraid to let us decide our own destiny."[8] The Panamanian and Mexican delegations tried to parlay the U.S. gaffe into an anti-U.S., anti-Somoza resolution. For a while, some of the Andean countries, led by Venezuela, were moving in that direction. Vaky and Christopher worked to avert a complete diplomatic disaster.

The resolution that emerged stated: "The solution to the serious problem is exclusively within the jurisdiction of the people of Nicaragua." It called for "immediate and definite replacement of the Somoza regime" and allowed OAS members to unilaterally "take steps that are within their reach to facilitate an enduring and peaceful solution to the Nicaraguan crisis." It was less than a full loaf, but under the circumstances easily acceptable. We could now move ahead with our plan.

Luis Pallais, Foreign Minister Julio Quintana (called "Negro" because of his swarthy complexion) and Ambassador Sevilla Sacasa met with Bowdler, Vaky, and me in Vaky's office on June 24.

Foreign Minister Quintana suggested that a clause in the Nicaraguan constitution could help facilitate the transition. The constitution permitted a president to resign and turn the presidential office over to a member of the National Assembly. We discussed the details and incorporated the constitutional process in the transition scenario.

Pallais added little, except to say that Somoza was concerned, among other things, about the future of the Liberal party and the Guardia Nacional. We had little to offer other than to question their viability. Pallais professed that the Liberal party had institutional strength and strong grass-roots support, a claim we did not believe.

At a Policy Review Committee meeting in the White House Situation Room the next day, we reported on our discussions. Quintana's and Pallais's responsiveness and the impression they left that Somoza might be more inclined to resign led to the consensus that it was time for me to go to Nicaragua and negotiate with Somoza directly.

I was prepared to travel immediately. It was also decided that Bowdler should fly to San José, Costa Rica, to open talks with the FSLN junta. The plan was for Bowdler and me to leave the afternoon of June 26 from Andrews Air Base on an air force executive jet. We would refuel at Homestead Air Force Base, near Miami, then fly to Panama City, where we would spend the night. I would be flown into Nicaragua on a small piston aircraft the following day, while Bowdler met with Panamanian strongman Omar Torrijos, who would introduce him to members of the junta, at the time visiting Panama City.

Bill and I were to work as a team, keeping each other abreast of developments in our respective capitals. The administration was hoping to moderate the junta and, at the same time, negotiate the establishment of an executive committee that could become an alternative source of power when Somoza left.

As the White House meeting was coming to an end, a minor incident offered an interesting insight into Somoza's contacts within the U.S. government. The affable, capable chairman of the Joint Chiefs of Staff, General David Jones, asked if I would like to take a military aide along with me to Managua. He had in mind someone who knew Somoza from a previous assignment. I agreed.

Later in the day, as I was preparing to leave for Nicaragua, I received a call from a Colonel Dent. Within an hour he was in my State Department office. A strapping fellow in his mid-fifties,

Colonel Dent informed me that he had served as commander of the Military Advisory Group to Nicaragua in the late sixties. He said he was willing to accompany me. I asked if he had any problem with the fact that I would be asking Somoza to step down. He said no, he would be supportive. We left it at that, and he went to put his affairs in order.

That evening I packed for my trip, with my wife, Jo, trying vainly to conceal her anxiety. We spent the night as quietly as possible trying to make little of the fact that I was walking into the throes of a civil war. Such was my single-mindedness in the weeks ahead that, while she and my children were constantly in my thoughts, I had almost no direct communication with them.

The next morning Pete Vaky asked me to accompany him to a meeting with Deputy Secretary Warren Christopher. As we walked the tunnellike corridors of the State Department, Vaky turned to me and asked if I really wanted to take along a military aide. "Wouldn't you be better served by a career foreign service officer, and one who has been dealing with the Nicaragua issue for years, like Malcolm Barnebey?" It made sense.

Informed of my change of plans, Christopher put a call through to General Jones. I would not be taking Colonel Dent. Vaky, meanwhile, alerted Barnebey to get ready to leave in a few hours. Four days later, as I was leaving Somoza's bunker following our third meeting, Somoza turned to me and asked: "By the way, where's Colonel Dent?" I shrugged and said I didn't know a Colonel Dent.

Of course, that wasn't true. But it made me wonder. There had been only ten people in the White House Situation Room when General Jones had made the suggestion. No doubt, General Jones had contacted Colonel Dent, who had probably discussed his new assignment with others. But all this had taken place in less than two days. And Somoza had found out. What else did Somoza know about our internal discussions and plans?

With Barnebey on board, Christopher, Vaky, and I discussed my mission. Somoza was the key. We had received some indication from Pallais and Quintana that Somoza was considering the idea of resigning. Still, no U.S. official had spoken to him directly since early in the year, when he had been hostile and obstinate. We expected him to try to play us, as he had before.

It was agreed that I would not present diplomatic credentials to Somoza, even though I had already been confirmed by the U.S. Senate and formally sworn in as ambassador to Nicaragua. Bow-

dler argued that this gesture would send a clear signal to Somoza—I was not going to Managua to perform the traditional
ambassadorial duties. Indeed, diplomatic protocol was being cast
aside. It wasn't the normal state of affairs for an ambassador to call
on a chief of state and suggest that he leave the country. But the
bloody crisis in Nicaragua demanded unusual measures.

6

The Sandinistas are everywhere. The Frente appears even in the
dictator's soup.
—Luis Rocha

The infamous Comandante Cero, Edén Pastora, looked grim as
artillery shells exploded in the mud around them. "It's a war," said
one of his aides.

On the morning of Tuesday, May 29, 1979, Pastora had led a
well-armed column of 300 Sandinistas over a rusty barbed-wire
fence marking the border between Nicaragua and Costa Rica. The
Benjamin Zeledon Column now occupied the farming community
of El Naranjo, just ten kilometers across the border.

A Guardia Nacional radio post was overheard reporting excit-
edly to Somoza: "They're entering from La Cruz. They're crossing
the border with confidence, well armed with heavy equipment.
They seem strong."[1]

Somoza's son El Chiguín was heard shouting back: "Those sons-
of-bitches don't know what they're asking for!"[2]

El Naranjo was a breathtakingly beautiful site—rounded wind-
swept hills overlooking the Pacific on a narrow strip of land that
separates Lake Nicaragua from the ocean. Hugo Spadafora, a doc-

tor who had resigned as Panama's deputy health minister to aid Pastora, had led the initial eighty-man column. Its members included Panamanian, Argentine, Chilean, Costa Rican, Peruvian, Swedish, German, Cuban, and U.S. volunteers.

Somehow the artillery had gotten lost. The Chileans who did the training had not been able to instill much discipline. Pastora lay down his AR-15 and picked up the wireless and called his commander, Humberto Ortega, in Costa Rica. He needed more artillery and mortars. This wasn't a guerrilla war. His troops and the Guardia were already locked into a battle for positions. He held up the microphone to the battle sounds to make his point.

Following Pastora's daring takeover of the national palace in August 1978, he had become the most recognizable and charismatic Sandinista. Because he was a social democrat in a group in which Marx, Mao, Castro, and Guevara were the models, Pastora had emerged as a favorite of Panamanian strongman Omar Torrijos and of the presidents of Venezuela and Costa Rica, Carlos Andrés Pérez and Rodrigo Carazo Odio.

In their judgment, the seductive and charming Pastora was the man to lead the broad coalition of forces against Somoza and rid Central America of the menace they had grown to despise. Since September, the three leaders had been supplying Pastora's forces in Costa Rica with arms flown in from Panama, Venezuela, and Cuba. Given the impetus of money, arms, and events in Nicaragua, Pastora's force had swelled to over 2,000.

Although Pastora was undoubtedly brave, dashing, and democratic, he was severely lacking in political skills. In the Sandinista movement where political alliances often counted for more than deeds, Pastora had been pushed aside. A part-time fighter, he had been married numerous times and had fathered some twenty-two children, for whom he had occasionally left the movement to provide. He had missed Pancasan and the Christmas party raid and the jailings and repression of the middle seventies.

While Daniel Ortega was in jail and Tomás Borge was in Cuba in the 1960s, Pastora moved from Mexico to Los Angeles to Italy and Switzerland, where he worked as a kitchen helper. In 1973, after some time in the mountains, he retreated to the fishing village of Barra del Colorado on the northeast coast of Costa Rica along the border with Nicaragua. He told a reporter:

I lived on the beach in a fisherman's hut, with my woman and my children, on the sand of the beach. The roof was made of straw, the floor of sand. I was a fisherman and lived on fish.

I didn't know how to catch them, didn't know how to gut them. Hell, the first shark I hooked, I gaffed it and brought it into the boat alive. And it damn near ate me, the son of a bitch, in the bottom of the boat.

After two years I wasn't a fisherman, I was a businessman. I bought shark. I bought coconuts. One day one thing, the next the other. And I'd built my house in town. . . . I was getting things together. . . . And one day [in early 1977] I was surprised to see, coming into Barra, Sergio Ramírez and Carlos Coronel.[3]

Ramírez, the writer, had been sent by Humberto Ortega. Coronel, the son of one of Nicaragua's most distinguished poets, was a conspirator, gun smuggler, and old friend. "The boys want to talk to you," said Ramírez. "What boys?" asked Pastora. "The Directorate." "What Directorate?" "The Directorate of the Sandinista Front."[4]

So he went to see the Ortegas, who talked about a new approach to the war against Somoza. They were going to move quickly and build a mass movement capable of rising up all over the country. Pastora, with his contacts in Nicaragua and Costa Rica, could play a role as leader of the Tercerista faction. He joined immediately.

Even after his spectacular success at the national palace, Pastora's fellow Sandinistas did not name him to the National Directorate. Nor was he invited to the reconciliation talks in Havana at the end of 1978. Tomás Borge, who was freed after the national palace takeover, considered Pastora melodramatic and unreliable. Borge's political guru, Fidel Castro, made it known that he didn't like the emotional Nicaraguan whom he referred to as "the peasant."

The forty-two-year-old Pastora was born in the village of Dario, thirty-seven miles south of Managua. His grandfather had been a follower of Conservative caudillo Emiliano Chamorro, and his mother, who had been educated in New Orleans, had once served as a translator for the U.S. Marines. Although his father was shot in a land dispute, Pastora liked to tell reporters that he had been killed by the Guardia Nacional.

While Pastora possessed an instinctive understanding of the Nicaraguan love of flamboyant romantic gestures, he lacked the

Edén Pastora with National Guard prisoners shortly after the revolution. Credit: Agencia de Comunicación Internacional, Managua

organization and leadership skills needed to fight a pitched battle with artillery, coordination, and positioning. The current thrust into El Naranjo was bearing this out. Pastora's objective was the departmental capital of Rivas, where the Sandinistas hoped to establish a provisional government on Nicaraguan soil. After Rivas he hoped to storm up the Southern Highway to Managua.

For the time being, Pastora's force was pinned down in this mountainous coastal strip only a few kilometers from the Costa Rican border. His troops were hanging tough despite the punishing bombardment of the *M.S. Managua* (a Somoza freighter with 400-millimeter Bofors mounted on its decks), T-33 jets, two giant Argentine-made 42-tube 70-millimeter rocket launchers mounted on the backs of flatbed trucks and heavy-caliber mortars.

"We had a forty-foot Coast Guard ship which was normally stationed in Lake Nicaragua," Somoza remembered.

> It was decided to use this small Coast Guard vessel in repelling the invaders. The vessel was operating in the Sapoa River. . . . We were surprised when it was reported that the Coast Guard vessel had exploded. Later, however, we learned the boat was hit by a 103-millimeter recoilless gun.

When I received that authenticated report, I reported this fact
to the OAS [Organization of American States]. I pointed out to
those people that this was prima facie evidence that we were not
fighting an internal uprising, as the OAS claimed. I stated that
we were fighting organized armies. . . . Of course, this evidence
made no difference to the OAS.[5]

Because of his renown and the size of his force, Pastora had
drawn the best of Somoza's army—the elite EEBI (Basic Infantry
Training School) strike force. It had been quickly airlifted into El
Ostional along with the Guard's best commander, Major Pablo
Emilio Salazar, known as Comandante Bravo. Daring and charismatic in his own right and also a good strategist, Bravo was a powerful deterrent to the less trained and equipped Sandinista force.

But across the border in the FSLN command center of Palo
Alto, chief military strategist Humberto Ortega was ecstatic. Everything was going according to plan. Two problems had neutral-
ized each other. Pastora had taken and was holding Nicaraguan
territory and had tied up Somoza's most mobile and reliable
troops. Now the call could be sounded for a general strike and insurrection in the cities and towns.

"The way we saw it, the insurrection had to last, at a nationwide
level, at least two weeks to make the enemy's situation untenable,"
Ortega recalled.

What was planned was that when the Southern Front went into
action in El Naranjo, the uprising was to be launched a few days
later in the Rigoberto Pérez Western Front (León), which would
create a very difficult situation for the National Guard: major
blows in the north, blows in the west, and more blows in the
south. Several days after the battles in El Naranjo, our forces in
Masaya, Granada and Carazo were to go into action, cutting off
the means of communication to Somoza's forces on the Southern
Front. The uprising in Managua was to start as soon as fighting
had begun on all those fronts.[6]

Humberto Ortega understood that a major difference between
this offensive and that of September 1978 was improved communication. "The means of communication were of vital importance:
wireless for communication among the various fronts, and the radio. Without them it would have been impossible."[7] Radio Sandino
operating out of Costa Rica played a vital role.

"After the success of El Naranjo we gave the order," Ortega reported.[8] It was broadcast on Radio Sandino on June 4, 1979: "From the National Directorate of the Frente Sandinista de Liberación Nacional. To workers, campesinos, students, public workers, businessmen. . . . The hour for the decisive battle has arrived!" It ended with Sandino's battle cry: "Patria libre o morir!"

The next day, city streets throughout Nicaragua were deserted and stores closed. Some Managua gas stations and a few banks linked to the government remained open. When government-run television showed a Managua marketplace teeming with people, reporters rushed there to find the place deserted. Two days later, Somoza declared martial law.

"The call for a general strike got a complete reaction with fires, riots in the streets, barricades and so on," recalled Ortega. "By this time our people had practice."[9] And the *muchachos* were better armed. But after over a year of strikes, insurrections, and other disruptions, many middle-class Nicaraguans were fed up. "Let whatever comes come," said a twenty-eight-year-old furniture wholesaler to Guy Gugliotta of the *Miami Herald* as he sipped his vodka on his patio in June 1979. He had bought a new Managua tract house the year before, but now couldn't sell it. "Whether it's the government or the guerrillas, just let it be over."[10]

A thirty-two-year-old Managua divorcee had a similar feeling. "I went to the supermarket last Saturday, just before the strike, and you can imagine it was packed with people," she told a visitor. "But nobody was depressed; everybody was joking, relieved. We all felt the end has come at last."[11]

So did Virginia Sanchez, the oldest daughter of an upper-middle-class family in the Altamira section of Managua. "Even though my parents were nonpolitical, my father decided to close the family hardware store. We knew this was it. All of us, my two brothers, my sister, and my parents, moved into a back bedroom. It was the one with the fewest windows."[12]

On the sixth of June, Somoza declared a state of siege. An 8 P.M. to 4 A.M. curfew was imposed in cities throughout the country. And the government ordered *La Prensa* to stop its presses. Fighting broke out in Managua the evening of the eighth. Some 300 Internal Front guerrillas led by Carlos Nuñez, Joaquín Cuadra, and William Ramírez were quickly joined by an estimated 1,200 *muchachos* who took control of the eastern and western barrios.

Poet Luis Vega described his role in the fighting:

> I started the first day
> of the Big Strike
> putting up barricades
> in my neighborhood.
> I stayed up that night
> with just a machete,
> while the "beasts" with modern
> rifles waylaid us.
> We kept the neighborhood awake
> and the dawn found us
> taking up bricks
> and putting them one on top of
> another
> a meter high
> so the "dogs" couldn't pass.
> But, in spite of everything,
> they entered
> and the horror of the O.C.
> forced me and my young compañeros
> to retreat to El Dorado
> where for twenty-two days Somoza's National Guard
> couldn't enter in spite of the planes,
> the rockets, the 500-pound bombs,
> the tanks, the M-50s,
> the Uzi machine guns
> the high-powered FAL rifle,
> the silent Galil,
> the destructive mortars,
> and the thousands, thousands and thousands
> of canisters which remained strewn
> like yellow worms around San Cristóbal,
> El Edén, El Pasaisito,
> Larreynaga, and Bello Horizonte.[13]

The fourteen police sectors covering every neighborhood and barrio of Managua came under siege. "Sol," the central headquarters, started receiving distress calls from across the city. Broadcast unscrambled over single-band radios, these communications were avidly monitored by many Nicaraguans, among them César Sanchez and Mendieta Alfaro:

"Sol, this is Sierra 13. . . . They're attacking us from all sides. We need help."

"I'll send reinforcements," answered Sol. "Stand firm. And remember to discipline your fire."

"Sol, this is Las Américas, we're being attacked by about 300 guerrillas."

"Sol, in Monseñor Lezcano there are armed people all over the barrio!"

"Sol, it's Sol 22, we're being attacked from all sides."

"Sol 22, I'm reading you. . . . We're sending the Combat Battalion General Somoza into barrio Monseñor Lezcano and the EEBI into Las Americas," responded Col. Nicolás Valle Salinas, commander of the Managua police.[14]

Guardia soldiers found themselves fighting more confident and better trained opponents. This time the *muchachos* weren't wearing masks. Mendieta Alfaro overheard one Guardia patrol leader in Managua reporting to his squadron commander: "Alfa Uno, this is Sparrow Hawk. Alfa Uno, this is Sparrow Hawk!"

"Sparrow Hawk, this is Alfa Uno. I copy."

"Alfa Uno, we've encountered a group of bad boys in the riverbed."

"Kill them, man! Drive them out. I'll back you up."

"They're shouting. They're calling us. They're telling us to advance!"

"What?!? Be careful of an ambush, Sparrow Hawk. Watch your asses!"

"The sons-of-bitches are waving us forward!"

"Maybe it's better to back up. . . . Be careful of an ambush! Look out for mines!"

Over the transmitter Alfa Uno heard the *muchachos* screaming:

"Come on, assholes. Now you're going to die! We're not women that you can rape, you faggots. The Sandinistas don't run. We don't surrender! *Patria libre o morir!*"[15]

By Sunday, June 10, many of the police *cuartels* in Managua were still under siege.

"Are you advancing, 47?" asked Sol.

"I can't," came the reply. "I'm fighting in Belo Horizonte."

Fifteen minutes later, Sol (central command) called again. "Have you advanced, 47?"

"We're still fighting! We can't move."

"How is it possible that fifty men can't advance a couple of blocks? Advance, goddammit! Sierra 13 needs your help."

The next day, Sierra 13, near the Mercado Periferico, still hadn't been relieved. "When are you going to help me, Sol?"

"Soon!"

"They've just shot our commander, Lieutenant Gaitán. Right in the face; they shot him! Please, send us help!"[16]

Meanwhile, a Guardia unit in another part of the city was calling for the truck (the "Blue Lady") used to cart off bodies of dead guerrillas. "Sol, what happened to the Blue Lady? I have nine little faggots here."

"Leave them to the vultures, goddammit."

"Sol, is the Blue Lady coming? The families of these faggots are here and they want to take them. Should we let them bury them, or not?"

"Let them take the rotten dogs."[17]

At noon, Sol was back on the radio to besieged Sierra 13: "I'm dispatching some airplanes, Sierra 13. I'll put them in contact with you so that you can direct the pilots." Over the Guardia Nacional radio frequency, Sierra 13 could be heard directing the pilots of several push-pulls. "At the entrance of the cemetery they have a machine gun."

Rockets flew everywhere, but Sierra 13 wasn't happy. "The pilots missed. The rockets are falling on the graves and on the nearby houses. They haven't done a thing to the guerrillas."

At 2 P.M., Sol had another idea. "Sierra 13, the Ball of Iron [Sherman tank] is headed your way."

By five, the tank still wasn't there. "Hold on! Hold on!" pleaded Sol. "Help is coming. But if something happens, shoot the radio so that it doesn't fall into the hands of those bastards."

"I've got a prisoner here, from before. What should I do?" asked Sierra 13.

"Shoot him!"

Soon, a new voice came on the line. It was Colonel Valle Salinas, commander of the Managua police. "Sierra 13, this is Sol 22. . . . I want to tell you from all the Guardia that you're heroes. In the name of the president of the republic, General Somoza, I want to congratulate you all."

"Thank you, sir, but—"

"Hold on, Sierra 13, the Ball of Iron is only a block away. Resist!"

"What for, sir? . . . The *muchachos* are here! They're coming in—"
Sierra 13's radio went dead. "Sierra 13, this is Sol. Respond!"[18]

As the fighting continued, Managua experienced widespread
looting. Hungry people and thieves took advantage of the chaos
to sack markets, hardware shops, and department stores. Men
were seen trying to push new tractors away from a torched farm
equipment showroom.

Virginia Sanchez and her family used a pickup truck to move
the contents of the family hardware store into their house. "The
rooms were filled with bales of wire and pipes and fittings. As we
were moving the last of the inventory we saw the *turbas* [mobs]
coming. They were taking everything, looting one store after another. We just stood outside in front of the shop and defied them.
We weren't armed or anything. To our surprise, they went down
the road to the next place. It was a drug store. I saw a girl I knew
from school in the crowd. She came out of the store carrying a
couple of mops. I just stared at her. She didn't need those things.
I could understand if people were desperate to eat. But people
were taking everything. It was disgusting. When an orange BE-
CAT [Batallón Especial Contra Ataques Terroristas] jeep arrived,
the crowd parted. Two of the soldiers hurried into the store and
came out with armfuls of toilet paper. They threw them into the
back of the jeep and took off."[19]

On the night of June 13, Somoza appealed for calm. "I never
thought there would be so much disorder and pillaging in our capital. I never thought people would have to face the embarrassment
of having to take things that are not theirs in order to feed their
children. Please confront the situation calmly. . . . Please, don't
force me to apply the law, because above all things, I love my
citizens."[20]

As they did in Monimbo, Matagalpa, and León in 1978, Somoza's forces used their combat aircraft, tanks, and artillery to bom-
bard rebel-held cities before trying to retake them. "Somoza's
beasts," the people called the Guard.

Somoza, directing the war via radio transmitter from his bunker,
was heard shouting orders to his air force: "Bomb everything that
moves, you hear me! Bomb everything that moves, until it can't
move anymore!"[21]

Some Guardia officers felt themselves being forced into an
impossible position. "To save our lives we have to kill our own peo-

ple," said one Guardia colonel. "We know that everyone sympathizes with the rebels. It is we who are in real danger, not the boss. He has millions and his airplanes ready to fly at any moment. But we are the ones who will face the firing squad."[22]

Against Managua's rebel-held barrios of Open Tres, Luis Somoza, and El Dorado, the Guardia used a constant barrage of mortars. "In the mountains mortars threw up dirt," remembered one seasoned FSLN fighter. "In the city they sent flying pieces of rock, glass, and metal. The mortars drove me crazy. The noise . . . the shrapnel . . . and you never knew where they were coming from. Every day the attacks grew more intense."[23]

An exodus of refugees could be seen leaving the city. Clutching a few valuable belongings, their children, and white flags, they traveled by truck, bus and foot. Virginia Sanchez remembers seeing groups of them leaving by the Southern Highway. "They were staring ahead or at the ground. They seemed in shock, totally defeated. When we asked them where they were going, they shook their heads."[24]

By the second week of June, the fighting in Nicaragua was more savage and widespread than ever. Sandinista commanders struggled to keep abreast with the tide of change. Father Ernesto Cardenal captured some of the danger and excitement of the time in his poem "Final Offensive":

It was like a voyage to the moon
with complexity and precision in all details
accounting for all that was foreseen and also what was not.
A voyage to the moon in which the slightest mistake
    could be fatal.
"Workshop here"—"Come in, Assumption"—"Come in Cornfield."
"Workshop" was León, "Assumption" Masaya, "Cornfield" Estelí.
And the calm voice of Dora María, the girl from "Workshop,"
    saying that enemy reinforcements were circling in dangerously,
    the voice singsong and calm,
"Workshop here. Do you read me?"
And the voice of Rubén in Estelí. The voice of Joaquín in
"Office."
"Office" was Managua.
"Office" would be out of ammunition in two more days ("Over").
Precise instructions, in code, where the landing would be made . . .
And Dora María: "We don't have the rear guard well guarded. Over."
Serene, calm voices intermixing on the Sandinista frequency.

And there was a time when the two forces stayed even, and the danger
   was growing and growing.
It was like a voyage to the moon. And with no mistakes.
So very many coordinating their work in the great project.
The moon was the earth. Our piece of earth.
And we got there.
Now it begins, Rugama, to belong to the poor;
this earth
(with its moon).[25]

"The insurrection began in Chinandega, but went bad," remembered Humberto Ortega. "It continued in León with the actions of
the Rigoberto Pérez López Western Front and quickly went from a
little to a lot. In the south where there were no cities and no
masses we fought a conventional war. But the fighting was difficult. It was a thin neck of land with only one highway. But if the
Southern Front hadn't tied up Somoza's elite forces it would have
been difficult for us."[26]

After routing the Guardia at El Naranjo, Edén Pastora's troops
captured the town of El Ostional. The plan was to take a back road
into the provincial capital of Rivas and cut off the southern part of
the country. But El Naranjo and El Ostional were hill country with
no forts, towns, factories, or geographic positions to hold. Then a
fierce storm broke.

After a week of constant rain, the *compas* were sleeping in
trenches two feet deep in water. The Guardia, meanwhile, was hitting them with 500-pound bombs, push-pulls, artillery, and everything else.

It was still raining on the eighth when Pastora gave the order to
retreat. The withdrawal turned into a disaster when the Guardia
spotted the 300 *compas* moving. Los Angeles native Alejandro
Murguía was in the rear guard when the *compa* next to him was
picked off by a Galil. "Piing! here below the eye. The *compa* cried
out, 'Ayy! They've hit me,' and fell down dead at my feet. . . . We
lost a lot of good *compas* in that retreat in the rain."[27]

Hugo Spadafora's column was the last to leave. Beneath a hail of
bullets and mortars, the Panamanian doctor left behind a knap-
sack containing his personal effects.

On the Costa Rican side of the border, Pastora's forces repaired
their weapons and tended to the funguses that had grown on everybody's feet. Somoza claimed victory in the south. On June

ninth reporters were flown down for a tour of the battlefield. "They were equipped with sophisticated equipment and they commanded ten kilometers of territory," said the confident, mustachioed Comandante Bravo. "We killed about one hundred and twenty of them and the rest are in Costa Rica. We won the battle this morning at nine A.M."[28] Reporters were shown captured Chinese-made RPG-2 rocket launchers, Garand M-1s, Galils, and Belgian FALs that had been shipped from Panama with the serial numbers filed off.

Six days later, Edén Pastora was back with a force of between 1,200 and 1,500. Supported with newly arrived artillery, they took the border town of Peñas Blancas in a surprise attack.

The funguses were gone, but coordination was still a problem. When FSLN veteran Leonel Poveda reached the front lines, he found chaos. "They [Pastora and his commanders] had put their artillery up front, and I said, 'How can that be? It ought to be behind us.' The National Guard almost took the artillery away from us. I arrived just as the National Guard was about to circle the artillery. Some of the *compas* had already given up to the National Guard. That's how the sad things began. We were there through June and into July."[29]

7

Through the fatal pages of history, our land is made of vigor and glory; our land is made for humanity.   —Rubén Dario

After my ten years' service in Latin America, Nicaragua offered many surprises. For one, the largest Central American country in area (57,000 square miles, roughly the size of North Carolina), is the most sparsely populated (2.5 million). It's a hot, wet, poor country of unpredictable natural phenomena that have periodically brought destruction in the form of earthquakes, volcanic eruptions, droughts, and even hurricanes.

In the words of native poet Pablo Antonio Cuadra: "Like Botticelli's Venus, Nicaragua rose from the sea—young in comparison to the rest of America—lifted on the shoulders of that line of volcanoes . . . —which are pivots of our slender geographic bridge, land which from that time on was to serve as a pass and a link between the two Americas."[1]

Culturally, this "place of much water" has been a bridge between North and South America, Spain and the Indians, the United States and Latin America, the real and the fantastic, the known and the unknown. It's this convergence, this sense of different lev-

els of experience operating at once that vitalized the verse of Nicaragua's world-famous poet, Rubén Dario, who wrote,

> My pick is working
> deep in the soil of this unknown America,
> turning up gold and opals and precious stones,
> an altar, a broken statue. And the Muse
> divines the meaning of hieroglyphics.
> The strange life of a vanished people emerges
> from the mists of time.[2]

Dario, who was born in León in 1867, spent most of his creative
life in Buenos Aires and Paris. Writers as diverse as Federico
García Lorca, Octavio Paz, and Pablo Neruda have given him
credit for lifting the Spanish language out of the dark corridors of
the medieval, Roman Catholic court and infusing it with new life.
He said that "words should paint the color of a sound, the aroma
of a star; they should capture the very soul of things."[3]

Even in English translation, Dario's poetry works directly on the
senses—

> Noon is burning the whole island
> The reef is in flames,
> The blue sky pours down fire.
> . . . Far off,
> Rough with antiquity, solemn with myth,
> Stands the stone tribe of old volcanoes
> Which, like all else, await their
> Instant of infinity.[4]

Dario's poetic sensibility has influenced poets from the French
symbolists to Spanish modernists. It's been said that he spawned a
whole country of poets. In fact, it's not unusual to find a market
vendor who can quote him, or compose verses of her own. World-
class poets like Salomón de la Selva, José Coronel Urtecho, Ernesto Mejia Sanchez, Pablo Antonio Cuadra, and Ernesto Cardenal
have followed in his literary footsteps.

Most inhabitants have lived and worked on the slender strip of
land that separates Lakes Managua and Nicaragua from the Pacific. It was on this natural bridge that the first known meeting of
North and South America took place—between the Nahua-

speaking mountain tribes who built the Aztec empire and the Chibcha-speaking hillsmen from beyond Darien. As far as anyone can tell, it was on this spot that Nicaragua became a colony.

Since then, Nicaragua has been visited by Cortes's lieutenants, English pirates, Sir Francis Drake, Admiral Nelson, Cornelius Vanderbilt, William Walker, American filibusters, U.S. Marines, Howard Hughes, and foreigners of all stripes eager to exploit it for wealth or glory.

Having been despoiled so often, it's no wonder Nicaraguans are jealous of their virtue. While a prisoner of Somoza in the early sixties, *La Prensa* editor Pedro Joaquín Chamorro made a discovery: "I had my first notion of what 'country' meant. The pure land, wounded a thousand times by dominating tyrants; her simple peasants, my brothers, left illiterate by the ambitious, taught me to read the truth without letters. . . . I knew that no one had the right to snatch a people's destiny from them."[5]

On this sensitive consciousness, the imperialist credo stung like a knife. Carleton Beals, a reporter for the *Nation* in 1932, characterized the imperialist at a time when U.S. Marines were hunting Sandino:

> The imperialist never stops to try to reconcile his inner conviction that backward, dark people are incapable of progress, efficiency, honesty, or democracy with his belief that the only way for a foreign people to be happy is to be standardized in the mold already created in the United States. Because of his faith in the value of lightness of skin, he hobnobs with the aristocratic Creoles who have exploited and betrayed their countries since the first days of independence.[6]

Rubén Dario pointed to this hypocrisy in his poem "To Roosevelt":

> You think life is fire
> that progress is eruption,
> that where you put the bullet
> the future blooms.
> No.
> The United States is great and strong.
> When it trembles a deep tremor
> passes through the enormous vertebrae of the Andes.

If you scream, it resounds like a
lion's roar.
You are rich.
You merge the cult of Hercules with
the cult of Mammon;
and Liberty lights the way to
easy conquest;
raising her torch in New York.[7]

For the better part of the twentieth century, the United States
was seen as the greatest threat to Nicaraguan identity. Much of the
enmity we inspired seems to have derived from our support of the
Somozas. In 1960, reporter Marvin Alisky made the following observation: "Anti-Somoza Nicaraguans range from Communists,
rootless political adventurers, followers of Castro, and terrorists on
one side to priests, Conservative landowners, idealistic students,
and disgruntled businessmen on the other. The one thing they
have in common at the moment, aside from their hatred of Somoza, is a dislike of the United States for what they think is our
unquestioning support of the dictatorship."[8]

Due in part to the instability of its geography, Nicaraguans had
a way of looking to greater forces to explain their oppressed condition. Before Lake Nicaragua had a name, it had been a gulf of
the Pacific. Then an earthquake closed it in, entrapping sharks,
swordfish, and seahorses. The choice was extinction or a painful
adaption to freshwater life.

Like the sea life in Lake Nicaragua, the Nicaraguan people have
found ways to adapt. Despite their misgivings about U.S. government policy, I found them to be open, warm, and hospitable. Even
the heavy yoke of the Somoza dictatorship hadn't stifled their ex-
pressive, independent spirit.

They are predominantly mestizo, of mixed Spanish and Indian
blood. A smattering of Miskito, Sumu, and Rama Indians live
along the Atlantic coast. While Somoza and his friends had prof-
ited, the majority of people lived in squalor. By the end of the seventies, life expectancy (fifty-five years) for Nicaraguans, the
nation's per capita income ($590 per year), literacy rate (52 per-
cent), annual growth (0.9 percent), and gross national product
were the lowest in Central America—and the lowest in Latin
America, with the exception of Haiti.

Before the 1972 earthquake, almost a third of Nicaraguans lived
in and around Managua—a city that was never rebuilt afterward.

All that remained of the downtown when I arrived in 1979 were the ruined hulks of the *palacio nacional* and post office, the towering Bank of America building, a beige bunker that housed the Rubén Dario Theater, and the gray facade of the cathedral, which loomed like a ghost over the landscape of the polluted lake and bulldozed hills.

While weeds and brush grew over the downtown rubble, the city had been added to, with new white and pastel suburbs for the rich and settlements of tin and cardboard squatters shacks for the poor. Rancid Lake Managua often overflowed its shores, inundating the barrios of Quinta Nina, Acahualinca, and Open Tres.

I was on my way to the U.S. Embassy. Expensively imported cars and small trucks swerved around holes in the roadway where cement blocks had been pulled up to make barricades. As I showered and shaved earlier, I had relived my meeting with Somoza the afternoon before. The fact that a U.S. congressman had been acting as an adviser to the dictator struck me as even more bizarre in the light of day. Rereading the cable I had sent to Washington, I was convinced that I hadn't been emphatic enough in stating my impression that Somoza was prepared to step down.

In my office, with the whine of a noisy air conditioner in the background, I composed a follow-up cable. "At this afternoon's meeting with Somoza, I would like to establish a departure date so that we can have something specific to point toward. I was thinking of next Tuesday. I will insist that he abide by the understanding reached yesterday that he resign and work out precise details of his resignation with us."[9]

A few hours later, I was sitting across from Somoza again at "La Curvita." Malcolm Barnebey and military attaché Lieutenant Colonel McCoy came with me to record their impressions. Somoza was accompanied by Foreign Minister Quintana, Minister of Interior General Samuel Genie, and Luis Pallais. He was dressed in combat fatigues instead of the gray pinstripes of the day before. Having just returned from inspecting his troops, he said: "I think we're winning." Then without a moment's hesitation he blurted out: "You are asking me to surrender unconditionally. I am ready to; the only thing I have is the moral voice to tell you: don't sacrifice people who have been your tools in your hands and props in your foreign policy."[10]

By now I was familiar with his unique way of stating things. Malcolm Barnebey sat up. I told Somoza that it was not our intention to "sacrifice" anyone.

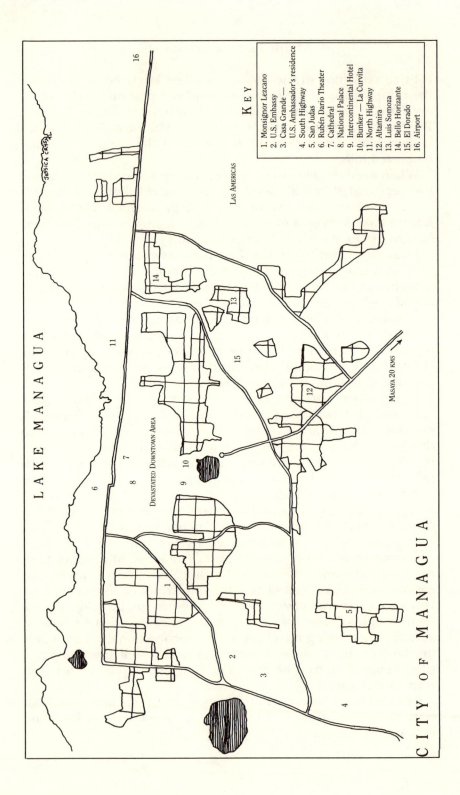

LAKE MANAGUA

JESSICA CREEK

CITY OF MANAGUA

DEVASTATED DOWNTOWN AREA

LAS AMERICAS

MASAYA 20 KMS

KEY

1. Monsignor Lezcano
2. U.S. Embassy
3. Casa Grande —
   U.S. Ambassador's residence
4. South Highway
5. San Judas
6. Rubén Darío Theater
7. Cathedral
8. National Palace
9. Intercontinental Hotel
10. Bunker — La Curvita
11. North Highway
12. Altamira
13. Luis Somoza
14. Bello Horizante
15. El Dorado
16. Airport

He was being dramatic, making speeches for the record. I could almost hear the tape recorder whirring in the background. "From now on every drop of blood that's going to be shed in Nicaragua is going to be the responsibility of the United States!"

"We don't accept that," I shot back. "We just don't accept that." His aides seemed surprised by my tone.

Somoza lowered his voice. "If you don't accept that, I want to know."[11]

I was anxious to move on. "Look, Mr. Ambassador, I have a conscience to live with. . . . I think I have done what's best for my country."[12]

Getting him to focus on the details of his departure was not going to be easy. Maybe it was because he had a new audience in the persons of Barnebey and McCoy. Whatever his reason, he couldn't refrain from making speeches. "Let me go back in history. . ." I let him go. His interpretation of events was simplistic and paranoid. Basically, the United States and President Carter were out to get him. He said he didn't understand why.

"Please, Mr. President," I interrupted. "When we were at the point in the discussion last year on the plebiscite issue, we saw an imminent clash. . . . The plebiscite was your idea. We accepted it even though the FAO and the moderates were very skeptical. They thought it was a device to avoid the issue. . . . Still, we put in a great deal of effort because we thought it would test the popular will of this country, and eventually we failed them."[13]

"It wasn't my decision," countered Somoza.

"It was a last opportunity. Political forces have become polarized, because of you."

"I'm glad that I've done it! Because most of the time the United States is naive about the appreciation of things."

A minute ago we were taking advantage of him and his people. Now we were being naive. I said, "I think you do us a disservice."

He turned humble. "This is the time for friends to be frank. If I am screwed up, I want to be proven that I'm all screwed up. So let's get down to brass tacks. This is what we call here 'el derecho del berreo.' You don't have me 'checkmate,' you have me checked."

"We don't want you checked or checkmated."

"But I feel myself being checkmated. . . ." He lowered his head. "My dear friend, that's why I'm saying to you: I am ready to leave."[14]

I told him I was glad to hear that. But the modalities of his departure had to be worked out. "We don't want to see bloodletting by a group of Marxist ideologues sweeping in and holding kangaroo courts and killing people indiscriminately."[15]

He agreed. I told him we would like to preserve those elements of the Guardia that could be salvaged. But we needed his help.

Once again, he changed the subject. "I have been able to identify the enemy, which was not quite identified in September. In September it was total anti-Somocismo, and then after September the things came out, and we identified the enemy as being: one, the communists; two, the moderates; and three, the Baptist [Jimmy Carter]."[16]

I was running out of patience. I suggested that maybe I could come back tomorrow and we could concentrate on the constitutional procedure for him stepping down.

Foreign Minister Quintana spoke for the first time. It might be difficult to call Congress into session, he noted, because so many Conservative deputies have left the country. He said the U.S. Embassy knew where they were. I told him I would look into it and rose to leave. Somoza hung his head, sadly. "I'm already a spent round."[17]

As I bade farewell I asked if he would consider releasing Edmundo Jarquín, an economist who wrote editorials for *La Prensa,* as a gesture of goodwill. Jarquín had been taken from his home on June 7. He was alleged to have "contacts" with the FSLN.

Jarquín's case had been brought to my attention by William Dyal, a friend from our service together in Colombia in the late sixties when I was assigned to the Political Section of the embassy. Dyal, a Texas Baptist minister who entered the Johnson administration with fellow Baptist minister Bill Moyers, had been assigned as Peace Corps director in Colombia while Moyers went to the White House. Dyal subsequently served in Brazil before becoming the first director of the innovative Inter-American Foundation (IAF) in the early seventies. While director of IAF, Bill had worked with Jarquín on several projects in Nicaragua and had developed a high opinion of him. When I raised Jarquín's name with the embassy staff, I got no reaction.

Somoza asked: "Why do you want Jarquín's release?" I explained how his name had come up. As far as I knew, Jarquín had committed no crime.

Somoza didn't hesitate. "I'll order his release."[18]

Late that afternoon, on June 28, I went to call on the archbishop. Since Vatican Council II of 1962 and the Latin American Conference of Catholic Bishops in Medellín of 1968, the Catholic church in Latin America had been redefining its mission. "If the demands of justice and equity are to be satisfied," read the Vatican Council II proclamation, "vigorous efforts must be made . . . to remove as quickly as possible the immense economic inequalities which now exist."[19]

Following a long tradition of encouraging submission to and acceptance of poverty and the political order, the Catholic church in Latin America shifted to an activist program of grass-roots religious organizations to help the poor promote themselves and to demand social and economic reform from their governments.

The emerging "theology of liberation" took root in Nicaragua during the late sixties and early seventies, coinciding with the appointment in 1968 of Miguel Obando y Bravo of Matagalpa as archbishop of Managua. His predecessor, Alejandro Gonzalez y Robleto, often cited Pope Gregory XVI's encyclical *Mirari Vos* in support of the Somoza regime—"All authority comes from God, and all things are ordered by that same God. Therefore he who resists authority resists God."[20] One of Obando y Bravo's first acts as archbishop was to sell the new Mercedes Benz sent to him by Tachito as a present and donate the proceeds to the poor.

In 1971 Archbishop Obando y Bravo refused to register to vote in upcoming municipal elections and "dignify" electoral fraud. And in 1972 he and other members of the Nicaraguan Bishops Conference boycotted the inauguration of Tachito's hand-picked triumvirate. For these acts and his outspoken opposition to repression, Obando y Bravo had earned the alias "Comandante Miguel" from Somocistas.

While Archbishop Obando y Bravo was raising the banner of social justice, Jesuits, Maryknolls, Capuchins, and Trappists were organizing hundreds of study groups and youth clubs to promote spiritual growth through social action. Trappist priest Ernesto Cardenal, for one, founded a peasant community called Solentiname on an archipelago in Lake Nicaragua. In the barrios of Managua, Spanish priest Father José de la Lara created Ecclesiastical Base Communities where the poor were asked to relate Bible teaching to the suffering and deprivations of their own lives. The Jesuits, in the meantime, founded the Ecclesiastical Committee for Agrarian Progress (CEPA) to help rural campesinos articulate their political and economic demands. And in Zelaya Province, Capuchin fathers sent out 900 lay people as "delegates of the word" to teach literacy, health and consciousness raising in hard-to-reach rural areas.

This political activism brought Christian organizers up against the repressive face of the Somoza regime. Their activities were branded subversive and, increasingly during the 1970s, church lay workers began to be harassed. The political repression further radicalized many Christian activists, driving them to the conclusion that social change would come only after the Somoza regime was replaced. Many joined the FSLN, including several priests. The most renowned, Sacred Heart Father Gaspar Laviana, the parish priest of Tola, Rivas, tried to answer many people's questions in his brief essay "Why a Priest Fights."

"It fell to me," Father Gaspar wrote, "to see perhaps the most shameful, the most oppressed of Nicaraguans. I tried to save this situation in a Christian way, peacefully; seeking to raise these people by their own means, or with the means of their government. But I realized that this was a lie, a deception. I began to lose heart seeing that so much work was completely useless, that so many dreams were left in the air, because the people kept on living as before. That is why I joined this violent movement, since I realized that nothing peaceful was possible. Any other way would have been dishonest to an entire people and to myself."[21]

While some priests took up arms, others turned to the pen. In 1976, thirty-five Capuchin priests wrote a letter to Somoza complaining about human rights abuses and documenting cases of torture by Guardia Nacional patrols. When the letter was publicized internationally, it created problems for Somoza with the newly elected Carter administration.

The following year, a pastoral letter drafted by Nicaragua's Episcopal Conference concluded: "The confusion and ills of the nation are growing. On the one hand, the accumulation of land and wealth in the hands of a few is growing. On the other hand, the powerless are deprived of their farmlands through threats and are taken advantage of because of the state of emergency. Many crimes are ignored without the corresponding legal sanctions which diminishes respect for fundamental rights."[22]

On February 9, 1978, following the assassination of Pedro Joaquín Chamorro, Archbishop Obando y Bravo published a letter in *La Prensa* legitimizing armed resistance to injustice as a last resort. "I have always believed that we must first exhaust all non-violent means. That we must use nonviolence actively, within the bounds of civil society. But I must recognize what some moral and theological authorities have, that collective armed resistance is acceptable when the following three conditions are fulfilled: (1) the existence of a self-evident injustice of extreme gravity that would legitimize an undisputed situation of self-defense; (2) the proven failure of all concrete peaceful solutions; (3) that armed struggle caused by injustice will cause less suffering than the perpetuation of that injustice."[23]

Archbishop Obando y Bravo came out to greet me as I stepped out of the car. He lived in a rustic, tree-shaded house on a dirt road behind the church of Santo Domingo. The hulking shell of the downtown cathedral had been declared irreparable, so the archbishop was using the parish in Santo Domingo as his cathedral church.

He hadn't changed since we first met in 1973 after the earthquake. His only sign of age was a bristle of gray hair at his temples. He was solidly built, broad-faced, and swarthy, evidence of his mestizo ancestry, and had a man-of-the-soil quality that I found compelling. I knew that some found him rigid and overbearing because of his strongly held convictions. Since I prefer the company of those who know what they believe in, I felt myself drawn to this deeply religious man and valued his judgment.

His rustic compound was a serene sanctuary after the charged atmosphere of downtown Managua. Lush banana fronds bowed over flowering bushes. A musty sweetness rose from the bougainvillea and damp earth. Away from the grit of cruel conflict, the tightness in my stomach eased.

We settled into wicker rocking chairs on his breezy veranda and sipped iced tea. Obando described the human tragedy that gripped his country. Guardia soldiers had become brutalized and merciless. He received a daily stream of mothers, widows, and orphans who came to voice their grief. "It has to end," he said, gravely. "In the name of God and humanity, this terrible bloodbath has to stop."[24]

I asked what he thought of the Sandinistas. He said he knew some of their leaders and many of their soldiers and operatives. While he sympathized with their cause, the ideological tone of their rhetoric concerned him. He was afraid that once in power they would try to impose their ideology. The people were fed up with Somoza and that's why he would fall.

As I began to describe my mission, semiautomatic fire erupted in the distance and drew nearer. The archbishop was pleased that the United States put a high premium on preventing reprisals and promised to do what he could to help. He said Somoza wouldn't step down without major pressure, which he doubted the United States would apply. I tried to reassure him of our determination to end the conflict. He listened, but wasn't convinced.

The firing grew closer. I asked if he saw any possibility of the Executive Committee arrangement working at this late date. He was impressed by the individuals named, but offered no encouragement. "The divisions in my country are so great," he said, "that a reconciliation would be difficult to achieve under the best of circumstances."[25] He didn't need to remind me that present circumstances weren't ideal.

The shots were so close that they seemed to be coming from the trees behind us. I started to ask about the possibility of arranging a cease-fire, when he interrupted me. "They won't harm me," he said. "But you're not safe."

On our return, as we wove through various Guardia checkpoints manned by weapons carriers with .50-millimeter machine guns, I asked my security officer, Frank Juni, if he had reviewed the security situation on the Masaya Highway before leaving the embassy compound. From the shotgun seat he nervously admitted that he had only checked with the CIA station chief. I let him know that he had never warned me of the danger. His face turned red. I wished him to understand that I wanted to make the decision whether or not to go into a dangerous situation—not him, or the station chief. "Never make this mistake again," I said.

Before my first meeting with Somoza, I had instructed my staff to arrange for me to meet with the "wise men." It turned out that Ismael Reyes, head of the Nicaraguan Red Cross, was the only one who was readily available. On the morning of June 29 I was sitting across a coffee table from a grizzly bear of a man who had settled himself comfortably into the center of the black naugahyde couch in my office at the embassy. I extended greetings to Reyes from Ambassador Bowdler, who, I said, was in Costa Rica conferring with the FSLN junta. Reyes seemed surprised.

I asked for his assessment of the current situation. He was brief and to the point. "The Guardia cannot hold much longer. Somoza cannot recover. All he can do is inflict more pain on the people."[26]

"Would the junta in San José permit popular participation?" I asked.

He had read their Plan de Gobierno, but was skeptical. "It sounds good, yes, but will they use it?"

There was earnestness and solidity about the man. I could see why Bowdler held him in such high regard. Reyes had seen the agony of Nicaraguans from rich to poor. Lives had been radically disrupted; people's plans and dreams had been destroyed. The pillars had been knocked out from under their society and it was falling on their heads. Responding to the tragic suffering of his people, Reyes had entrusted his cosmetics business to subordinates in order to devote himself to his job as president of the Nicaraguan Red Cross.

He reported that the Red Cross was seriously overburdened. I promised to try to help fill the shortage in food and medicine. Reyes explained that their limited and overworked staff presented the main problem. Working in collaboration with the International Red Cross, they were not only risking life and limb to attend to the wounded on both sides, but also visiting prisons, hospitals, and staging areas to ensure that prisoners were cared for and not mistreated. Given the proportions of the conflict, it was a mammoth task.

I filled Reyes in on recent events in Washington and the OAS conference. He looked at me quizzically, wondering where this would lead. I told him that I had been sent by my government to see if we could organize a transition of power that would avoid reprisals and include the participation of a wide spectrum of political forces.

He sat upright. "Did Somoza say he will resign?" I told him that I had initiated the dialogue with Somoza only last evening. There were still many details to work out.

Reyes wasn't satisfied. I continued: "I have been asked to explore the possibility of of forming a transitional government composed of highly prestigious individuals like yourself who would govern for an interim period, while electoral and constitutional structures could be established as a necessary prelude to popular elections."

I had his full attention. "Is the United States prepared to send in troops to stop the fighting and support this transitional government?"[27] Reyes asked. "No," I said, beginning to make the case that we would first negotiate a cease-fire.

He interrupted. "Then it won't work. You see, it's too late to try to patch things up."

I tried to push the case further, but he cut me off. Looking at me sadly, he asked whom else I planned to approach. I listed the others: Emilio Alvarez Montalbán, Mariano Fiallos, Felipe Manteca, Adolfo Calero.

Reyes offered no encouragement. He got up to leave. "I hope you don't consider me rude, Ambassador Pezzullo. I have met you today for the first time and I respect your willingness to try to help my country. We need help, believe me. But, please understand . . . it is too late, 'way too late to be devising schemes. You see?" He stopped at the door. "Besides, and don't take this personally, there is little respect left among us Nicaraguans for the United States. You raised our hopes during the mediation, but you failed us, you know. Good luck."[28]

In the next two days I met with the other "wise men" who could be reached. Mariano Fiallos was sequestered in León, which was controlled by the Sandinistas, and Felipe Manteca, we were told, was out of the country. Emilio Alvarez Montalbán, whom I later came to treasure as close friend and astute observer, was less outspoken than Reyes, but conveyed the same message. Adolfo Calero, a tall, gregarious graduate of Notre Dame University who was very much at home with Americans, was intrigued by the idea, but curious about how it would work.

I was convinced that the situation had deteriorated too far for the Executive Committee ("wise men") plan to succeed and cabled my views to Washington: "It is apparent that we have little if any chance of putting together an Executive Committee of any size. The opposition figures we identified have either openly supported the Provisional Junta or are fearful of playing an independent role."[29] But the idea didn't die easily in Washington.

8

We'll keep struggling so that someday all our people will dream in color.   —FSLN leader Doris María Tijerino

The Frente Sandinista had been founded unceremoniously in 1961 by three veterans of student protests of the 1950s—Carlos Fonseca Amador, Tomás Borge, and Silvio Mayorga. Carlos Fonseca, the illegitimate son of an administrator of Somoza agricultural properties in Matagalpa, was the dominant political thinker of the group. He had studied and written about Sandino, whom he regarded as "a kind of path."[1] He had also traveled to the Soviet Union and recorded his impressions in a booklet, "A Nicaraguan in Moscow." Circulated clandestinely in the universities, it advanced the Soviet system as a model for Latin America. His views were naive and uncritical: "Because production is planned . . . they never have to suffer economic crises, nor do they suffer from overproduction, and, consequently, never have been obligated to throw tea into the sea, burn cotton, or allow apples to spoil."[2]

In the mid-fifties, both Fonseca and Tomás Borge, the socially outgoing son of successful Matagalpa shopkeepers, were enrolled in the law faculty of the UNAN (Universidad Nacional Autónomo de Nicaragua) in León, where they experienced great alienation. To Borge, "The university was a roof, some walls, an indifferent, obscure corridor, without familiar nostalgia and smelling of dissected dogs: the pits."[3] Both young men participated in the student uprisings that followed the elder Somoza's assassination and were jailed.

In 1959 Fidel Castro overthrew the corrupt Batista regime in Cuba. "The victory of the armed struggle in Cuba," Borge wrote, "more than a joy, was the lifting of innumerable curtains, a flash of light that shone beyond the simple and boring dogmas of time."[4]

In July 1961, Borge and Fonseca, along with Silvio Mayorga, met in Tegucigalpa, Honduras, and formed the Frente Nacional de Liberación. "Sandinista" was later added to the name at Fonseca's insistence. According to Borge, the FLSN was "born not as a guerrilla group but as a revolutionary organization that used guerrilla warfare as an instrument of struggle."[5]

Adopting the Che Guevara *foco* theory—creating a guerrilla base in a hard-to-reach area among sympathetic peasants—they led sixty mostly poorly trained students across the Rio Coco into the heavily forested mountains near the Honduran border. But their efforts to politicize the Miskito Indians failed. Despite the guidance of Sandino veteran Colonel Santos López, the group managed to get lost and ran into a strong Guardia patrol. They quickly lost a third of their force. The remainder retreated to Honduras, where many were arrested.

Throughout the mid-sixties the group struggled against extinction. They had roughly twenty activists in the cities of Managua and León trying to infiltrate unions and another ten or so in the mountains trying to organize a peasant base. When Fonseca was deported from Honduras in 1965, he traveled to Guatemala, where he met FAR (Fuerzas Armadas Revolucionarios) leader Luis Turcios Lima. Lima, who had been studying the Asian guerrilla concept of prolonged warfare promulgated by Mao and Vo Nguyian Giap, convinced Fonseca to return to Nicaragua to test the new strategy.

This time Fonseca chose a remote mountain peak called Pancasán in Matagalpa for the guerrilla base. He planned for a gradual buildup of material, human, and ideological resources. This would be the start of a slow, patient struggle that would gather momentum against the crumbling dictatorship.

"Pancasán lasted nine months, from December [1966] to August [1967]," recalled Borge. "Our work was slow: organizing the farmers, establishing conduits. We set up a good communications and intelligence network. We gained political control of the area; we had a lot of support. But we had a lot of firefights [with the Guardia] and our military capability was limited.

Furthermore, we made tactical errors that were of a strategic nature. We divided into three groups. One was led by Carlos Fonseca, who was the guerrilla leader. Another was led by Silvio Mayorga, who was to make incursions into the mountainside. I was in charge of the third group near Matagalpa to open conduits. The Guardia came between us like a wedge. When I found out what was happening, I moved toward Carlos's position. I arrived, but Silvio could not—he and his whole group died. Rigoberto Cruz also died there—a heroic death, really. Even the Guardias recalled that Rigoberto, horribly wounded, held his intestines with one hand and fought with the other."[6]

A jubilant Tachito Somoza claimed that the Sandinistas no longer existed. The surviving militants fled to the cities. Twenty-three-year-old organizer Daniel Ortega was one of the those arrested in Managua. His younger brother Humberto fled to Costa Rica where he wrote, plotted, and organized. Borge, Fonseca, and others went to Cuba for further training.

As Borge tells it: "After Pancasán we began the silent accumulation of forces that gradually formed an organized structure in the barrios."[7] The process was not so smooth. Urban cells proved to be particularly vulnerable to Somoza's extensive network of *orejas* (spies). On July 15, 1969, one FSLN safe house in Delicia del Volga, a few blocks from the old city center of Managua, was surrounded by Guardias with Staghound armored cars, heavy weapons, and tear gas. Four Sandinistas were killed immediately, and another two captured and tortured. Julio César Buitrago, head of the Frente's urban guerrillas, was the only one in the house who remained alive.

Omar Cabezas, who was a Frente activist in León, recalled,

> The Guard, in a total screw-up, broadcast this battle on television. Sitting in front of the screen at the University Club in León, we could see a huge number of Guardias staked out in various spots, in twos and threes, standing behind trees or cars, kneeling behind walls, or lying flat on their bellies, all firing at the house.

There was no sound. We couldn't take our eyes off the screen—
the automatic weapons were spitting out spent cartridges at an
incredible speed; we strained to see bits of concrete, wood, glass,
and paint flying off the impact of hundreds of bullets hitting the
house. We saw the barrel of Julio's submachine gun at the balcony window, and the smoke of his gun bursts when he fired
back. Then he was at the basement window, or at another window on the first floor, or at the door of the second floor that
opened onto the street. Then Julio wasn't anywhere to be seen,
and the Guard wasn't moving, and nobody was firing. The officers of the Guard were conferring outside. The Guard started
advancing on the house. Then, Julio suddenly appeared, shooting from one of those places I mentioned, and the Guardsmen
turned tail and shot off running in the other direction. . . .

A small tank rolled up; you could see how it cheered up the
Guard. . . . A small plane appeared. Then all hell broke loose—
the whole Guard started shooting, and the tank, and the plane,
almost grazing the roof, and in a matter of seconds the house was
a pile of rubble. Hunks of iron, zinc roofing, bits of wood—all
hurtling through the air with glass showering everywhere. We
couldn't imagine how Julio could possibly be alive. But the
Guardsmen were ducking; Julio's bullets were zinging past them;
they fell down wounded; and then . . . we saw Julio come burst-
ing through the front door, running and firing his submachine
gun, and seconds later he started to double over; still firing he
doubled over more, firing and doubling over until he fell to
the ground. We felt like crying, but at the same time we felt that
we had an indestructible force.[8]

Doris María Tijerino was one of the Sandinistas captured in this
battle. She reported,

They had orders to kill me, and had decided to do away with me
slowly so that I would suffer more, and they began the brutal
beatings. They even sent out an international cable saying that I
had been captured in combat, wounded and taken to the military
hospital where I had died in surgery. But they did not realize
that a journalist had been there when I was captured, that he
had taken some photos and recorded a brief conversation with
me, in which I said I was not wounded. He asked what the blood
was on my clothing, and I told him it was from a Guardia who
had fallen in combat. After the notice came out about my supposed death, this recording began to circulate in all the churches

and schools, because, of course, the media were censored. And that's what saved my life.

But they had already tortured me horribly, inflicting bruises and wounds in the genital area from forcing me to open my legs, and injuries on my face from beatings. I had deep cuts on my knees because they made me fall down on finely ground stones that they had put down on the floor. They would make me get up, brush my knees off, and fall down again. This they called the Vietnamese torture. I was naked and hooded the whole time, and they manhandled me; it was their way of degrading the person.[9]

By the end of the 1960s, young Nicaraguan activists trained in Cuba and at the Patrice Lumumba Friendship of the People's University in the Soviet Union began returning to Nicaragua. Some, led by Henry Ruiz (Modesto), joined the remnants of the Sandinista Front in Matagalpa determined to help the movement recover from Pancasán. Modesto's motto was: "In the mountains we will bury the heart of the enemy."[10]

It didn't seem like a real possibility to Omar Cabezas, who was one of those sent to join Ruiz. He recalled:

You joined the Frente because you believed in its political line. . . . You believed that the Frente was capable of overthrowing Somoza and the Guardia. We went up to the mountains with the idea that this was were the power lay, that myth of the compañero in the mountains, the unknown, "Modesto" . . . arms, the best men, indestructible power. And when you get to the mountains, you find there's "Modesto" and 15 others split into small groups. You almost reach the point of saying, my God, I've made the worst decision of my life."[11]

While Nicaraguan students were, in the words of Modesto, being "freed of their vain desires in the montaña," others, like the Ortega brothers—Daniel, Humberto, and Camilo—were radicalized while giving Bible lessons in the poor barrios of Managua. "Did you know Danielito was such a diligent, serious student that the brothers invited him to join their order?" asked their mother Lidia Saavedra de Ortega. She remembered:

Danielito and Humberto were always involved in the political struggle. So was their father. About the time of the Cuban revolution, my husband would defy the Guardia every afternoon by sitting in his rocking chair on the sidewalk in front of the house with the radio at full blast listening to Radio Havana. The two oldest [Daniel and Humberto] dedicated themselves completely to the revolutionary struggle. They were both jailed while they were still in secondary school for participating in student protests against the dictatorship.[12]

When Daniel was jailed again in 1967, he studied, read Victor Hugo's *Les Miserables* several times, and wrote letters and poetry which he sent to his family and Archbishop Obando y Bravo. While many of his poems were political, one of his most moving, "I Never Saw Managua When Miniskirts Were in Fashion," is a bittersweet commentary about his years in jail. Meanwhile, his brother Humberto trained in Cuba. On December 23, 1969, Humberto lost most of the use of his right arm when he was shot by Costa Rican police in an unsuccessful attempt to free Carlos Fonseca from jail.

One night in 1972, about a dozen youths from affluent families went into spiritual retreat with a priest named Uriel Molina. During their hours together, they reflected on religious convictions and how they related to the social and political inequities around them. Emerging with a heightened sense of political commitment, they formed a group—Movimiento Cristiano Revolucionario (MCR)—led by one of their members, Luis Carrión Cruz. "Christianity gave me the ideological tools to break with the bourgeois ideology that had been inculcated in me by my family and studies," said Cruz years later. "Because when you read the Bible honestly, you see that it's a revolutionary book, 'subversive' as they called it under Somoza."[13]

For over a year they lived in a commune behind Father Molina's church in the Riguero section of Managua, working with the poor and continuing their studies. "In the morning we read the Bible and in the afternoon we tried to organize the barrio so that the neighborhood could start solving its problems," remembered Carrión. "In the evenings with our friends and girlfriends we would play guitars around a campfire and argue about poetry and politics."[14] In 1973 the group merged with the FSLN.

Meanwhile, Carlos Fonseca, living in exile in Costa Rica, wrote extensively and continued organizing the resistance movement. In

1969 the first National Directorate of the FSLN was formed with Fonseca as secretary-general. It announced a Historic Program that was strongly anticapitalist and anti-U.S. Among the Frente's stated goals were "replacement of the constitutional theory of elected representation—never effectively implemented in Nicaragua—with a revolutionary government that would promote direct popular participation in its structures."[15]

The late sixties and early seventies were "a period of silence" for the FSLN. Direct confrontations with the Guardia were avoided. Instead, militants worked alone or in small groups to recruit individual campesinos. Slowly a chain of contacts spread through intermediary organizations like the Frente de Estudiantes Revolucionario (FER). Bank robberies continued to be a major source of funding.

Omar Cabezas, in *Fire From the Mountain*, characterized this period:

> Our practice of compartmentalization . . . meant that none of the compañeros knew the details of the organization as a whole. All you knew is what you heard, and the Frente made a lot of noise. We had posters plastered all over the streets, on the walls; we robbed banks, which all the radio stations reported while the whole country hung on to the beep-beep-beep-beep-beep of those famous flashes. With news like that going out to the whole country we saw ourselves as much bigger than we really were through the magnifying glass of publicity.[16]

When Tomás Borge returned from exile in 1971, he estimated that the group consisted of about seventy cadres working mostly underground. In the countryside around Managua, Borge and Oscar Turcios went to work training new recruits from the campuses in guerrilla tactics they had learned in the field and Cuba.

Then, on December 23, 1972, Nicaragua's political landscape shifted suddenly when an earthquake devastated Managua. The shameless greed of Somoza and his cronies in profiting from the crisis turned many middle-class merchants and farmers, who had up until then accepted government corruption as a cost of doing business, against the regime. Middle-class alienation became increasingly widespread. "Family conversations seemed to always turn anti-Somoza," remembered one daughter from a well-to-do family. "More and more I heard about friends joining or collaborating with the Sandinistas. For the first time we felt it was inevitable that Somoza had to go."[17]

With the mood of the country changing in their favor, the Sandinistas responded with bolder actions—like taking the cathedral in León for the ransom of guerrilla Comandante Chico Ramírez and a Salvadoran professor who had been taken prisoner by Somoza. Six unarmed Sandinistas, including Omar Cabezas and Manuel Calderón, seized the cathedral on December 23, 1973.

> It was beautifully decorated for a wedding, [remembered Calderón]. We made some decorative banners and stayed a month, until January 23, 1974. We would leave at times to coordinate with other compañeros who were organizing in the barrios and with the students. That was very important because at the time students were on vacation, and we were able to mobilize 8,000 people, students and residents of the working class neighborhoods. The Guardia responded with shots, jail, rifle butts, beatings. For example, I saw a woman, a simple vendor in the cathedral square, who began to argue with a guardia. He threw a smoke bomb which landed in her bag of yucca. So the woman grabs it, and throws it back at him. There were three Guardia together, and when the first one caught it, he threw it to the second, and the second one to the third, and then it exploded. They beat that woman, dragged her away and took her prisoner. The next day there was a demonstration of all the mercaderas, the women vendors, in León, and the Guardia released her.[18]

At the end of 1974, in a dramatic gesture to bring themselves to the attention of the world, the Sandinistas seized the house of former minister of agriculture and close friend of Somoza, José María (Chema) Castillo, who was throwing a party in honor of United States Ambassador Turner Shelton. It was an hour before midnight. Ambassador Shelton had already left. Ten men and three women commandos, including Joaquín Cuadra, raided the house, killing Chema and three guards. They captured Somoza's brother-in-law, Guillermo Sevilla-Sacasa, his foreign minister, the mayor of Managua, and thirty other prominent Nicaraguans.

Somoza and the country were stunned. Negotiating through Archbishop Obando y Bravo, serving as intermediary, the commandos were able to win the release of fourteen political prisoners (including Daniel Ortega, who been seven years behind bars), more than $1 million in cash, and the broadcast of a 12,000-word communique explaining their political and military goals. Two and a half days later, when they were bused to the airport for a flight to Cuba, people gathered on the streets of Managua to cheer.

Archbishop Obando y Bravo rode the bus that carried the commandos to the airport for their flight to Cuba. "It was a miracle that we didn't have an accident. Vehicles of all kinds drove along beside us to gawk. Many people on motorcycles and bicycles came up close to show gestures of support and love for the guerrilla commandos."[19]

Despite the raid's success, it immediately came under attack by a faction of the Sandinistas. Calling it "a petit-bourgeois deviation," they argued that because of the martial law and crackdown imposed by Somoza, more people were arrested than freed as a result of the raid. The leader of the theoretical attack, Jaime Wheelock, the son of a wealthy landed family from Jinotepe, had recently published a book—*Imperialismo y Dictadura*—which analyzed Nicaraguan history according to the classical social-class model of Marx and Engels.

Wheelock rejected the strategy of a peasant revolution, calling the peasantry "an anachronism." He argued instead that agrobusiness and industrial development had turned the Nicaraguan peasants into a real working class that could be mobilized into proletarian class struggle, as Marx had predicted.[20] Those who sided with Wheelock began to call themselves the Proletarian Tendency (TP) and to devote their energies to organizing militant unions and educating barrio dwellers in the populous western highlands.

The defenders of the Prolonged War strategy (GPP), especially Tomás Borge, fought back angrily, saying that Wheelock and his followers "cannot endure the rigor of guerrilla campaigns."[21] At meetings held in October 1975, Wheelock, Luis Carrión Cruz and other Proletarians were expelled from the Frente and threatened with assassination. Wheelock took refuge in a church. Borge explained: "We said that all this could be discussed, but at the same time there were disciplinary faults. We took measures, sanctions. And these sanctions were interpreted as reprisals for the political statements that were being made."[22]

Hoping to heal the split in the movement, Carlos Fonseca returned to Nicaragua in late 1975. After holding meetings with many of his lieutenants, he blamed Wheelock and his group, call-

Jamie Wheelock, Tom O'Donnell, and Ambassador Pezzullo at the U.S. ambassador's residence in 1980. Credit: Agencia de Comunicación Internacional, Managua

ing them "pseudo-Marxists" and attacking "the sterile dogma of their economic materialism." He also singled out Wheelock, claiming he was out of touch with Nicaraguan realities because of years spent in Chile and Europe.[23]

Siding with the Prolonged War faction, Fonseca went to the northern mountains to join Henry Ruiz. The man who many saw as the reincarnation of Sandino was killed there by a Guardia patrol on November 8, 1976.

"[Fonseca] was making his way to Modesto's group with a group of comrades," wrote Borge.

> Just beyond dusk, in the rain and along one of those pathways where calm is always suspect, they heard three revolver shots. The group took cover. Claudia, Carlos Aguero's lovely comrade, was able to observe—in sharp black and white—the light-footed

step of a peasant man. They could all hear the shouts: the guy was drunk on *cususa*. . . .

Carlos decided to wait twenty-four hours, and they resumed their march the following sundown. At the head of the group, the guide, then Carlos, and bringing up the rear of seven men, Claudia. The first shot of a Garand was heard and there was an immediate flush of birds. Seconds before the darkness was broken by machine gun fire, Carlos threw himself to the ground and shot his M-1, ordering the rest of the squadron to retreat. The combatants managed to crawl and take cover a short distance away. The explosion of numerous grenades and then total silence translated the painful fact: our leader was dead.[24]

The story at the time said that Fonseca's head was cut off and brought to Somoza, who declared the Sandinistas were finished. However, when Fonseca was reburied as a hero of the revolution in 1979, his body was intact.

Tomás Borge, who had been arrested in Managua, remembered hearing the news. "The commandant of the Tipitapa jail came to our cell, jubilant, with *Novedades* in his hand. 'Carlos Fonseca is dead,' he told us. We responded after a few seconds of silence: 'You are wrong, Colonel. Carlos Fonseca is one of those who never die.' The Colonel told us: 'All of you are really unbelievable.' "[25]

In the vacuum of leadership created with the death of Fonseca and arrest of Borge, a new, less dogmatic strategic line began to emerge from a group of exiles living in Costa Rica. Calling themselves Terceristas, they saw their way as a third evolutionary stage of the struggle.

As far as they were concerned, Jaime Wheelock's notion of building a mass party of the working class before seizing power was ridiculous. They were more practical and less patient. In their view, the backward, underdeveloped Nicaraguan economy and the weakness of the working class had to be compensated for by an advanced level of ideological and organizational development among the revolutionaries.

Led by the Ortega brothers, Daniel and Humberto, they sought to accelerate the pace of revolution by creating alliances with non-Marxist groups and nationalist elements of the bourgeois and private sector who opposed the Somoza regime. Humberto Ortega, in *Fifty Years of Sandinista Struggle,* pointed out that "a favorable correlation of forces was developing in which the Sandinistas could count on help from other Latin American countries and from sectors within the United States itself."[26]

The differences in strategy among the three FSLN tendencies were summed up by his brother Daniel: "I would say that the GPP proposes the accumulation of forces. They go to the *montaña* and isolate themselves from the daily struggle of the masses. The TP does not transcend propagandizing, although it is strong in the centers of production. We place ourselves at the front of the popular insurrection in cities, and carry out actions in the *montaña* and countryside."[27]

As the level of frustration with the Somoza regime grew exponentially, the Terceristas with their advocacy of popular insurrection proved to be the right group, with the right strategy, at the right time. As Humberto explained: "In order for the insurrection to be implemented nationally, it was necessary for us to unite the whole nation in all sectors that had conflicts with the Somoza regime. Without that very broad policy, we would not have achieved an insurrection."[28]

To this end, the Ortega brothers asked writer Sergio Ramírez in early 1977 to recruit a group of prominent opponents among members of the bourgeois opposition to support the Tercerista program. Known as Los Doce (the Twelve), they included an aristocratic corporate lawyer (Joaquín Cuadra Lacayo, father of the guerrilla leader), a millionaire owner of a supermarket chain (Felipe Manteca), the manager of the country's largest coffee-producing company (Emilio Baltodano Pallais), a banker (Arturo Cruz), a former rector of the national university (Carlos Tunnerman), two priests (Fernando Cardenal and Miguel D'Escoto), an agricultural engineer (Ricardo Coronel Kautz), a lawyer living in Costa Rica (Ernesto Castillo), a dental surgeon living in Mexico (Carlos Gutiérrez), and an architect living in California (Casmiro Sotelo).

Joaquín Cuadro Lacayo explained why he joined: "My son made me see the need for change in Nicaragua. We can't ignore the lesson of the sacrifice of our children if we are to see any progress in our country."[29] According to Arturo Cruz, "Los Doce was intended as an opposition government to be headed by Felipe Manteca. What Felipe and I didn't realize at the time is that most of Los Doce were already secret members of the FSLN."[30]

With the isolation of Henry Ruiz (Modesto) in the mountains, the imprisonment of Tomás Borge, and the death of Carlos Fon-

Brothers Daniel and Humberto Ortego carry the body of fallen comrade Germán
Pomares with the earthquake-damaged Managua Cathedral in the background.
Credit: Peter Schmid Camera Press, London 30802-9 (97) Globe Photos, Inc. 1993

seca and others, the Ortega brothers and Victor Tirado of the Terceristas began to dominate the leadership of the FLSN.

The first efforts of the group to incite popular insurrection failed. They began their operations in October 1977 with a coordinated attack on the towns of Ocotal, San Carlos, and Masaya, with skirmishes, bombings, and ambushes throughout the country. The Prolonged War faction and the Proletarians accused the Terceristas of militarism and adventurism.

Ironically, the first popular insurrections were spontaneous without leadership or direction from any faction of the FSLN. On February 26, 1978, the Indian district of Monimbo in Masaya revolted. Indians armed with hunting rifles, pistols, shotguns, and homemade explosives fought the Guardia Nacional for a week.

Archbishop Obando y Bravo traveled to Monimbo to offer to mediate the dispute. When he reached the Indian insurrectionists, he was surprised by what they asked. "Listen, we've been fighting with homemade bombs and any arms we could find in the neighborhood, but we're convinced that it won't be sufficient to stop the National Guard much longer. Because of this, it's necessary for you to obtain arms so that we can continue defending ourselves."[31]

Camilo, the youngest Ortega brother, and other Tercerista commandos rushed to Masaya to try to lead the Indians, but were killed. His brother, Tercerista strategist Humberto Ortega, called the uprising "premature" and "lacking vanguard direction."[32]

Six months later, on August 27, armed *muchachos* overran the streets of Matagalpa. This time it took days of aerial bombardment and armored assault by Somoza's elite EEBI units to crush the 400 ill-equipped teenagers and handful of Sandinistas who had rushed to join the uprising. When Obando y Bravo asked the combatants who was leading the revolt, they answered: "Sir, here there is no leader. It's only the people who have taken up arms, and we are the ones responsible."[33]

Once again the FSLN was caught as unaware as Somoza. Said Humberto Ortega: "We certainly could not oppose that mass movement, stop that avalanche. On the contrary, we had to put ourselves at the forefront in order to lead it and channel it to a certain extent."[34]

Over the objections of the Prolonged War faction and the Proletarians, the Terceristas called for a mass uprising one week after the retaking of Matagalpa, September 9. Led by the Terceristas, large numbers of armed civilians joined the revolt in Managua,

Masaya, León, Chinandega, and Estelí. In the latter four cities, the Guardia Nacional was besieged for days in their garrisons. Somoza, who called the attacks "a very big riot, but not a war," struck back savagely. When guerrilla units withdrew, their ranks had increased threefold.

Although few FSLN cadres were killed, the Red Cross estimated that 5,000 civilians died due to National Guard bombing and mop-up operations. Jaime Wheelock of the Proletarians called the Tercerista tactic of inciting towns to revolt and retreating "an act of scandalous political irresponsibility."

He explained: "When the offensive actions failed, leaving people ready to fight, what developed was a war of emplacement where most of the people exposed their lives and left themselves trapped and on the defensive without having prepared a retreat. I heard some reports that made me angry, which said something like: 'Our squads retreated without casualties.' And who was responsible for the dead who could not retreat so grandly?"[35]

It was clear after the September offensive that if the Sandinistas were going to succeed they would have to reach a reconciliation. To this end, Fidel Castro summoned leaders of the three factions to Havana. In early March 1979, they reached agreement to merge their forces politically and militarily.

A nine-person directorate was named, comprised of three men from each faction. From the Prolonged War group came Tomás Borge, Henry Ruiz, and former *La Prensa* reporter Bayardo Arce; from the Terceristas, the Ortegas and Victor Tirado; and from the Proletarians, Jaime Wheelock, Luis Carrión Cruz, and Carlos Nuñez.

On May 28, 1979, the FSLN's final offensive had begun with coordinated attacks from Costa Rica and Honduras, followed by uprisings in all the major cities. Popular revolt was the crucial element of the FSLN strategy. Without the Nicaraguan people fighting with them, the Sandinistas had no hope of defeating Somoza's 14,000-man Guardia Nacional.

9

Somoza is the National Guard. —An opposition leader

After my first two days in Managua, the Guardia Nacional remained an enigma. From the relative safety of the U.S. Embassy, I asked: "Now that their leader is in trouble, what are Guardia officers thinking? Will they remain loyal to *el jefe* to the bitter end?" And, most important, "Can the Guardia Nacional survive the Somozas as a professional army?"

When I posed this last question to Somoza in his air-conditioned residence on June 29, he seemed more interested in stories that had begun to appear in the *New York Times, Washington Post,* and *Miami Herald* speculating on his resignation. His minister of the interior, General Samuel Genie, pointed out one of these to me at the start of our third meeting.

Somoza reiterated: "I'm ready to resign. I would be crazy to think I could ignore the will of governments that lead 300 million people," he said in reference to the OAS resolution of June 23, which had clearly stung him.[1]

Once again I asked him to concentrate on the future. "How do we end the bloodshed?"

124

But Somoza was too busy feeling sorry for himself. "I guess you understand that right now my life is worth nothing, and the longer I stick around here, it will be worth less."[2]

I urged him to focus on the lives that were on the line for him in the cities and barrios of Nicaragua. I didn't expect him to be sympathetic to the Sandinistas. He had already shown the world his blatant disregard for the lives of the common citizens. "Aren't you interested in the survival of the National Guard?"

"Of course I am," he answered as his eldest son, Anastasio Somoza Portocarrero (El Chiguín, "the kid"), entered in camouflage fatigues. El Chiguín had come from the field, where he was directing much of the fighting under the code name "Alfa Sierra Papa." As director of the EEBI (Basic Infantry Training School), housed directly across from the bunker, Colonel Somoza was largely responsible for the character and outlook of the army. While his father had become morose and withdrawn, El Chiguín had seized the military initiative. At this point it was hard to say whether father or son commanded more respect in the Guardia.

A tall, good-looking man of twenty-seven, El Chiguín had been born in Tampa, Florida, like his mother, Hope. His interest in the military took him from Harvard Business School to the Royal Military Academy at Sandhurst in England, to training courses with the United States Army at Fort Benning, Georgia. At the age of twenty-one, he forfeited his U.S. citizenship by joining a foreign army, the Guardia Nacional. He had been director of the EEBI since 1977.

During the uprisings of 1977 and 1978 he had developed a reputation for being brutal. Even friends admitted he was "mercenary and bloodthirsty." He was also reputed to have won huge commissions from business deals with the government in fishing, tobacco, lumber, and distribution of heavy vehicles. In the words of one young woman who knew him, "Each generation of the Somozas was a little bit more corrupt."[3]

"I'm purported to be lots of things," said El Chiguín in his own defense, "among which I'm a sort of economic monster gobbling up every contract that the government can let loose, which is false."[4] He admitted that he had won some contracts, but only after open bidding.

With El Chiguín in the room, the atmosphere changed. While he always addressed his father respectfully as "Mr. President," El

Chiguín was not afraid to disagree. He began by saying that he was very interested in the idea of preserving some elements of the Guardia. I said that if the Guard hoped to survive, officers who had somehow been tainted by too close an association to the Somozas would have to be retired.

Somoza immediately balked: "These men are professional soldiers—"

El Chiguín broke in: "He's right, Mr. President. Some of these people just wouldn't make it." He went on to note that from the rank of lieutenant colonel and up, about 70 to 80 percent of Guardia officers were at retirement age. The younger officers, he felt, "are more used to a different, more flexible style of leadership . . . and they have more leeway in their decision making."[5]

Finally we seemed to be getting somewhere. "It's crucial that the man selected to head the Guardia be someone who can command the loyalty of the army and at the same time deal with a completely new political environment," I added. "Is it possible to find someone with those qualities?"

"I believe so," El Chiguín answered without hesitation. I thanked him for his input and told him that he could be instrumental in making the transition work. His father, however, had a different agenda.

"These people, Mr. Ambassador, are not fighting for Somoza, they are fighting the enemy they have fought for the last eighteen years—Communist Castroites. That's why you have not had any success in getting these people to turn against me, even with the overtures the United States has made."[6]

I stopped him right there. "Wait a minute," I said. "What overtures?"

"When you say that I should leave, that's an overture to the army!"

"Please, please . . . we have never sought to undercut you!"

"You have done that publicly, which is a way of doing it."[7] His mood changed suddenly. Before our eyes he seemed to deflate. Clearly, the pressure and the long nights of gunfire and vodka were having their effect. His son looked sad as his father continued: "Someday I'm going to have to die. . . . I'm dead for all intents and purposes. But what are these officers going to do? Because philosophically, these people are democratic."

El Chiguín took the floor. "Whatever happens in this damned country, let's hope that within a couple of years people can go out and vote for what the hell they want."

I agreed. "That's the key."

"Because that's the only way there'll ever be peace in this damned country," added El Chiguín.[8]

Back at the embassy, I asked military attaché Lt. Col. James McCoy if he could confirm El Chiguín's assessments. He couldn't. Over the years the Somozas had jealously guarded contacts with their army. According to the unwritten protocol, any communications between outsiders and Guardia officers had to be approved by Somoza or his son. To the detriment of their own policy makers, U.S. military attachés through the years had honored the understanding. Consequently, we knew damned little about the Guardia.

Lieutenant Colonel McCoy admitted later that had he tried to initiate contact with Guardia officers, "it would have looked like we were trying to replace Somoza."[9] Apparently, at one point El Chiguín had even warned him that there could be "an accident" if McCoy contacted a Guardia officer without informing him first. But McCoy never shared this with me.

It was ironic. While most of Somoza's officers had trained in U.S. schools, we had practically no understanding of their thinking at this critical time. To redress this shortcoming, I instructed McCoy and the CIA station chief to begin to subtly sound out Guardia officers. Not only were we interested in their feelings about the conflict, but also we had to begin to identify officers who could lead the Guardia after Somoza's departure.

On the morning of June 30, McCoy met with five lieutenant colonels at the Campo de Mayo in Managua. He was surprised by their responses. They admitted that there had been much discussion of the political future of their country among officers stationed in Managua. The mood had shifted dramatically in recent days. Most now agreed that Somoza had to leave. Only a few still believed that the fate of the Guardia Nacional was tied to that of the Somoza family.

This might have been wishful thinking on their part, but it gave credence to the theory that a cleansed, reconstituted Guard could survive and even win acceptance from the Nicaraguan people. As a result of their discussions, McCoy and the station chief composed a list of officers who might be able to command the Guardia Nacional during the transition period following Somoza's departure. Interestingly, it included Col. Enrique Bermúdez, Nicaragua's military attaché to Washington, Col. Nicolás Valle Salinas, chief of Managua's police, Major Emilio Salazar (also known as Comandante Bravo), and an officer I had never heard of, Lt. Col. Federico Mejia, an executive officer with the police department.[10]

Before McCoy was able to finish his report, the repercussions of his visit were felt in Washington. One of the Guardia officers attending, Lt. Col. Alberto Smith, had informed El Chiguín, who told his father, who called his friend Congressman Murphy in Washington, who put a call through to Army Chief of Staff General Edward Meyer, who cabled the embassy to ask what McCoy was up to—the implication being that the embassy was plotting a coup.

In my answer to Washington I suggested that "someone inform Murphy we are seeking ways to reconstitute the Guardia Nacional so that it will survive, that I have held discussions with Somoza and his son on this very subject, and that this in no way constitutes planning a coup. Why should we be coup plotting when we have Somoza's commitment to resign?"[11]

An independent assessment of the Guardia's state of mind came to us unexpectedly on the afternoon of June 30 when Edmundo Jarquín stopped by the embassy to thank us, only hours after Somoza released him from jail. He had used his forced contact with the Guardia to make some inquiries. According to Jarquín, Guardia officers were indignant that Somoza had gotten them into such a mess. While unity and morale appeared to be high, the officers he spoke to complained of poor intelligence and communication.[12]

Practically everything we were hearing supported the view that the Guardia Nacional was a professional institution that in some form could weather the transition from Somoza to a new government. While some (most notably Pete Vaky) had doubts, none of us—either in Washington or at the embassy in Managua—appreciated how corrupt and loathed an institution the Guardia Nacional had become.

In a conversation years later, Arturo Cruz, who entered the military academy created by the Somozas but never served in the army, explained: "The strategy of corruption was intentional. When it was formed back in the thirties, the Guardia attracted very capable people from the finest families. Eventually the Somozas realized they didn't want that. Independent, intelligent officers were a threat. Thereafter, they only wanted people who were completely loyal to them."[13]

With few exceptions, the Somozas recruited the most venal and corrupt. "Those officers were like valets, they were below valets," said Cruz.[14] Those willing to play the game were greatly rewarded. "The commander of the town of Chinandega can expect to pick up $20,000 a month in kickbacks from the bars, prostitution rings, smugglers, traffic fines, and farmers in his regions," said Lt. Col. Bernardino Larios, a Guardia officer who defected to the FSLN.[15]

"Every commander had his collector," reported Pvt. Antonio Mendina Leiva, "and he collected from the bars, the billiard halls, the gambling dens, the houses of prostitution. . . . And the commanders, Alesio Gutiérrez, Nicolás Valle Salinas, and the others put those fees that were collected into their pockets. That's why many commanders and colonels owned up to ten or fifteen cars and fifteen buses. General Alesio Gutiérrez had twenty-four taxis."[16]

And the soldiers learned from their superiors. "I didn't like what many of my companions were doing," continued Private Medina. "They were always looking for ways to shake down people to earn a couple bucks, or some way of paying less. . . . We privates earned 650 cordobas a month, and someone with kids, a wife, and a house to look after . . . well, they looked at how they could rob. . . . They'd take away someone's driver's license at the slightest infraction to see what the person would pay to get it back."[17]

Not only were there opportunities in the army and police force, but also the Guardia ran the prisons, the post office, and the telegraph system. The civil service and many of Somoza's businesses were also staffed with retired officers. Their main qualification was loyalty. "The Guard runs the country," explained Richard Millet, author of *Guardians of the Dynasty.* "Over half the directors of the national bank, for example, are retired officers whose knowledge of banking could be written on the head of a very small pin."[18]

Somoza paid his soldiers well, by Nicaraguan standards—$75 a month for recruits to $263 for colonels, plus generous food, housing, and medical subsidies. "I was from a campesino family north of Chinandega," said former corporal Efren Mondragón. "At fifteen I came to the capital to look for work. The Guardia became a form of survival. It offered me economic stability."[19]

"I was like all the others: an illiterate campesino kid," recalled former lieutenant Rigoberto Betancourt, who defected to the Sandinista forces in Costa Rica. "For the first time in my life, I got three meals a day, shoes, clothes, a gun, and self-respect. That is

A National Guard deserter is led off by Sandinistas during the battle for León.
Credit: Benoit Gysembergh Camera Press, London 30410-6 (97) Globe Photos, Inc. 1993

why some guardsmen would rather kill their own mothers than think of getting out."[20]

Somoza, his illegitimate half brother, General José Somoza, and his son, El Chiguín, commanded the Guard. "When a recruit refers to Somoza as 'el jefe,' " wrote Gabriel García Márquez and his collaborators in *The Battle for Nicaragua*, "he's not just alluding to his formal title as commander-in-chief, but something much more complicated and more profound. Tachito is, like his father before him, the patriarch, the natural ruler, the protector. It is he who gives promotions, bestows the infinite privileges and prerogatives, who apportions consumer articles at special prices, who provides medical attention for the whole family, who lets you taste a piece of the pie of corruption."[21]

"The officer's status symbols—their Mercedes, their houses, their *fincas*—were all gifts from Somoza," said Arturo Cruz. From the highest officers to the lowest recruits, "all the Guardia understood that their fate was tied to that of *el jefe*."[22] He looked after officers' widows and was the godfather to many of their children. One general's daughter remembered attending Somoza's birthday parties: "We were all in white dresses as if they were some kind of special family gathering. He was always very, very charming and knew all the kids."[23]

"Somoza is a real godfather type," said Lt. Col. Guillermo Mendieta, who fled to Costa Rica after being demoted to private for criticizing the Guard. "He can pass an ordinary soldier and say, 'I hear your mamma is sick.' Then he'll reach into his pocket and peel off thousand-dollar bills and say, 'This is for the airfare, and this is for the clinic in Miami.' You cannot talk against him, but you feel that if he likes you, he'll never let you down."[24]

The price for such privileges was blind loyalty to Somoza. It meant accepting the tactics and actions that compromised many a soldier's sense of right and wrong.

"The mission of an army is very delicate when it comes to the people," commented ex-Guardia infantryman Efren Mondragón. "They have to defend the people and the sovereignty of the country. Their role depends on which government is in power. In the time of Somoza, Somoza involved the army in all the bad things he was doing."[25]

Lt. José Antonio Robleto Siles participated in many of the early counterinsurgency campaigns against the Frente Sandinista in the northern mountains. On September 1, 1975, before reporting to duty near the Rio Blanco, he was summoned to a meeting with Somoza in the bunker. "He made his entrance and everybody stood and remained absolutely quiet," Robleto remembered.

> He took a seat at the end of the table and ordered us to sit. He quickly glanced at all the faces and began: "I want to be brief with you. . . . I'd like to spend more time with you officers but I have difficulty finding time to sleep. I've asked you here to bid you good luck and tell you that you have a difficult job ahead. It brings with it a great deal of sacrifice and sleepless nights. But the people have entrusted you to safeguard peace and order. . . . I think I should remind you what to do with people you find who have been suspected of aiding the guerrillas. We don't want prisoners. We want to have nothing to do with prisoners."[26]

When Lieutenant Robleto arrived at the camp, he saw firsthand what this meant. One night he met the custodian of an improvised graveyard. "How many people are buried here?" he asked.

"They say there are many. There are days when they kill as many as five people."

"Women?"

"Everyone, even young kids."

"They're legitimate guerrillas?"

"No, they're Indians who have been accused of cooperating with the guerrillas. There were times when the helicopter arrived full. Now it doesn't bring them. The colonel has ordered the patrols to shoot them on the spot."[27]

Later that night, Lieutenant Robleto arrived at the tents where the Indians were being held. "I was struck to see children of all ages," he remembered, "with frightened eyes full of innocence, with emaciated bodies, without a stitch on. Two women had recently given birth and were nursing their babies. . . . The scene I saw made me think of the concentration camps of Hitler."

"Why are you being held?" he asked one of the prisoners.

"We're accused of giving food to the guerrillas."[28]

As Lieutenant Robleto was leaving, a soldier who had been listening said: "Lieutenant, these poor Indians will spend the whole night in turmoil. It's better if we kill them now. They're going to die anyway. This way they won't suffer."[29]

Days later when Lieutenant Robleto was introduced to the colonel, he asked: "Sir, don't you think it would be better if the campesinos under suspicion be brought to justice before civil courts? That would cleanse the image of the army, because in the city people are already hearing rumors of a massacre being carried out by the Guard."[30] The colonel told Lieutenant Robleto that he was acting under orders from General Somoza.

As the political situation in Nicaragua deteriorated and more people openly opposed the Somoza regime, repression at the hands of the Guardia became more open and brutal. In 1978, following the assassination of Pedro Joaquín Chamorro, uprisings spread from towns to cities. The Guardia's mop-up operations directed by El Chiguín were fierce.

The Inter-American Human Rights Commission took the following testimony from a woman in Chinandega during their inspection of Nicaragua in October 1978:

It was Thursday, September 14, when the airplanes began to strafe our houses in Barrio La Libertad. My husband, my five-year-old daughter and I were crouching in a corner of our house, crying and thinking that we would die right there because the bullets and shrapnel were destroying our small wooden house.

We decided to go out and seek shelter in a safe place; we left our kitchen, my husband with our daughter in his arms. A plane flew very low, it seemed as if it was coming straight at us, and fired some rockets which hit my daughter's shoulder and my husband who was carrying her. Everywhere I looked I could see the heart and intestines of my child; she was in pieces, destroyed. My husband, who had already lost an arm, took about thirty steps, with blood spurting everywhere, until he fell dead. He had a wound in his chest; he had part of a still smoking rocket stuck in his leg. The left leg was bare to the bone. I wanted to lift my child, but she was in pieces. I didn't know what to do. I ran and got her little arm and I tried to put it on her, I tried to put everything that was coming out of her back but she was already dead.[31]

In Matagalpa at the end of August several rebels fleeing the Guardia entered through the main door of the Hotel Soza and immediately went out the back. Shortly thereafter soldiers arrived, and the sole survivor gave the following account:

Some thirty soldiers shot their way into my house, known as "Hotel Soza" and said they belonged to the EEBI, and ordered us all in the house toward the back with our hands in the air, in the direction of the principal room in the house. In the house there was my elderly mother, Tina Arauz de Soza, my brother-in-law Harold Miranda, the maid Nubia Montegro, and a guest, Alfredo Lacayo Amador, and the undersigned. As they were coming out they were also being machine-gunned. I was behind my mother and I jumped to the neighboring house and I was able to hide in the trash bin, hidden by the body of my mother.

I spent the whole day hidden in the trash bin, that is, twenty-four hours, hiding behind some rotten beams a few feet from the soldiers who continued shooting to break down the doors. I could hear them shouting, "There were five, where is the other one?" And I could see how my mother was butchered after they machine-gunned her, opening her abdomen with a bayonet. My brother-in-law had his genitals cut off and put in his mouth.

They took my mother's clothes, my brother-in-law's watch, and even the keys to his car. And from the house they took about 8,000 cordobas [$1,143] that my mother had hidden under a mattress. After having looted the whole house and not finding any guerrillas or weapons, a member of the guard said, "We screwed them for the fun of it."[32]

To carry out such operations required a special kind of soldier. "The EEBI [directed by Colonel Somoza, El Chiguín] were the most dangerous," said former EEBI private Geraldo Medina Leiva. "They were young boys, young boys who were antisocial in a sense. . . . They learned to murder, torture, stab, beat, and all that. Their lives were killing."[33]

"They took young boys like me who were seventeen, fifteen years old," explained former EEBI private Norberto Mojica Paz. "You could say we were boys who were impressionable. Because a person like me was very easy to influence. . . . You see, I didn't know anything and I didn't think I was very good. . . . And I entered the school and liked the things there. . . . The school was pretty. The uniforms, the boots, the training, the good food . . . the result was that they could get you to do lots of things. . . . It was a dangerous combination."[34]

"El Chiguín gave everything to the EEBI," recounted recruit Denis Nuñez. "He had American ideas. In the EEBI we had movies, beer in cans, a very good club, recreation rooms, everything in the style of an American army."[35]

"Colonel Somoza embraced all the Guardias that were there," added Norberto Mojica Paz. " 'My boys,' he would say. . . . '*Mis muchachos,* you don't know what you mean to me.' " And God forbid anyone should mess with an EEBI. An EEBI was respected in all commands."[36]

"They put it into our heads that we were the best, the elite," said Denis Nuñez. "It was also drilled into our heads that the people were the enemy and that we had to kill the people."[37]

The stated enemy was always communism. "We're the only force capable of impeding the cancer of communism from our country. From our commander in chief to the last private, we're the elect; we're a special breed," read an editorial in *El Infante,* the internal newspaper of the EEBI.[38]

"The assault of international communism has been brutal," wrote El Chiguín in December 1978, "without parallel in our national history. During 1978 and especially during the bitter successes of September, our soldiers, young and old, imbued with patriotism, serenity, valor and professionalism, have salvaged the well-being of the nation."[39]

According to *El Infante:* "Christ was not a revolutionary nor a man full of hate like the communists who exist within the urban guerrillas and among the campesinos. Furthermore, the plan of Christ was not based on social justice. In other words, they forget—or they pretend to forget—that Christ did not come to proclaim social justice or elevate the conditions of the poor, or to take up the cause of the oppressed. He came for another reason: to save humanity for spiritual redemption."[40]

"Most soldiers can barely read, let alone understand politics," said former private Mendieta. "It's enough to tell them that the communists will take their little farms and their money and turn them into slaves."[41]

Blind loyalty was expected throughout the ranks. "In the Guardia we would say, 'He's grumbling,' " declared Efren Mondragón. "He who was 'grumbling' was not in accord with what was going on."[42]

In 1973 Sublieutenant Robleto was assigned to the security detail at Las Mercedes Airport. One day, after inspecting the kitchen, he asked his soldiers if they were satisfied with the food. "Sir, they're going to starve us to death," answered a private. Apparently, soldiers outside the EEBI were not treated with the same high regard. "In the morning we eat bread, an egg and black coffee. We have meat two times a week that's pure gristle. And for supper we have the same as in the morning."[43]

When Sublieutenant Robleto brought this to the attention of the cook, the cook explained: "Sir, it's not our fault, but that of the lieutenant who gives nothing for the kitchen. The bean soup we're serving is pure water. They give us a dozen eggs and a couple of onions for a soup for sixty-two soldiers. The rice is of the cheapest and poorest quality."[44]

The lieutenant's defense was even more surprising: "You're a fool to be worrying about those drunks and thieves. These jerks don't deserve anything. . . . None of of the officers speak up for them, because they know what they are. If you're not careful they'll rob you, too."[45]

For his efforts Sublieutenant Robleto was transferred to another post and accused of reading Karl Marx and Mao Tse-tung. "Many of my friends," wrote Robleto, "including companions in the Guardia, started to tell me that the Guardia Nacional wasn't for me, and they were right. After so many corrupting years of the Somoza dictatorship, the Nicaraguan military was rude, hypocritical, impudent, without conscience, and full of machismo. As time went on, it lost all of its principles and moral convictions, causing an intellectual and spiritual decay that wrought increasing inhumanity and degradation."[46]

10

Blessed are the poor, for they shall inherit the moon.
—Leonel Rugama

The decision to attack the capital city of Managua where the Guardia had all the advantages of command, supplies, armor, air power, and artillery had been forced upon the FSLN command. Sandinista leaders knew from experience that once uprisings began in other cities, the inhabitants of Managua's barrios would take to the streets. In order to maintain their claim that they were the "vanguard of the revolution," the FSLN directorate called for the Managua uprising to begin June 9, 1979.

Later, Humberto Ortega would state that this decision was part of his strategic plan "to bring the war to Somoza's front yard."[1] But others in the movement were opposed. Jaime Wheelock of the Proletarians thought it was a mistake. With no downtown to fight in, he felt, the city was not suited to urban warfare. Moises Hassan called the attack on Managua a "Tercerista blunder." Despite his reservations, he was ordered by Henry Ruiz (who, according to Hassan, also found fault with the action) to represent the GPP in Managua. Upon entering the besieged northeastern barrios, Hassan became even more convinced that the attack was a tragic

136

miscalculation. "We couldn't even move because of the incessant bombardment by Guardia planes, mortars, and artillery," Ortega complained.[2]

Nineteen-year-old Omar López, who had traveled to the capital from Estelí as an FSLN courier, was trapped by the fighting. He recalled:

> There was no way to get back. The insurrection was starting and I wanted to be united with the guerrilleros. I went to a trench and talked with some of the muchachos. I told them to take me to their chief, whose name was Chombo, a pseudonym for Walter Ferrety. They took me to someone in charge, and I explained that I was a guerrillero with the Frente in the north, He asked me some dates and then said, "Okay, go with that column. You have more experience than they do, so help them."[3]

The rows of tin-roofed cardboard and adobe shanties that made up the northeast barrios of Managua provided little shelter from Somoza's artillery and bombs. Omar López continued:

> One day I was behind a barricade near my sister's house, when the Guardia bombarded a church opposite her house with a tank and planes. Approximately twenty people died and some children were wounded. The day after that, I was ordered to retreat to El Edén bridge, where we fought the Guardia for eight hours. One of Somoza's planes was dropping 500-pound bombs, and one of the bombs fell at the end of the bridge. It buried most of us and a whole family. Almost a whole block of houses disappeared because of that bomb.[4]

"The Frente gave us leaflets telling us how to make bomb shelters," explained housewife Rosa Alilia.

> We have twelve children, so my husband made us squat down two by two in the living room, to make sure we would all fit. We dug it there—five yards wide and three yards deep. We put wooden planks and corrugated iron sheeting over the top and used parts of the kids' iron bed frames as supports. We didn't want to die because we hadn't made it right.

At five in the morning neighbors started screaming that a
rocket had fallen nearby. The shrapnel ripped apart a door
across the street. It was awful. We spent the whole day counting
the mortars fall.[5]

From the roof of his stucco house in the upper middle-class
suburbs that overlooked the city, fifty-three-year-old Manolo
Gutiérrez had been watching the fighting for over two weeks.
Through a pair of binoculars he followed one of Somoza's push-
pull Cessnas as it dropped bombs on the barrio of Open Tres.
Manolo had timed the explosions and found that it took an aver-
age of four seconds before the big boom reached him. Sometimes
he went across the street and listened on his friend's radio scanner
as Alfa Sierra Delta (Somoza) directed the bombing attacks from
his bunker.

It had been a month now since Manolo had gone to work. His
engineering firm had been shut by the strike and heavy fighting in
Managua. Several days before, he had driven by and found it in a
shambles. Gone were the typewriters, chairs, desks, and files. Even
the telex machine had been ripped out of the wall.[6]

Manolo Gutiérrez had realized Somoza was finished three
nights earlier, June 24, when he and his sister, María Eugenia, had
listened to him address the nation on television. With the same
disgruntled expression he always wore when speaking to the people, Somoza had read his speech. He was dressed in a business suit
and looked very tired. Though his high-pitched voice was more
pinched than usual, his tone was calm.

A majority vote of OAS foreign ministers had called upon him
to resign. He called this "a flagrant violation of the internal affairs
of Nicaragua." It was the "by-product of strong communist influence." Even so, he said he was "open to dialogue" and willing "to
receive the initiative of member governments of the OAS which
have a real interest in resolving the Nicaraguan crisis through
democratic, just and permanent formulas."[7]

When Somoza finished, an announcer came on and pleaded—
"Your country needs you; we must join to defend it. Report to the
National Guard commander. Have faith in Christ."[8] He went on to
denounce the communists, charging that they had perverted the
nation's youth with an orgy of blood, sex, and drugs.

When the television announced a repeat of the rodeo competi-
tion that had been playing for days, Manolo's sister had switched

off the set. The huge groundswell of resentment toward the Somoza regime didn't surprise her. As a Catholic nun, she had
worked with the poor on the Atlantic coast and in the barrios of
León and Matagalpa. After the earthquake of 1972, the archbishop had sent her to Granada to help cope with the streams
of refugees who were arriving there. They had expressed their
disgust with the corruption they had seen in their own government in the wake of the disaster. Tents, blankets, medicines, and
foods meant to be distributed freely were put into warehouses
and sold.

All Manolo could do now was pray that his children were alive
and the fighting would end. Whatever the outcome, he knew their
lives would never be the same. His wife was staying with her sister
in Honduras, and his daughter Lucía ("the rebel") and his son
Gustavo were mixed up in the fighting. On June 1, eighteen-year-
old Gustavo had left a note on the dining room table saying he was
on his way to San José, Costa Rica, to join Edén Pastora, hero of
the national palace takeover. Under his signature, Gustavo had
written "Patria libre o morir."

Manolo didn't realize that his son was less than three miles away
in the barrio of El Dorado. Gustavo and his friends had tried to
drive to Costa Rica, but with the Highway Sur patrolled by
Guardias, they returned to Managua just in time to join the uprising there. Nothing his father had taught him had prepared
Gustavo for this. He sat behind a barricade made of bags of sugar,
leaning against a pink wooden house. The last three weeks seemed
a lifetime.

The smell of gunpowder mingled with the smell of decaying
corpses and garbage. In the muddy street in front of him, women
were lining up to receive cupfuls of rice and beans from a Sandinista truck. They were the same women he had seen run from
their houses and litter the streets with garbage, bottles, broken
furniture—anything so that the Guardia tanks couldn't pass. And
they were the women who had run out between battles to bring
food, water, and cigarettes to the rebels. A month ago they had
been anonymous faces of the *pueblo* on buses and in the market.
Now they were his *compañeros*.

Around him in all directions were rows of barricades and
trenches. Although the fighting had let up, an occasional rocket or
mortar would still land nearby. What disturbed him more this
morning were the moans of the two little girls who lay on a plastic

sheet in the muddy yard across the street. Yesterday they had been hit by shrapnel from one of Somoza's 500-pound bombs.

Gustavo heard voices through the slats of the wooden house. A jeep rounded the corner and stopped in front of him. Out jumped a man in an aqua sports shirt and two bodyguards with M-16s. He had seen the muscular, dark-skinned man before. Some called him "Professor" and others "the Arab." He was Moises Hassan of the Movimiento del Pueblo Unido (United People's Movement), who a few days earlier had been named to the FSLN junta.

"Tavo, come inside," one of the bodyguards said to him. "Guard the door." The room was crowded with Sandinista leaders sitting and leaning against the walls. Some were smoking cigarettes. A skinny old man was curled in one corner asleep. Hassan listened to their complaints:

"We're running out of supplies."

"Guardia morale is finished, but we need ammunition."

"What about more guns?"[9]

Only two days before, a FSLN supply plane had arrived from Costa Rica. When it circled to land, the *compas,* mistaking it for a Guardia bomber, had opened fire. Gustavo had screamed at them to stop. After the plane eventually landed on a highway, Gustavo and his unit unloaded only a small faction of the supplies before a Guardia helicopter firing rockets chased the little plane away.

Hassan listened intensely for several minutes, then in a soft voice he said: "The leadership has reached a decision."

The room grew quiet. The men and several women sat up.

"We have to leave Managua. We will retreat tonight."

There were shouts of "No!" "We're betraying the people!" and "It will be a massacre!" Some of the *compas* had tears in their eyes. A young, attractive female leader named Monica Baltodano spoke up. "What will happen to the people who are left behind?"

They knew from experience what the Guardia would do.[10]

"The civilians can come with us," answered Hassan.

The news spread quickly through the barrios. Families debated whether or not to follow the Sandinistas to Masaya or stay behind. César Sanchez, a freelance reporter and photographer, traveled to the barrio of El Edén from his home in Belo Horizonte to inquire after his brother, Jorge, and his family. "All the houses in El Edén were closed," he remembered. "Where my brother lived, there was no one home. I knocked on the door once, and then again. No one answered. 'Where is everyone?' I shouted. There was no answer. It was only early afternoon and everyone had already left."[11]

The *compas* spent the afternoon bathing, resting, eating, and changing clothes. From outside the Church of the Sagrada Familia in the barrio of El Dorado, Gustavo Gutiérrez watched as units from the other barrios arrived. "Can I have your attention?" yelled Mayra González (known as "Venancia"), who was in charge of the *compas* from Bello Horizonte. "All of you wearing light clothes or shoes, watches, shiny buttons, anything that can be detected by the enemy, will have to remove them."[12]

At five in the afternoon, a group of rebels were ordered to create a diversion at the north end of the barrio. The Guardia counterattacked and were trying to penetrate the barricades behind a Sherman tank. People ran like crazy toward Gustavo's position near Sagrada Familia. There were naked children and women without shoes. Their faces were masks of terror.

A very tall *compa* strode past them toward the barricades with an RPG-2 rocket launcher at his side. Minutes later, Gustavo heard a "whoosh" as it fired, then the blast and the cheers of relieved *compas*. The Sherman tank turned and fled.

Gustavo was always surprised at how swiftly the mood could shift from terror to exultation. Near his position they were organizing a convoy to carry the wounded. About forty stretchers were being improvised from planks of wood, sheet metal, and plastic sheets. Already more than twice that number of wounded men and women had gathered. Some were missing legs; others with bloody bandages wrapped around their heads were pleading to be taken. They knew that any wounded fighters taken by the Guardia would be shot. Moises Hassan and William Ramírez estimated that the retreat would involve 1,000 people. In the end almost 6,000 *compas* marched.

The Church of the Sagrada Familia was crowded with refugees. A lone priest ran back and forth in his white robe trying to find space for the frightened people begging for sanctuary. There were whole families whose houses had been destroyed by bombs. Having lived for days on meager rations of seed and water, they were tired and weak. Sick and wounded children lay on the floor and waited.

The retreat was organized into three groups—vanguard, center (with the convoy of wounded), and rear guard. "The order came from the military staff, Carlos Nuñez, William Ramírez, and Walter Ferrety," Omar López remembered. "My squad, the Pérez Cassar Squad, was put in front, because we were the only ones who knew where we were going. They sent us ahead since we'd been given the best arms and ammunition. We all thought that by going to Masaya, we'd die."[13] Everyone understood that a Guardia ambush or pincher could produce a massacre.

Earlier in the day some *compas* had ambushed and captured a jeep with a .50-millimeter machine gun. It led the way. "Camión [the code name for Masaya], we're coming to your house," Comandante Joaquín Cuadra said over and over into the radio so that the rebels there would be alerted.[14]

Gustavo Gutiérrez was one of 130 cadres selected to serve as guides. Marta Lucía Corea was giving them last-minute instructions—"Advance with care. Keep the columns in order. Don't talk; no noise. Don't waste ammunition. When you hear a voice say 'Halt!' stop quickly."[15] Many *compas* carried only two rounds for their guns.

The vanguard started to leave at six. There was so much shouting and disorder that Gustavo was certain that the Guardia could hear. In barrio Schick some guerrillas reported that they had passed three Guardias standing behind an old truck. They didn't shoot or try to stop them, they just watched the rebels pass. "Their morale must be very low," William Ramírez remarked.

Everyone was coming—old people following their children, children following their mothers and fathers. Gustavo started toward Masaya at seven, at the tail end of the vanguard. He followed two captured EEBI soldiers carrying a .50-caliber machine gun with all its ammunition. The last *compas* didn't leave until eleven P.M.

From the beginning, the retreat was chaotic. Some *compas* didn't listen to orders. In some cases, orders weren't clear and groups of rebels walked off in the wrong direction. It was impossible to keep track of everyone.

Gustavo's group marched east until they got to Four Corners. Somebody said there was a *compa* there who could serve as a guide. Nobody could remember where he lived. When they knocked on the red door of a little store, a little old lady stuck her head out. Her lips trembled as a small white-haired man came out behind her. "Give me a shotgun and I'll take you," he said, proudly. The *compas* offered him a pistol, which he was glad to accept.[16]

They walked in the dark following narrow roads and crossed freshly plowed fields. The terrain was rough and mountainous. At three in the morning as they crossed a cornfield, a shot rang out. Half of the rebels dived for cover. The other half kept walking. There was a steady chorus of curses, especially for the mud that sucked off boots and shoes.

There were several stops to repair and readjust stretchers. Particularly burdensome was one tall, fat man with a fractured knee. Once, when the *compas* dropped him, he cried out: "Cowards! I'd like to see you wounded! Are you thinking of dumping me here, you lousy shits?"[17]

Moises Hassan led his group with a pistol and a lantern. They passed Santiago volcano belching sulfurous clouds of steam. Green parakeets sang in the distance as Gustavo remembered the story of David Tejada, a lieutenant in the Guardia and a spy for the FSLN. After resigning his commission, he became a guerrilla. When the Guardia caught up with him, they beat him to death right before his terrified wife and son, then dumped his body into the mouth of Santiago volcano.

At kilometer 11 of the road to Masaya, the Sandinista units abandoned the labyrinthine mountain paths and took the highway. William Ramírez ordered them to march in two long columns along either side of the road. That's when one of the *compañeros* dropped a grenade. "The Guardia has found us!" screamed a panicked *compa*.

As sunlight crept over the mountains, the climb to Masaya began. Looking back, Gustavo saw a line of people he'd never forget. A convoy of trucks and buses arrived from Masaya to help with the wounded. People gathered along the highway to watch the *compas* pass. "Do you want a little water? Are you tired?" they asked.

The news passed through the column like electricity—"A Guardia convoy is coming. We're going to have a fight!" William Ramírez instructed the *compas* to set up an ambush. "Everyone with weapons, advance to the front!" he shouted. "We'll form a wall to stop the beasts! Come quickly!"[18]

Gustavo heard shots. Just a few at first, then all hell broke loose. He readied his Garand. Up ahead, a .50-millimeter machine gun crackled through the dull explosion of grenades. *Compas* near him were already shooting, spending their ammunition. Very few were heeding orders.

Within minutes there was total disorder. *Compas* were running forward toward the fighting, others were running away. Gustavo watched a thin boy with long hair hurry toward him. He was holding the place near his eye where he'd been wounded.

Summoning all his courage, Gustavo pushed forward. He was sure he'd find a massacre, with hundreds of well-equipped Guardias with tanks. But as soon as the fighting started, it was over. A helicopter passed overhead and veered off. Someone said that the Guardia had fled, that they were mostly women and young boys in five or six trucks.

In the gold light of dawn, the *compas* scurried back in place and the column inched forward like a huge snake. "It was only a patrol," *compas* whispered back through the ranks. Now they were passing the place where the encounter had taken place. An abandoned, bullet-riddled Guardia jeep lay on its side. *Compas* struggled to remove its .50-caliber machine gun.

The column passed the bodies of a dozen *compas* lined up in a gully. Some were lying on their sides with half-closed eyes; others with their mouths half open. Some had looks of surprise; others seemed to be laughing as though they had enjoyed death when it came. Gustavo made the sign of the cross as two rebel leaders argued over what to do with the bodies. Tired *compas* filed past without looking up. They were stooped with fatigue and covered with scratches.

It was morning when Somoza's planes came. Gustavo was surprised that after twelve hours of walking he still had the energy to run. The girl *compa* beside him tripped and hit the mud. He picked her up, but she slipped again as a rocket exploded in the trees behind them. An injured *compa* screamed, "Shoot me! Please, shoot me!" Gustavo couldn't make his legs stop shaking.

A Sikorsky helicopter was giving positions, and the planes made passes, machine-gunning and shooting their rockets. "Bastards, don't be cowards! Dogs!" the pilots shouted.[19] Gustavo thought he heard a voice in English. He counted six planes.

The captured .50-caliber machine gun fired back: "Poom, poom, poom," as a rocket whizzed in the direction of the column and exploded in a huge cloud of smoke. Through half-opened eyes, Gustavo saw *compas* getting up, brushing themselves off. Some were stunned, but no one was dying.

The push-pull veered up sharply and came back for another pass, with its wing-mounted machine guns spitting fire. Miraculously, it was hit by the machine gun. A cheer rose from the column. The push-pull launched all its rockets in one huge gasp as *compas* screamed—"Take that, you son-of-a-bitch! We got him!" The plane lost altitude, but picked up speed again and limped off into the clouds.

In spite of the planes and helicopters, the column advanced. Gustavo passed Moises Hassan holding his side. Blood was seeping through his sport shirt. "What happened?" the youth inquired.

"Some shrapnel from a rocket, brother," Hassan replied. "But let's keep walking."[20]

Compas were so hungry that they ate green pineapples. Before long, they had stomachaches and sore noses and lips to add to their miseries.

Passing a group of adobe huts, Gustavo heard campesino women and children screaming with fear. "Help us! Please, God, get us out of this hell!" Just then a rocket hit the little earthen path between the houses. Thousands of shards of hot shrapnel whistled through the air.

A running *compa* was hit in the back and fell. He writhed on the ground as though struck by lightning. A group of young rebels looked on as his chest heaved violently and his eyes begged for mercy. In the shade of a mango tree the *compa* exhaled his last breath.

When they arrived in Masaya, people started taking the rebels into their houses. "We were the first to arrive," remembered Omar López. "The people received us well, but there were thousands of us and not much food. We stayed in a house that belonged to a minister of Somoza's and it became our commando base."[21] There were now 6,000 hungry people to feed in Masaya.

For the first time, Gustavo Gutiérrez was convinced the revolution would triumph. Someone yelled—"This is Monimbo! You're in free territory of Nicaragua!"[22] The retreat, organized in desperation, would prove to be a major strategic victory for the FSLN.

Back in Managua, César Sanchez arose at sunrise to find a few civilians milling around the barrio of Bello Horizonte. At nine-thirty or ten, the planes arrived, as they had every morning for the last two weeks. But this time when they fired their machine guns and launched their rockets, there was no return fire from the ground. At noon Guardia troops entered the barrio. "The soldiers spread everywhere," César Sanchez remembered, "running and continually firing their M-16s and Galils. It gave me the impression that every house in the barrio was being demolished by bullets."[23]

"You," screamed a Guardia seeing César and his fourteen-year-old son Eduardo, "grab some shovels and fill in those trenches."[24]

A few miles away, the Guardia was entering El Dorado for the first time in three weeks. Anyone who could walk was ordered to clear away the barricades. "How many wounded are there here?" screamed a major with a thick belly as he entered the Church of the Sagrada Familia. He had perspired through his uniform in three dark circles—one in the front and two below his arms.

Families were ordered to stand together. Anyone who wasn't with a family was led outside with the wounded. So were the teenage boys who had pants ripped at the knee or any type of scrapes.

The poor families that huddled together were trembling. They knew the Guardia was looking for revenge. The major was inspecting the graffiti that had been painted on the church wall. He pointed his automatic pistol at one of the walls and fired.

"All right, you sons-of-bitches," he yelled. "Let me hear you sing. 'El pueblo unido jamas será vencido!' (The people united will never be defeated)," he quoted from the graffiti. Then, changing it, he added: "El huevo podrido jamas será cocido. (The rotten egg will never be cooked)."[25]

From outside the church, the priest heard automatic weapons fire. He rushed to the door to look. "They're killing the *muchachos*," he thought and remembered the lines from the poem by Father Ernesto Cardenal:

You, the ones taken by the guards. Those 'loved by the gods.'
The Greeks said that those loved by the gods die young.
It's true, I think, because they stay young forever.
Others can age a great deal, but those who died will be young and fresh,
    their brows smooth, their hair black.
The Roman girl with blond hair will always stay blond in our memories.[26]

The priest looked out at the barrio in a shambles. Families walked half in shock, trying to remember where they lived amid the rubble. They passed trenches hastily covered with earth. Arms and legs of fallen guerrillas stuck out. The smell of rotting corpses made the air sweet and putrid. They passed other trenches filled with burned-out cars that had been pushed in by the *compas* to protect them from the bombs, mortars, and rockets that had rained for weeks.

A little girl led some Guardias to a rebel cemetery. In her sweet voice, she told them she had seen seventeen guerrillas buried there last week. On the fence nearby were the initials CCFA—Cementerio Carlos Fonseca Amador.

Craters left by the 500-pound bombs had already become playgrounds for emaciated children. When the families found their homes, they had to chase out packs of dogs and swarms of insects.

A father sorting through the rubble of his bombed-out home was bitter. "It's always the workers who have to pay when this happens. It's always the people with nothing. The people with money just get on a plane and go where they goddamn please."[27]

11

*Even the most courageous among us rarely has the courage for that
which he really knows.*   —Nietzsche

On June 30, 1979, I received a flash cable from Washington:
"You should not, repeat, not try to establish a departure date at
this time. What follows after Somoza's departure is too uncertain
at this time."[1] I asked myself, what the hell are they thinking? The
answer was close behind.

That afternoon, Pete Vaky called, summoning me to Washington. President Carter, National Security Adviser Brzezinski, and
Secretary Vance had just returned from an economic summit in
Tokyo. In their absence a rift had developed between State and the
NSC over how to proceed in Nicaragua. The president was being
asked to decide. First, he wanted to consult his ambassadors in the
field and seek the advice of his friend General Torrijos of Panama.

The military attaché's King Air Beechcraft stationed in Tegucigalpa, Honduras, would pick me up at Las Mercedes Airport and
fly me to Howard Air Force Base in Panama, where I would board
a military flight to Washington.

To reach the airport, my driver, Security Officer Jerry Wilson
and I had to pass through an eight-mile industrial strip on the

148

northern edge of the city. As we wound around the debris and barricades left from the recent fighting, scenes of destruction greeted
us from every side. What had once been a thriving center of small
factories, warehouses, and businesses was now a graveyard of gut-
ted buildings and twisted steel.

We passed the blackened wall that had once protected *La Prensa*.
Somoza had used the recent fighting in Managua as a cover
to punish his enemies. On the afternoon of June 11, *La Prensa*
employees had watched with horror as a Guardia Nacional
Staghound armored car pulled up to the front gates and fired
point-blank. Fifteen of them had escaped through the back fence
as several Guardias scaled the padlocked gate and poured gasoline
over the presses. As flames licked the afternoon sky, a Cessna rock-
eted the newspaper to ensure that it would never speak again.

The next morning the building was a smoldering hulk. Pedro
Joaquín's brother and editor, Xavier Chamorro, looked on sadly.
"We can rebuild the paper," he said. "We have done it before. But
the thousands of people who are dying in Nicaragua and will continue to die cannot be replaced. We have to rebuild the paper because the paper will be needed to rebuild the morale of this
country."[2]

At the military terminal, the Beechcraft was waiting with its engines on. We passed over resplendent Lake Nicaragua, crowned
with volcanoes, before veering west over the Pacific. The last three
days seemed like years. I was leaving a job half done. I wanted to
impress this on the president. Before drifting into slumber, I scribbled a note to myself—"Get the goddamn guy out. Stop the killing. The faster the knife goes in the better."[3] It was as though I
had entered a strange nightmare to find myself an actor in a tragedy by Euripides.

I arrived at Andrews Air Force Base near Washington around
midnight. Awaiting me was an urgent message from Bob Pastor of
the NSC. A drowsy Pastor answered the phone. He asked me
about my progress in putting together an executive committee. I
felt the blood surge up my neck. "Didn't you read my cables!?
There's a war going on down there, Bob. It's too late! They're not
interested in our harebrained schemes."[4]

I was under the impression that the executive committee idea
had been iced. Apparently, I was mistaken. At the Special Coordinating Committee (SCC) meeting the next day, I made it clear.
Quickly the attention of the president's frustrated advisers shifted

to the FSLN junta. Bill Bowdler, who had been meeting with them, reported what we should have known. The junta did not trust us. He had been unable to establish a rapport.

It had to be a difficult assignment for Bowdler, returning to face many of the same opposition figures who had felt betrayed by the mediation of 1978. A towering, taciturn man, Bowdler was trying to keep his balance on the volatile, shifting landscape of politics wrought by the FSLN junta.

Nevertheless, on June 27, the day I flew to Managua, Bowdler had stayed behind in Panama. That same morning, Panamanian President Aristedes Royos dispatched a plane to Costa Rica to pick up three members of the junta—Violeta Chamorro, Alfonso Robelo, and Sergio Ramírez. Royo greeted them at the airport with a military band, honor guard, and thousands of Panamanians screaming, "Somoza parédon!" (Somoza to the wall!)

"The Nicaraguan people have known suffering for forty-five years under the family dynasty now headed by Anastasio Somoza," Royo said. "You are an example to all the countries of the world."[5]

Accompanying the junta was Dr. Hugo Spadafora, Panama's former vice minister of health, who had resigned the previous fall to organize an eighty-man volunteer brigade to fight alongside Edén Pastora on the southern front. Two weeks ago at a press conference in Managua, Somoza had offered Spadafora's driver's license and identification card as proof of international support for the rebellion. The doctor, he said, had been killed in a battle with the Guardia Nacional.

Spadafora responded to the cheers of the crowd. "Death to the dictator! 'Patria libre o morir!' "

Following the airport ceremony, the group traveled to the home of General Omar Torrijos, where they met the press. "The people of Nicaragua will never forget the brotherhood Panama is showing them," Violeta Chamorro said.[6] Although six Latin American countries had severed relations with Somoza, so far only two— Grenada and Panama—had recognized the junta as the legitimate government of Nicaragua.

That evening the three junta members slipped into the house of Gabriel Lewis, a Torrijos confidant and Panama's former ambassador to the United States, on Fiftieth Street in Panama City. There they were joined by Daniel Ortega for a meeting with Special U.S. Envoy Bill Bowdler and Ambassador Ambler Moss. The meeting, arranged by Torrijos, was the first between U.S. officials and the Sandinista junta. Bowdler remembers that Daniel Ortega was particularly quiet and reserved. Sergio Ramírez characterized the meeting as "disappointing."[7]

The next day Bowdler followed the junta to San José, Costa Rica, where they had established their headquarters in the home of Sergio Ramírez. So far Bowdler had not disclosed the United States' four-point plan: (1) the resignation of Somoza; (2) the appointment of a constitutional successor by the Nicaraguan Congress; (3) the immediate appointment of a broad-based provisional government made up of distinguished Nicaraguans (the Executive Committee); and (4) immediate contact between the provisional government and the FSLN junta to form the most widely based provisional regime possible.

When it appeared that morning on the front page of the *New York Times*, the junta was miffed. "We consider it dirty politicking," said junta member Alfonso Robelo, "that they should tell the press about it but not us." When the junta met with Bowdler that afternoon, Sergio Ramírez expressed surprise that the United States was confident that Somoza would resign. "Mr. Bowdler was so sure it was going to work, but we said, 'Why?' It's the same demand he's turned down before.' "[8]

The next day, June 29, the FAO (Broad Opposition Group) and COSEP (Superior Council of the Private Sector) reiterated their support of the junta, declaring that they would not participate in a competing administration. "The Americans are mistaken in their fears of a radical takeover here," said one FAO and COSEP member still living in Managua. "The junta will definitely need strong American support. Instead of first ignoring it and then trying to undermine it, the United States ought to be working with the junta and showing their real desire to help our country."[9]

On the hot, humid morning of July 2, Washington was in a quandary. Having finally convinced the Special Coordinating Committee of the NSC that the Executive Committee idea was unworkable, I listened as they debated U.S. options. Brzezinski, Defense Secretary Harold Brown, Pastor, and others continued to be obsessed with the power vacuum that would result from Somoza's departure. They were loath to consider the possibility that the Sandinistas would fill it.

I argued that the best we could do was to force Somoza to resign quickly, bring about a quick cease-fire, cleanse the Guardia of officers closely associated with the Somozas, and appoint a new

Guardia commander in an effort to hold the vestiges of the Guard together. Bowdler agreed. It would end the bloodshed and force the still disorganized Sandinista army to negotiate.

Vaky and Deputy Secretary Christopher had less faith in a reconstituted Guardia Nacional. After forty-some years of identification with the Somozas and all the recent bloodshed, how could the Guard, however reformed, gain legitimacy with the Nicaraguan people? They argued instead that the United States should use the carrot of future economic assistance to try to influence the junta in San José. As always, Brzezinski and his staff wanted assurances that Nicaragua would not become a Soviet satellite. The specter of Cuba hung over our heads.

After two hours of debate, Brzezinski on his own, drafted another four-point strategy: (1) The United States would actively seek a new Guardia commander and gain the acceptance of Panamanian strongman General Torrijos as a first step toward gaining wider support of the new leader in the region. (2) The United States would seek to replace the junta with a different one that included Sergio Ramírez, Alfonso Robelo, Ismael Reyes, Mariano Fiallos, and the new Guard commander. (3) The president would insist that Torrijos stop the arms flow to the FSLN, or the United States would reserve the right to resupply the National Guard. (4) After Somoza's departure, the United States would provide humanitarian aid to contribute to the stability of the new regime.[10]

I never saw Brzezinski's four-point draft, nor did it reflect what was discussed in the meeting.

When we met with President Carter in the House Cabinet Room that afternoon, he quickly became annoyed. It didn't take him long to sense that the Brzezinski plan was unrealistic. "How can I ask the Sandinistas to accept a junta that excludes them?" he asked.[11] I remember being impressed by his sagacity and thinking how poorly he was being served by his staff.

Brzezinski was immediately on the defensive, arguing the need to preserve spheres of influence. Carter didn't look pleased. According to Brzezinski's notes: "The State Department types were absolutely delighted by this exchange. One of them grinned openly. My own judgment is that we were about to produce for ourselves another Iran but close to home."[12]

President Carter seemed to grasp intuitively that our options were few. He said that anything that the United States did alone at this point brought with it "the kiss of death." If Torrijos and President Carazo of Costa Rica were willing to support a reformed Guardia headed by a new commander and the expansion of the junta, Carter said he would go along. Without a reformed National Guard, he understood that there would be little to negotiate with the FSLN.

Overnight, Bob Pastor drafted the plan to be presented to General Torrijos the next day: (1) Panama, Costa Rica, Venezuela, and the United States should reach agreement on specific names to be suggested to expand the junta. (2) Agreement should be reached on whether General Gutiérrez or General Guerreo would direct the Guard in Nicaragua during the transition. The new commander should serve on the junta and as minister of defense. (3) The junta would agree to a cease-fire once peace is restored. (4) No arms would be transferred to the FSLN or to the Nicaraguan government during this period. (5) The United States would facilitate Somoza's departure and organize a humanitarian aid program. (6) The Nicaraguan Congress would name a caretaker president, call a cease-fire, and approve the new Guardia commander. (7) The caretaker president would then step down and transfer power to the junta, which would call for organized elections.[13]

The next morning at 9 A.M., President Carter received General Omar Torrijos in the Oval Office. According to U.S. Ambassador Moss, Torrijos expected to be chastised for supporting the Sandinistas. The Panamanian strongman had grown to admire President Carter for the courage and sincerity he had demonstrated during the politically difficult Panama Canal negotiations and struggle for Senate approval. Given his nervousness and Márquezian sense of drama, Torrijos had guzzled pink champagne all the way from Panama City to Miami. He ended up sprawled on his back in the center aisle of the small jet, causing a minor incident when U.S. customs inspectors were not permitted to board the plane.

On the morning of July 3, Torrijos remembered, "Like a schoolteacher, [President Carter] told me to sit down. Then he spoke to me amicably, as if I had not done anything."[14] Carter was pleased that the Panamanian enthusiastically endorsed the new plan. Using the recent air disaster in Chicago as a metaphor, Torrijos compared the president's plan to taking the bolt out of a DC-10 while the plane was in the air. "The trick," he said," is to keep the plane flying."[15]

Although he seemed vague on details, Torrijos claimed he would only "need a few hours to sell the list" to the Sandinistas.[16] As a member of the Central American military fraternity, he had also become convinced of the need to save parts of the Guard and use it to balance the Marxist-Leninists within the FSLN.

Names of potential Guardia leaders were discussed. The leading candidate, General Gutiérrez, a former Guard general serving as ambassador to Japan, had already been approached by Secretary of State Vance during the recent trip to Japan. Gutiérrez said he would be interested only if invited by a new government. Word of the meeting had apparently gotten back to Somoza, who called Gutiérrez in Tokyo. When Gutiérrez gave the State Department a list of officers who would make up his general staff (all Somoza cronies), we at the embassy in Managua became suspicious. I warned the State Department: "Based on Gutiérrez's list, I suspect some arrangement between Somoza and Gutiérrez has been reached." I recommended caution regarding the Gutiérrez candidacy.[17]

Another Guardia candidate, Col. Inocente Mojica, was posted in Guatemala City as Nicaragua's military attaché. Bowdler and I were asked to meet with him on our way back to San José and Managua. Vaky was dispatched to Venezuela, Colombia, and the Dominican Republic to recruit their support for the new plan.

I left Washington with as many reservations as when I arrived. Despite my efforts and those of Bill Bowdler, the president's advisers were still unwilling to grasp the realities. Furthermore, they seemed to have misread Torrijos's enthusiasm for the new plan. While Brzezinski and Pastor were excited by the prospect of expanding the junta, Torrijos was encouraged by the administration's commitment to end the Somoza regime.

Torrijos put little stock in the junta. Given Nicaragua's political history, he understood that power in the new government would shift to those who controlled the army. Therefore, the composition of the junta, or its size, was of minor importance.

Los Doce member Arturo Cruz had communicated exactly the same message to Vaky and Pastor on June 28 after a trip to San José. "A broadened junta will not be effective. As long as the FSLN has the guns they will dictate policy," Cruz predicted.[18] Vaky didn't need convincing. The NSC did. As the situation deteriorated in Nicaragua, the NSC was still trying to stage manage a

smooth transition to a moderate, pro-U.S., democratic government. It wasn't in the cards.

Arriving at the home of Colonel Mojica in Guatemala City, Bowdler and I found a man quietly recovering from a heart attack.
Colonel Mojica was not well informed about events in Nicaragua,
nor had he kept in touch with his colleagues in the Guardia. He
was the picture of a comfortable retired military officer content to
watch events from the sidelines. He expressed little interest in returning to Nicaragua to command a reformed Guardia Nacional.
Bowdler cabled our impressions to Washington. Much to my surprise, Colonel Mojica remained a leading candidate until the eleventh hour.

When I returned to Nicaragua the next day, the pilot of the
Beechcraft flew high over Lake Managua because of fighting on
the North Highway, not far from the airport. He dropped the
plane practically into nose dive before leveling out. Turning to me,
he asked if I minded if he kept the engines running when we
landed in Managua. My stomach was still settling as I answered, "I
don't mind."

12

In war you cover yourself with glory or you cover yourself in shit.
—Saying popular among the Sandinista fighters
on the Southern Front

As I shuttled between the two promontories of Managua and policy makers in Washington searched for ways to keep Nicaragua from turning into another Cuba, the realities of the civil conflict continued to define the political future.

On July 1, Manolo Gutiérrez's daughter, twenty-three-year-old Lucía Gutiérrez, was in León, the country's second largest city, where the fighting had been fierce. She had been assigned there by the FSLN directorate to support field commander Leticia Herrera of the Rigoberto Pérez López Western Front. Leticia was one of seven Sandinista leaders in León—four of the seven were women.

Lucía had lived in León before. She had traveled there in 1975 to attend the humanities branch of the UNAN, the national university. She had met a young psychology student named Leonel who introduced her to the Student Revolutionary Front (FER), which was allied to the FSLN. Together they had organized resistance committees in the Subtiava barrio. Later she became a coordinator for the Christian base communities in the León-Chinandega region.

156

In early 1977, just weeks after Leonel confessed to her that he was a member of the FSLN, he was picked up, tortured, and killed by the Guardia. Lucía, fearing for her life, fled to Honduras. While she was in Tegucigalpa she called her father and told him she was becoming a Sandinista. He said she was a traitor and hung up. From Honduras she had helped organize the September 1978 insurrection.

Lucía and her father had never agreed about politics. Even so, they had a lot in common. She thought of him as a clever, outgoing man, bold and confident like herself. He knew how to get around people. And like his daughter he had big dreams.

Lucía's father was in love with development and progress and loved the United States. She often said that he had an engineer's perspective because he admired the North Americans' conquest of space. In terms of culture and understanding, the things that nourished people, she considered him stupid. He had a *Reader's Digest* mentality, she would say. He bought the magazine every week.

Since March, Lucía had been in León helping to organize the insurrection. There was a lot of work to do and few resources. From the beginning, she found the cadres badly organized and security arrangements sloppy. Everyone spoke of victory as though it was a foregone conclusion. How to achieve that victory was something they did nothing about.

On the night of April 16, the Guardia raided a safe house where the top leadership were meeting. Lucía and her superior, Leticia Herrera, had been asked to attend. Leticia had a bad feeling that night, so they didn't go. Subsequent rumors said that she had been part of a plot. Despite unification of the tendencies of the FSLN, there was still bad blood.

A government spokesman said that the guerrillas, hiding in the house of a prominent León resident, had fired on a passing Guardia convoy. But area residents said the troops burst into the home with their guns firing. Five FSLN leaders were killed immediately, including Edgard Lang, whose mother was a cousin of Somoza's mother. Edgard's father was one of the wealthiest men in the country.

After this tragedy, the top leadership in León had to be rebuilt. When the call for insurrection went out on the fourth of June, there were 180 cadres divided into thirty-six squads. Poet Juan Velázquez captured the mood in the city:

A Sandinista *muchacho* receives some anxious words of warning from a León housewife. Behind him on the wall are pictures of wanted Guardias. Credit: Benoit Gysembergh Camera Press, London 30410-2 (97) Globe Photos, 1993

Suddenly the *muchachos* knocked on our door,
a rainy night, the second of June, 1979,
They came from out of their hiding places onto the street
like a wild animal that first searches
for a scent in the air and quickly goes.
The sparks of raindrops shining in their beards.
Jets of water falling from the brims of their hats;
the mahogany butts, the steel like lead,
each one like a storm hammered into rage.[1]

By the morning of June 4, shooting could be heard from all directions—explosions, sustained automatic weapons fire, the *ping!* of handguns and small rifles. Streets were already filled with debris, and a light drizzle fell as Lucía made her rounds. All the doors of stores and houses were closed tight. On a bright green door scribbled in chalk she read: "Two old people and two children live here."[2]

Lucía's job was coordination—moving people, supplies, ammunition—and passing and giving orders so that the squads could support each other. She had been on her feet so much in the last three weeks that her feet had swollen like balloons. Lucía was also responsible for the distribution of arms. She could tell you that when the *compas* launched the insurrection they had twenty Garands, seventy-two FALs, four carbines, one Hornet .22, and four shotguns. Whatever else they needed had to be wrested from the Guard.[3]

About 600 Guardias were fortified in five positions—the "21" Jail, El Fortín, Command Central barracks, the exit to the highway, and El Godoy Airport, a concrete strip used mainly for small fumigation planes. The *compas* attacked first at the airport, because that's where the Guard was stockpiling supplies.

The battle went back and forth for days. The rebels would take it, the Guard would counterattack. By the time the Guardia retreated to Command Central barracks, there was nothing left for the *compas* to take. After fifteen days of fighting, Somoza's troops stopped venturing out onto the streets. Lucía could navigate the city freely.

One by one, the "21" Jail and the exit to the highway fell. The battle for the Command Central barracks turned out to be one of the pivotal struggles of the war. The *compas* used municipal backhoes to dig trenches.

"Most Spanish cities are alike," explained a Guardia captain, "with the local police or army *cuartel* in the center of town. It's easy to take over the approaches to a city, at least for a while, but unless you capture the garrison, you don't control anything."[4]

While Somoza's push-pulls and T-33s made bombing runs over the city, the Sandinistas blasted Command Central barracks apart piece by piece with Chinese-made RPG-2 rockets. Many of Somoza's bombs were left over from the Bay of Pigs.

"When we ran out of bombs," said one of Somoza's foreign mercenaries, "we concocted giant Molotov cocktails from fifty-gallon drums of gasoline. At first we made them like napalm with trip flares. Then we discovered that they were more effective if exploded at a hundred feet, which would create an igneous cloud that would burn the people below to a crisp."[5]

The fighting had been fierce. "When I talked to the department commander on the telephone," recalled Somoza, "I could hear the cries of agony in the background. My heart bled for those men. I searched for reinforcements . . . but all available troops had been sent to the southern front to battle the army which had come across from Costa Rica."[6]

After a week of fighting, the commanding officer in León, Major General Gonzálo Evertz, was badly wounded. Retired general Ariel Arguello and his son volunteered to take command. It seemed like a lost cause. A FSLN radio operator overheard Somoza exhorting the new general. "Hold on, my friend, we are with you all the time."

"We are like the French Foreign Legion," replied General Arguello. "We will fight to the last man."[7] Somoza remembered:

> Since no supporting troops could be sent to León, and since it was obvious that these men were in a death trap, the decision was made to evacuate central police headquarters (Command Central). The plan was to get out of the building and, if possible, make their way to El Fortín, a point of high ground overlooking the city.
>
> From the time those troops left the building until they reached El Fortín, it was a bloodbath. The revolutionaries had the protection of solid walls and the retreating detachment had nothing but guns and guts. The brave and loyal Brigadier General Arguello was killed and so was his son. Those who made it to El Fortín were fortunate.[8]

Lucía was one of the first to enter the Command Central barracks after the Guardia abandoned it. She had wished her father had been with her so that he could see. Prisoners taken before the insurrection lay dead and mutilated on the floor. She saw a woman with a bayonet thrust between her legs and men missing features and genitals. The faces were so badly disfigured that they were impossible to identify. The courtyard behind the barracks was ankle deep in ammo boxes and empty cardboard canisters that once held individual rounds for the Sherman tank.[9]

The bodies of four Guardias were being buried in a vacant lot across the street. Ten other guardsmen lay dead in the street. Some *compas* were holding a group of Guardias prisoner in a private house converted into a prison. Meanwhile, a C-47 with a machine gun in the cargo hatch was strafing FSLN positions.

By June 19, with the fall of Command Central barracks, León was virtually a liberated city. It marked a turning point that even

Sandinista fighters wind their way through the grotesque debris of fighting in León. Credit: Benoit Gysembergh Camera Press, London 30410-27 (97) Globe Photos, Inc. 1993

Somoza acknowledged. "In my opinion," he wrote, "the defeat at León marked the beginning of the destabilization of our military situation."[10]

The city had suffered acutely. The streets were strewn with bodies. The entire center of León was a mess. The elegant colonial arches of the central market lay in ruins, as did the main public buildings and the hospital. Whole neighborhoods had been cordoned off with barbed wire. Warning signs were posted at the entrances: CONTAMINATED. The stench of death told you why.

Even in the midst of death and destruction, Lucía and her *compadres* were excited. If her eyes were red with fatigue, she knew in her heart that the Sandinistas would prevail. Reports from around the country were encouraging. The Guardia was trapped in their *cuartels* in Estelí, Masaya, and Matagalpa. "If only it would end quickly!"

In her exhilaration and exhaustion, Lucía tried not to think ahead. But she couldn't help herself. She was a planner. The job they faced would be enormous. People were starving. There was no market, no running water, and no electricity. *Compas* like herself had been surviving on a soup made from chicken feed.

It was a different story on the Southern Front. There, Edén Pastora's men were still locked in brutal combat with elite units of the EEBI.

"At Peñas Blancas we hit the Guardia barracks with recoilless rifles in the middle of the night," wrote Alejandro Murguía. "When the smoke cleared, the Guardia had abandoned the town and *compas* were swarming all over the duty-free stores, the restaurants, and everything. It was like a movie, with *compas* sporting expensive sunglasses and toting imported whiskies looted from the dictator's stores."[11]

Pastora's men then advanced through Sapoa until they came to a river with a stretch of flat land on the other side and Hill 50. There they had to stop. "In terrain like this," Murguía wrote, "where one sniper can stop a whole column, you advance with your balls in your hands."[12]

Somoza's forces had control of the skies and used their helicopters to spot enemy positions. "We got into these artillery duels," remembered a Sandinista. "They'd hit us for a while and we'd hit them back."[13]

The smell of burnt gunpowder hung everywhere. "Sometimes the Guardia comes at us all hopped up on pills," wrote Alejandro Murguía, "their mouths foaming, eyes wild. You have to pop them a few times to stop them. Whoever says he's not scared is a liar."[14]

Leonel Poveda of the FSLN's Internal Front estimated that 300 rebels had died in the many battles for Peñas Blancas and a least 100 others had died trying to capture Rivas. That meant nearly a fourth of all the volunteers who had crossed the border from Costa Rica had died.[15]

The battle for Masaya was shaping up to be just as brutal. Gustavo Gutiérrez awoke the morning of June 29 to the sound of sharp explosions. Government-run Radio Nacional was announcing that the Guardia had begun "cleaning up" Masaya. Since dawn, mortars had been raining over the city from the Guardia's hilltop fortress of Coyotepe. Now the push-pulls and the AC-47 gunships made passes over the city, firing their rockets at Sandinista positions.[16]

Deputy Foreign Minister Harry Bodan explained to reporters that the National Guard decision to pull out of Masaya had been part of strategy to turn the tables on the rebels. "The city center has always been vulnerable. The Coyotepe fortress commands the city and the vital highway north and south. We are sending out patrols from the fortress to harass the FSLN which now has to defend the vulnerable positions."[17]

The town of Masaya was a mess. There was no water and nothing to eat but avocados and *zapotes*. The Sandinistas' stockpile of rice and beans in the nearby *finca* of San Miguel was too dangerous to reach.

From Gustavo's perspective, in a trench four blocks from the central plaza, there was destruction everywhere. There were pockmarks on every building. Walls were covered with graffiti urging the people to resist and pleading with the soldiers to lay down their arms. "The people are dying because of Somoza," read one. "Soldiers, don't kill your people."

Down at the corner, two cars and a Guardia jeep were scorched and overturned. Beside them lay the half-burned bodies of Guardias bloating in the tropical sun. They were covered with flies. The stench was sweet and heavy.

The *compa* next to Gustavo passed a cigarette. He took a drag and pointed up to the sky. Three helicopters were circling the city like vultures, descending slowly. A boy across from him had been shot in the foot. When he removed his boot, it was full of blood and pus.

"We'd better get you to the doctor," said Gustavo. The boy grinned back as an AC-47 came in low over the treetops with .50-caliber machine guns firing from its sides. The *compas* took aim and fired back. When the big round 500-pound rolled out, they covered their heads. The blast ripped through the air and shook the ground. Gustavo flew up two feet in the air and slammed down. He remembered to keep his mouth open so that his ear drums wouldn't burst. Word soon reached them that twelve *compañeros* died from the explosion near the Church of San Jeronimo.

Before they could catch their breath, the helicopters started dropping gasoline bombs and napalm. Gustavo and his unit spent the rest of the day shooting at the helicopters and fighting the fires that raged throughout the city. The townspeople had nowhere to run. They cowered in doorways and behind barricades with the few valuables they could carry, wondering which was more deadly, the fires burning around them or the machine gun fire from above.

In the afternoon, exhausted from the heat, the fighting, and the smoke, Gustavo saw some *compas* bring out a spy. He'd been turned in by his neighbors and was barefoot and unshaven. His eyes were red and wild, staring back at the crowd that had gathered.

A *compa* in a red beret made him get down on his knees while he tied the spy's hands behind his back. Asked if he had any last words, he answered "Viva Somoza!" The *compa* pulled out a fishing knife, yanking the spy's head back by his hair and with one quick motion sliced his neck from ear to ear. Gustavo watched in shock as the spy's eyes got big and he twisted. A terrible sound was coming out of his throat. People jumped back. There was blood spurting everywhere. After what seemed like an eternity, his body went limp. When the *compa* let go of him, he folded to the ground.[18]

Twelve miles south in the town of Diriamba, the Guardia was trapped inside their *cuartel*. From his position near a second-story window, Corporal Jorge Royo heard his major pleading on the radio: "I beg you, I beseech you. . . . If we don't get reinforcements, we are all screwed!"

Corporal Royo's boots were covered with brass casings from the spent rounds of his .50-millimeter machine gun. He saw a black beret in the smashed window across the street, quickly trained his sights, and fired. Chunks of glass and adobe filled the window with dust.

"They're coming," barked the voice on the radio. "They might get there tonight."

"Don't bullshit me."

"I can't promise anything," answered the voice on the other end.[19]

Corporal Royo was wondering if his commander was talking to El Chiguín or General José Somoza, the president's half brother. He didn't know that many of the Sandinista fighters who had retreated from Managua were aiding the rebellion in the Carazo area towns of San Marcos, Jinotepe, and Diriamba.

"Don't tell me they're coming if they're not," yelled the major. "I'm up to my neck in shit here. . . . If I don't get reinforcements I'm talking turkey with the guerrillas."[20]

"Fight like men!" barked the tired voice. And the radio went dead.

When Corporal Royo looked around him, he didn't like their chances. Morale was low; the soldiers were exhausted after fifteen days and nights of fighting. A group of soldiers crouched silently in a back room with their rifles. They wouldn't fight. Each day more and more soldiers were refusing to shoot at their countrymen.

With Corporal P.oyo and the rest of the Guardia holed up in their *cuartel,* the Sandinistas controlled the town of Diriamba. But they too were having problems. There were hungry mouths to feed and homeless families. A few blocks from the Guardia *cuartel,* the newly formed People's Assembly was trying to decide how to distribute the twenty bags of maize that had been liberated from a government storehouse. There was lots of revolutionary rhetoric and ideas.

"Everybody had to get used to making decisions beyond little routine things," explained a Sandinista named Milagros. "When a meeting ended, the crowd would continue the discussion in the street, thinking someone would solve the problems. They thought the answers would come from above. That was the hardest things to work against."[21]

Throughout the department of Carazo, Somoza's military situation was growing increasingly desperate. When Sandinista reinforcements reached Diriamba from Masaya on the fourth, the Guardia *cuartel* was quickly overrun. From Diriamba the *compas* moved south into Jinotepe. There the fighting went street by street.

On the afternoon of the fifth, Somoza put a call through to the besieged garrison:

"I want to speak to the commander. Am I speaking to the commander?"

"You're speaking to the commander. Yes."

"How's the situation there?"

"We're screwed, sir."

"Move the troops you have in Las Esquinas and those you have in the Social Security Building and get out of there."

"Those of Las Esquinas aren't there, sir. I think they've also been attacked in Social Security. They killed an officer."

"Well, do what you want, but abandon that old house."[22]

After two days of intense fighting, the *cuartel* fell. "In Jinotepe, when we liberated the *cuartel* and freed the prisoners," remembered Sandinista leader Walter Ferrety, "one prisoner was so euphoric that he ran into the plaza screaming: 'Viva el Frente! Viva el Frente!' We didn't have time to warn him that there were still

Guardias hidden in the park. They shot him."[23] "That's how it was throughout the first days of July," wrote FSLN comandante Carlos Nuñez; "you didn't know whether you should shout for joy or cry."[24]

13

God offers to every mind its choice between truth and repose. Take which you please—you can never have both.
—Ralph Waldo Emerson

In the early hours of July 4, 1979, the director of Latin American Affairs of the National Security Council, Robert Pastor, was awakened by a call from the White House Situation Room. Two letters had arrived for President Carter from the Nicaraguan embassy, and National Security Adviser Zbigniew Brzezinski wanted an immediate analysis of the letters to present to the president. Pastor dressed and drove to the White House, "exhausted, but moving on spurts of adrenaline, [his] mind racing through hundreds of permutations of what the two letters contained." What he discovered as he read anxiously were July fourth birthday greetings from Anastasio Somoza and his brother-in-law, Nicaragua's Ambassador Guillermo Sevilla-Sacasa. He remembered wondering whether it "was a grotesque joke, or a metaphor heralding the last act of a Pirandellian play."[1]

I discovered that events in Managua were refracted in the same warped mirror. I returned to find a city clenched in anxiety. Something big was going to break, and everyone was asking: When? How will my life change?

The estimated 600,000 refugees throughout Nicaragua added to the sense of urgency. Although the fighting had eased in Managua, the Nicaraguan Red Cross was concerned about the threat of starvation and disease. There were some 74,000 refugees crowded into Red Cross shelters across the country. An estimated 100,000 people in Managua alone were depending on the Red Cross for food. "We've been reduced to giving out half-rations this week," said J. Wilfrid Cross Urcuyo, vice president of the local Red Cross. "In some neighborhoods, people are close to starvation. They're having to beg or steal food. Some are breaking into homes for food and this will get worse if we don't get more in from abroad."[2]

In response to my request that we take immediate measures to assuage the critical food shortage, the Office of Foreign Disaster Assistance in Washington dispatched one of its veterans, George Beauchamps, to assess the need and submit recommendations to initiate an emergency food program. It didn't take Beauchamps long to size up the situation and explore sources of supply. Soon, approximately eighty tons of food a day were being trucked in from El Salvador, Guatemala, and Honduras to help redress the emergency shortage. Since supplies in those countries were running low, it had become necessary to fly food in from the United States. We were concerned about using U.S. military planes. The already suspicious Sandinistas might think that the United States was flying in military supplies for Somoza's army. It was decided that Beauchamps would contract a private cargo carrier.

Somoza's situation on the ground was growing grimmer by the hour. Bolstered by the 5,000 or so fighters who had survived the retreat from Managua, the FLSN had overrun one southwestern city after another. Masaya, Masatepe, San Marcos, Diriamba, and Jinotepe were all in rebel hands. Guardia Nacional defenders had retreated to Granada. Resupply routes between Managua and Guardia troops on the Southern Front had been cut off.

Although the Guardia still held the advantage in heavy equipment, its profligate use of ammunition, loss of garrison arsenals, and a cutoff of imports had severely cut into their supplies.

Of its original four Sherman tanks, only one was still operational. The rebels had destroyed one, captured another, and cannibalized a third for parts. Of the forty British-made Staghound armored cars the Guardia had at the beginning of the fighting, only fifteen were still operational. Its small forty-five-plane air force had been halved because of mechanical failures, losses, and at least one defection.

Furthermore, the Guardia commanders were careless and sloppy. In the early morning of July 4, an air strike was requested from "Massachusetts," the code name for the commander of Fort Coyotepe overlooking the FSLN-held city of Masaya. "Massachusetts" called "Buffalo," General José Somoza, to tell him that the "jackals" were unloading a twin-engine plane that had just landed on the Masaya highway. He was told by an aide that "Buffalo" was asleep. When "Massachusetts" asked to talk to "Alfa Sierra Delta" (Somoza), he was told the president was sleeping, too, and could not be awakened. So "Massachusetts" watched as the plane's cargo of ammunition was unloaded and carted away by the Sandinistas.[3]

When I met with Somoza on the afternoon of the fourth, he admitted that the military situation had deteriorated. El Chiguín reported that while the morale of middle-grade Guardia officers was still high, they were growing more anxious by the hour.

Ironically, the tables had turned. The Somozas were now pressing us to act quickly so that they could leave. "An early political solution is needed," argued Tachito, "or the Guardia won't be able to defend itself. I'll be forced to act on my own, sir, to save the people close to me."[4]

It was weird. I was asking Somoza to be patient.

Luis Pallais interrupted. He was having trouble keeping a quorum of congressmen in Nicaragua. His son had been given the task of ferrying Liberal congressmen back from Miami. Seeing the dire conditions in Managua, many quickly slipped back out of the country again. Conservative congressmen were sticking it out. The prospect of attending a session of Congress to accept Somoza's resignation delighted them.

The usually unflappable Pallais was frustrated. "I heard that President Carter met with Torrijos to work out a democratic solution and that Ambassador Bowdler was meeting with representatives of the Andean countries and with the junta, but you give us no details, and you ask us to wait."[5]

I assured them that we would soon be moving forward.

"I hope so," said a tired Somoza.[6]

Returning to the embassy, I drafted a flash cable to Washington with my analyses: "Our estimation of the fighting and the strains within the National Guard account in large part for the growing anxiety within the Somoza inner circle. . . . I am more concerned about the fears of the middle and lower grade officers at this point. . . . [They] will have to remain to prevent an FSLN sweep."[7]

Typically, Washington had its own preoccupations, namely the political fallout of the crisis and what the administration stood to gain or lose from it. At a press conference in Mexico City, after visiting his friend the shah of Iran, ex-President Richard Nixon said that President Carter "shouldn't grease the skids for our friends." Nixon said that the choice was "not between Somoza and somebody better, but between Somoza and somebody much worse."[8] Pastor of the NSC complained that "the United States was already in so deeply that it had a responsibility to see the project through."[9]

Bill Bowdler returned to San José, Costa Rica, on July 4 to find a FSLN junta as suspicious of U.S. intentions as when he left. They were also feeling bolstered by the military situation. "Somoza has already lost the war," claimed junta member Sergio Ramírez.

> It's impossible for him to take the military initiative again. He can't take the forces he has in Managua elsewhere. The moment he does, the Sandinista columns that left there will return. His elite forces at La Virgen [north of Rivas on the Southern Front] cannot move from there. In fact, all of his elite forces are in Managua or Rivas. There is no important Somocista force in the north or west of Nicaragua. We have control.[10]

Despite such talk from the junta, General Torrijos gave the plan he had agreed to in Washington a try. Summoning Sandinista leaders Tomás Borge and Daniel Ortega to Panama, he tried to convince them to expand the junta. After listening to the general, Ortega and Borge consulted Fidel Castro, who advised them to accept Torrijos's suggestion.

Meanwhile, Vaky was in Caracas, Venezuela, where former President Carlos Andrés Pérez suggested five names: General Julio Gutiérrez, Mariano Fiallos, Emilio Alvarez Montalbán, Ernesto Fernández Holmann, a leading Conservative economist, and Jaime Chamorro Cardenal, brother of the slain *La Prensa* editor.

The junta was feeling pressured. "We're willing to talk about expanding the junta," said Sergio Ramírez on the fifth, "but this should be done directly between Nicaraguans."[11]

A meeting between the junta and Ambassador Bowdler was scheduled for the afternoon of July 5. When Bowdler suddenly canceled and flew to Panama, the junta grew even more suspicious. What was the United States trying to pull? Characterizing the pressure as "blackmail," junta spokesman Father Miguel D'Escoto accused the United States of "trying to bargain with the blood of our people."[12] What they didn't know at the time is that Bowdler had been evacuated to Panama because of a sudden illness, which he told me years later was a "phosphorous deficiency." The junta, meanwhile, was being barraged with calls from Carlos Andrés Pérez, Torrijos, and members of the Andean Group. Costa Rican President Rodrigo Carazo Odio called the junta in and urged them to accept more members.

Ironically, it was the moderates who resisted the expansion. FAO leader and junta member Alfonso Robelo said he saw "no reason why the United States should lay down conditions on how we should run Nicaragua. We see no logic in broadening the junta when it has been backed by COSEP and the FAO."[13]

Violeta Chamorro called the effort to expand the junta "an unwarranted intervention in Nicaraguan affairs" and threatened to resign.[14] When the ex-president of Venezuela, Carlos Andrés Pérez, tried to change her mind, she broke into tears and said that if she were the hurdle to some kind of arrangement between the presidents of Costa Rica, Panama, Venezuela, and the United States, she would step aside, but she would not agree to the changes.

By the time Bowdler returned from Panama on the evening of the ninth, the junta had become more aggressive. The day before, junta spokesman Father Miguel D'Escoto telephoned Senator Edward Kennedy and asked him to send a letter to President Carter. The senator wrote to the president, quoting the junta representative as follows: "We have asked our friend Senator Kennedy to convey to you this message expressing our desire to have some members of our Government of National Reconstruction meet with you as soon as possible in Washington."[15]

Bowdler realized that the idea to expand the junta was dead. After repeated efforts to sell the scheme, Torrijos and other Latin leaders had backed away. They now referred to it as the "American plan"; as Carter had predicted, that meant "the kiss of death."[16]

When Bowdler finally met with the four junta members (the fifth, Moises Hassan, was still fighting inside Nicaragua) on July

10, they indicated that they expected power to be transferred directly to them. To assuage U.S. fears, the junta offered to incorporate reformed elements of the Guardia into a Sandinista army. It was also agreed that the junta would get a chance to approve the officer selected to head the new National Guard.

Talks in San José, Managua, and Washington now focused on the survivability of the Guardia Nacional. No one was taking bets. Assistant Secretary Vaky already had his doubts, which he expressed on July 10 to slightly dumbfounded policy makers at the NSC. Their attitude was that "it has to work," or "we'll make it work." But nobody was saying how. Instead, their focus shifted to the search for a new Guardia commander acceptable to all parties.

At a special coordinating meeting of the NSC on July 9, names were tossed back and forth. General Julio Gutiérrez was finally ruled out because of his refusal to return to the region. Several names suggested by the FSLN, including Col. Bernardino Larios who had left the Guardia to join the Sandinistas, were dismissed by the Defense Department. The concern was that they would not be able to win support within the Guard. Incredibly, Col. Innocente Mojica, the military attaché to Guatemala who had expressed no interest in the position when Bowdler and I met with him, emerged as the leading candidate. Brzezinski wanted to offer the new Guard commander assurances in the form of military assistance, but was quickly overruled.

Meanwhile, Somoza was planning to leave. His mistress Dinorah was already waiting for him in Florida. Four-year multiple-entry tourist visas had already been issued to members of his cabinet and entourage. When I met with him at "La Curvita" on the afternoon of the fifth, I noticed bulging suitcases waiting along the walls. Somoza asked if the people leaving with him could become legal U.S. residents. I explained that he had priority as the spouse of a U.S. citizen.

Once again, he asked how soon we could set a date for his resignation. He still feared assassination. I told him I was sure he knew how to look out for himself. "Then let me ask you this, Mr. Ambassador, as a bona fide ex-president, will I have diplomatic immunity in the United States or not?"

"Well, it's not a question of diplomatic immunity," I answered, referring to the guidelines issued by the legal advisers weeks before. "For instance, an ambassador has more rights than a citizen. You wouldn't have that immunity. But you will have all the protections of the law. Same as any U.S. citizen."[17]

On the morning of the seventh, Somoza telephoned me at the embassy to protest the assassination of a distant cousin, killed by the Sandinistas when they overran his father's hometown of San Marcos. That afternoon I received a cable from Pastor of the NSC. It began by stating, "Colonel Inocente Mojica may be the new Guard commander," and continued, "In your conversations with moderate leaders, you should make it clear to them that they will be making a mistake if they rely solely on the provisional junta to safeguard their rights. You may wish to consider urging them to establish contact with appropriate people in the National Guard."[18]

It was hard to believe. Somoza was practically begging us to leave; the country was on its knees; there were a handful of moderates left in the country. Didn't Washington understand there was a war going on? People couldn't move; there was a curfew from sundown to dawn. How were moderate leaders supposed to reach Guardia officers? What did Washington think was going on here?

While the diplomatic maneuvering continued, a confused and increasingly distraught Nicaraguan public looked on. Their country was bleeding and starving to death, and it seemed the whole world was playing politics. "The United States has always intervened when we Nicaraguans have tried to define our own future," said a wealthy young businessman. "Now it is willing to see Nicaragua bombed back into the Stone Age in order to maintain its system of domination."[19]

This feeling of hopelessness was exacerbated on July 7 by a front-page article in the *Washington Post*. Over a photograph of a weary, fatigue-clad Somoza screamed the headline: "Somoza Agrees to Quit, Leaves Timing to the U.S." Given Somoza's paranoia and insistence on secrecy, I was taken aback.

Since the assassination of *La Prensa* editor Chamorro in January 1978, an extensive press corps had set up shop in Managua. Mostly young and inexperienced when they arrived, the reporters had earned their spurs covering the convulsive events of 1978, the OAS mediation, and the outbreak of civil war. By the time I arrived in June 1979, I found them understandably suspicious of U.S. motives and anti-Somoza. After all, Somoza's Guardia Nacional had been responsible for the cold-blooded murder of ABC reporter Bill Stewart on June 20. Somoza, who had once enjoyed his salty banter with reporters, had grown defensive and hostile, accusing the press of being part of the communist conspiracy to overthrow him. On the other side, the Sandinistas, led by spokesman Miguel D'Escoto, were open and solicitous with reporters.

By early July 1979, Somoza—uncharacteristically—had not spoken to the press for weeks. Still, one aggressive young journalist, Karen DeYoung, had made it a habit of telephoning the bunker each day, hoping for an exclusive interview. On the afternoon of the sixth, she was surprised when the dictator came on the line.

"Señor Presidente, I'd like to see you."

"All right, come on over."[20]

She did. Somoza was drinking tumblers of vodka. "I'm like a tied donkey fighting a tiger," he said. "Even if I win militarily, I have no future."

Somoza went on to spell out the substance of our talks. He made it sound like he was thinking about everyone except himself when, of course, the opposite was true. "What I'm trying to do is lessen the suffering of the Nicaraguan people by getting an arrangement where everybody would feel sure. Right now, nobody feels secure, because the (FSLN) junta has been adamant about . . . wanting it their own way."

His generosity came with the customary threats: "There are two alternatives. One is to leave in an orderly manner, and the other is to take what we think we should and move out of here. Arms, goods, and money. Make a tactical retreat. Instead of holding a lot of small unimportant towns, we gather everything up, put it in a section of the country and stick it out."

As usual, he was most accurate when describing attitudes in Washington: "Your national interest is that Nicaragua keep going like it is, with different faces running it, with different attitudes. But not to fall into the hands of the Marxists, because you have problems if you let that happen."

When he spoke about himself, you could practically hear the violins. "I've got my education. I might find a job someplace. What can a retired general, a retired president, do?"[21] Left out was any reference to the hundreds of millions he had squirreled away in banks accounts in Switzerland and the United States.

Although Washington made little of it, the *Washington Post* article produced an outcry in Managua. In his Sunday, July 8, homily, Archbishop Obando y Bravo accused the United States of drawing out the fighting as a means to persuade the Sandinistas to accept a political solution more beneficial to Washington. "We are thankful of those governments who have shown an interest in our people's situation," said the archbishop in a statement that was distributed in churches throughout the country, "but at the same time we lament the ambiguity of those governments who have thought or continue to think of their own political interests before the common good of the Nicaraguan people."[22]

A week before, Somoza's air force had begun a brutal bombing of the Sandinista-held city of Masaya, twenty miles to the north. The archbishop went on to condemn this bombing and other flagrant acts of the Guardia. "The raids on churches, places of refuge and hospitals must be considered criminal. . . . The indiscriminate killing of women and children, even when there is simple suspicion that they have collaborated with the adversary, must be considered a war crime. War action that leads to the destruction of cities together with their inhabitants is a crime against humanity and God."[23]

As the archbishop spoke, government helicopters were rescuing troops from El Fortín in León. The Sandinistas declared Nicaragua's second largest city liberated. According to Somoza: "León is the first communist controlled city on the American mainland."[24]

In a July 8 cable, I tried to warn Washington about the changing mood in Managua:

> The Karen DeYoung article is hurting us here. COSEP gave a statement which accuses the U.S. government of prolonging the bloodshed. The article coincides with the bombing of Masaya. The net effect of these factors reinforces the perception that we have the means to end the conflict but have been delaying in order to prevent a leftist takeover. It would be unfortunate, now that we are so close to a political settlement, to have the psychological environment move against us.[25]

Adding to the surreal drama, Somoza's friends in Congress, the self-proclaimed "dirty thirty," mounted a public relations campaign, no doubt paid for by Somoza. On Saturday, June 30, representatives Larry McDonald (D-Ga.), George Hansen (R-Idaho) and my old friend John Murphy (D-N.Y.) took out a full-page ad in the *New York Times*.

> The sands of time are running out for liberty and representative government in Nicaragua. Cuba was surrounded by water; Nicaragua is not, and a Communist takeover would be a disaster not

only to the Nicaraguan people, but to their neighbors in Central America, and indeed to the Western Hemisphere.[26]

Congressman Murphy was in daily telephone contact with the bunker and the White House, arguing Somoza's case. On the sixth, the *Washington Post* ran an editorial criticizing Murphy's role as an "adviser" during my first meeting with Somoza. "Didn't this at least suggest impropriety?" asked the *Post*. "For a legislator to take up a part as a freelance negotiator, or, as Murphy put it, 'observer,' lending his presence and prestige and advice to a foreign party involved in a delicate adversary proceeding with his own government is very odd."[27]

Representatives Hansen and McDonald and their wives followed up the missive of the June 30 with a visit to Managua on July 10. Bearing fourteen boxes of food and medical supplies, they visited with Somoza and toured several refugee camps. They told the press that they had come on a humanitarian mission. But before an audience of members of Somoza's Liberal party, they blamed the lack of U.S. support for their regime on "distorted press accounts of Nicaragua and a failure to respond to threats from international Communists."[28]

Congressman McDonald charged that the press had painted "the authority element, the elected government as some kind of brutal, oppressive dictatorship" and the Sandinistas as "Robin Hood angels."

"Take heart, keep up your courage and stand fast," he said to the gathering at the Intercontinental Hotel. "The American people are beginning to understand your plea." Mrs. Hansen added: "The truth will prevail and ultimately Nicaragua will be a free country."[29]

In an emotional exchange with an ABC reporter, Larry McDonald claimed, "There was no question of distortion of news of Nicaragua in the United States." The ABC reporter asked McDonald to "walk down here on the beach at the lake and look at the bodies with their hands tied that the National Guard is burning in the morning. And you come down here and accuse us of distorting? Where the hell have you been, sir?"[30]

Six hours after they arrived, Somoza's friends departed.

On the seventh, my new Deputy Chief of Mission Tom O'Donnell arrived in Managua. He was met at the airport with a flak jacket. Tom, who had served as economic officer in Nicaragua from 1971 to 1974, was happily assigned to London when I called. Affable, intelligent, and clear-thinking, Tom was a stellar addition to the staff. His first assignment was to oversee the emergency food assistance program and take charge of plans for the possible emergency evacuation of the embassy staff.

The embassy had been operating in the middle of a civil war. Firefights still raged sporadically in and around the capital. Since both sides in the conflict had plenty of reason to take a shot at us, the United States Embassy was particularly vulnerable. Security at the "Casa Grande" (the ambassador's residence where most of the staff was staying) and the Chancery consisted of a six Marine guards headed by a superb Marine gunnery sergeant and three State Department security officers. Shortly after I arrived, the aged Guardia contingent assigned to watch over us suddenly and, without notice, disappeared.

O'Donnell's secretary, Pat Brania, had been working seven days a week since April. She had refused to be evacuated with the rest of the staff in June, because they wouldn't take her dog. While Pat remained perfectly calm through the hairiest moments, her dog had become paranoid. He followed her everywhere, spending most days curled safely beneath her desk.

We had one communications officer who virtually lived at the Chancery. Because of the twilight-to-dawn curfew, cables were often sent and received from Washington at night. O'Donnell and I often had to communicate between the residence and the Chancery via secure-line walkie-talkies supplied by the CIA. One night, our search for clear reception sent us out on the balcony of the second floor. As we were talking, shots popped in the distance. As the pops grew louder, one of the security officers came running out on the "Casa Grande" lawn. He was armed and wearing shorts. Bandoliers of bullets crisscrossed his chest.

"They're shooting at you, for Chrissakes! Get inside!"

Staying with us at "Casa Grande" was a special air force team from Panama to aid an emergency evacuation if it became necessary. Two Hercules helicopters had been stationed across the border at Liberia Airport in Costa Rica. We didn't know at the time that Liberia was the same airport the Sandinistas were using to resupply their troops. On the tenth, the Costa Rican legislature voted 29 to 20 to ask President Carazo to have the helicopters removed. They were subsequently moved to a navy ship offshore.

No. We weren't winning hearts and minds in Central America.

14

Change is not made without inconvenience, even from worse to better.   —Richard Hooker, quoted by Samuel Johnson

In their house in an upper middle-class Managua suburb, Virginia Sanchez, her two brothers, and their parents had been trying to while away the boredom.[1] Surrounded by the inventory of their family's hardware business, they played endless games of dominoes and monopoly and listened to the news reports on the radio. Their lives seemed to grind to a halt. There was no commerce, no classes at the university, no work, no social engagements, and often no electricity and water.

Confined to an inside bedroom for over two weeks now, they had run out of patience. On July 9, 1979, Virginia received an unexpected call from her employer. Citibank was evacuating all Nicaraguan employees to Guatemala. They offered to take immediate family (husbands, wives, or children). When Virginia refused to leave without her brothers, the bank offered to take them, too.

The next day the three of them bid their goodbyes. Parting was difficult and emotional, especially for the parents. Everything they had worked so hard for—a close family, a good life for their children, security for their last years—seemed to be going down the drain.

A Red Cross jeep with flashing blue lights escorted their white van to the airport. Scenes of devastation met Virginia and her brothers everywhere—pock-marked buildings, piles of charred bodies, barricades, looted stores, burned-out cars. It was worse than they had imagined. As they wove their way around the debris, artillery holes, and barricades of the North Highway, they were stopped at several checkpoints. Some were manned by the weary faces of the Guardia, some were manned by the tired but youthful faces of *muchachos*. The grim expressions of hatred told Virginia and her brothers how bad things had become.

At one Guardia checkpoint, their van was stopped. At gunpoint, the passengers were ordered to get out. "Roll up your pants and sleeves, we want to check your knees and elbows."

Virginia and her brothers experienced a moment of panic. "Did I fall recently?" she asked herself. "Did I scrape my elbow?" She knew that those who did not pass the test—whose bodies bore evidence of having participated in the fighting—would be detained and probably shot.

The airport was packed. Families with as many possessions as they could carry were camped out in the lounge. Many looked as though they had been there for days. Their faces were twisted into masks of fear and desperation. Guardias with automatic weapons prevented the crowd from spilling onto the tarmac.

Virginia and her brothers were relieved to see their small plane waiting on the runway. They buckled in. When the door to the cabin flew open, Virginia heard the pilot ask: "Do you think this piece of shit will make it?" Luckily for them, it did.

Back in Managua, Manolo Gutiérrez was listening to the birds. After each outbreak of shooting, a half minute of silence would follow. Then the birds would start singing. Their songs gave him hope.[2]

His sister, María Eugenia, had abandoned him to help the Red Cross. For a week now she had been feeding refugees in the Church of the Sagrada Familia in the El Dorado barrio of Managua. Women, young children, and old people lined up, looking stunned and hopeless. "What's the use of trying?" asked one old man pointing to his livelihood, his taxicab, a burned-out hulk down the street.

An estimated 9,000 people had died so far in Managua alone. Casualties across the country were estimated by the Red Cross to be as high as 50,000.

Manolo's son, Gustavo, was still in Masaya where the sky was the color of raw steel. A light rain was falling. It didn't rouse the exhausted young Sandinistas who slept behind brick barricades, or the stray dogs and pigs that foraged through the piles of garbage.

After a week of incessant bombing and counterattacks from the Guardia fortress of Coyotepe, the rebels had not given up. Almost every adobe house was pockmarked with bullet holes. Some had large chunks missing. The National Guard garrison in the central plaza was still smoldering. The charred brass plaque near the entrance read: *Built by the Government of General Somoza, 1941.*

Gustavo leaned against the entrance of the abandoned bookstore that was being used as a temporary jail. A pickup turned the corner and screeched to a stop in front of him. In the back were three men in dark pants and soiled shirts. Their hands were bound behind them. A fourteen-year-old girl wearing a green uniform and black and red bandanna pointed her M-1 at the men and ordered them inside.

Gustavo's sister, Lucía, was in León, where she had just learned that FSLN founder Tomás Borge and junta member Daniel Ortega were arriving that evening. She was sitting at a desk in the supply office. Three weeks ago, it had been the headquarters of the light and power company.[3]

From the supply office, over 200,000 residents of León were being provisioned with sugar, salt, cooking oil, soap, cereals, rice, and candles. Goods went from here to the United People's Movement, which distributed them to the popular committees and then to block organizations called civil defense committees. All those years of organizing had paid off.

Individual residents would go to their local civil defense committee every fifteen days to fill out a form. On it they would list the names of the people living in their home. Each person was entitled to four ounces of meat every two weeks.

The director of the supply office was a twenty-nine-year-old mathematics teacher named Oscar. With his combat boots on the desk, he offered a reporter an opinion: "I think that León can be a model for all Nicaragua."[4]

Like Lucía, Oscar had studied Marx. But Oscar and his mathematician's mind sought an interpretation of Marx's theories that applied to everything. While Lucía championed social and economic justice, she was also practical. She wanted a system that worked. To her thinking, a strict Marxist model was not realistic. She knew there were many like Oscar who hoped to turn Nicaragua into a Marxist state. She pointed out to him that the junta in San José had recently announced a program for a mixed economy.

Oscar shook his head. "No, No. . . . I think that sounds just like what we had before. We don't want reform, we want socialism. We want something better, something organized."[5]

The junta's fiscal planners in San José were beginning to paint a picture of that economic future. Led by the former secretary general of the Central American Common Market, Roberto Mayorga, they recognized that Nicaragua faced severe shortages of foreign exchange because of the disruptions in key crops, fiscal restraints because of the decline in revenues, and heavy unemployment. "It means austerity and sacrifice," Mayorga predicted. "We must create a very strong public sector for the expropriations and confiscations that will take place." He pledged that private property "fulfilling social functions would be left alone. . . . The state will be the temporary owner of property that will then be transferred to social types of cooperatives," Mayorga explained. "The state should not be administering farms and industries."[6]

So far, almost all the business people in León had been cooperative. Down the street in the devastated center of the city, a hardware store owner was wondering how she would be compensated. A representative of the supply office had ordered Margarita López de Lobo to open her store two weeks ago. When they requested paint, string, and nylon, she complied. Friends warned that the Sandinistas were bringing a disturbing new life. But Margarita López de Lobo was hoping for the best.

So was Lucía Gutiérrez. She couldn't complain. She and other FSLN leaders were living in a mansion complete with a swimming pool and beautiful gardens that had been left behind by a cotton planter. The owner had been in such a hurry that he left behind family pictures, books, a gilt-edged antique mirror, and even his children's toys.

At the "Casa Grande" in Managua, we were still camped out four and five to a room. One night we tried relieving the tension with a videocassette of the Mel Brooks movie, *Young Frankenstein*. Cleverly done and full of double-entendres, it had us laughing uproariously. The next morning, Tom O'Donnell was one of the first in the breakfast room. Joining him were the three-man air force team to help us in the event of an emergency evacuation—major, lieutenant, and sergeant. The sergeant kept his place and never spoke. "That was really a funny movie," O'Donnell said, as the three took their seats. He repeated one his favorite lines from the movie. "All of a sudden the Sergeant started spouting lines," remembered O'Donnell. "Before I knew it we went around the table and almost recreated the full dialogue of the movie."[7]

Back in Washington, National Security Adviser Zbigniew Brzezinski opened the Special Coordinating Committee meeting on July 10 by asking sarcastically whether the United States would be a willing or an unwilling tool of the destruction of the Guardia Nacional. The president's advisers were growing increasingly frustrated. The other actors in the Nicaraguan crisis weren't playing along with their scenarios. Unwilling to grasp the realities, the NSC Special Coordinating Committee decided to push their points one more time. They decided that: (1) The United States would seek the support of Torrijos, Pérez, and Carazo to ask the junta to expand their membership; (2) the United States, through the three Latin American leaders, would press for a new Guard commander; and (3) the United States would tell Somoza that it saw no reason for him to delay his departure.[8]

When Ambassador Bowdler met with four members of the junta at Puntarenas, Costa Rica, on the evening of July 11, they presented him with their own Plan to Achieve Peace. Conceived with the help of President Carazo, Carlos Andrés Pérez, and other Andean leaders, it called for Somoza to transfer power directly to the junta, which would then dissolve Congress and the Guardia Nacional. Members of the Guardia who had not committed crimes would be permitted to either leave the country or apply for membership in the Sandinista army.

The junta also used the meeting to announce a cabinet. It included Father Miguel D'Escoto as foreign minister, Tomás Borge as minister of the interior, Arturo Cruz as head of the Central Bank, Roberto Mayorga Cortés as minister of planning and economy, and Guardia defector Bernadino Larios as minister of defense.

To allay further doubts, the junta sent a letter to the secretary general of the OAS on July 12 pledging "full respect for human rights," a peaceful transition that would avoid "a bloodbath," and "the first free elections that our country will have in this century."[9] But they didn't say when.

In a morale-boosting speech before his National Liberal party the same day, Somoza sounded fierce, blaming the "destruction, looting, burning, and assassinations" in Nicaragua on "communism encouraged from abroad. We are facing a diabolical conspiracy against the people of Nicaragua to abolish our public freedoms and destroy our democratic institutions." To a confused and uncertain assembly, he issued a call "to every man and woman who believes in democracy, free enterprise, and individual freedom to stand up and fight for his home, his property, his family and the liberty of the Nicaraguan people."[10] He made no mention of his widely publicized agreement to resign.

On Thursday, July 12, I received the instructions from Washington I had been lobbying almost two weeks for: "You are authorized to see President Somoza as soon as possible and relay the following: This is a difficult situation and the decision to make is yours, but we think your prompt departure will help minimize bloodshed and the further loss of life."[11] I delivered the message to Somoza at his bunker that morning. He asked once again about diplomatic immunity, and I repeated that he would have "the full protection of U.S. law."[12]

Luis Pallais wanted to know if Somoza could choose his successor and the new commander of the Guardia. I said yes to the first and pointed out that the new commander would require the approval of Washington and the junta in San José. Somoza said he'd have to think it over; then, looking at me sadly, he added, "It's too bad your negotiations didn't succeed."[13]

I sat wondering what he was referring to when El Chiguín strode in wearing fatigues. He seemed perturbed. "Did you get the information that an American plane had been involved [in resupplying the Sandinistas]?"[14] I had heard that a push-pull had been shot down carrying shotguns and shells for the rebels, but had no details.

Before I had a chance to answer, El Chiguín changed the subject. "We finally tracked down the Chinese launchers, the RPG-2s that are being used to blast us to bits. They were bought by a Panamanian company in Lisbon from a Hungarian company in Budapest."

"It was in the name of Caza and Pesca," his father added. "Four million dollars worth of arms have been sold to Caza and Pesca

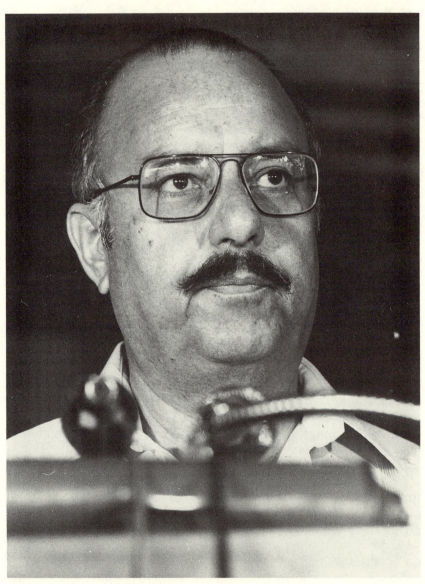

A beleaguered Anastasio Somoza faces the press. Credit: Benoit Gysembergh Camera Press, London 25813-11 (97) Globe Photos, Inc. 1992.

with an export license that was given to them by the Ammunition Board of the State Department."[15] I knew that Casa and Pesca was a hunting and fishing club in Panama and that a former Panamanian consul was under indictment. I told them so.

"I'm sorry to say that someone at the State Department must have been winking at this," said the elder Somoza, "because it's impossible for a club to buy four million dollars' worth of rifles."[16]

El Chiguín veered off onto another subject. He apparently had a lot to get off his chest. "The people themselves are beginning to wonder," he said. Then, continuing,

> The rebels went into Jinotepe and performed an against-the-wall type of shooting. Had it been an informant or something like that, I could understand.
>
> There was a captain with a family of four. Neither the captain nor his family had anything to do with the repression of any kind. His duty had been at the airport. They killed his mother, his grandmother, his father, his grandfather, and then they got his two sisters and two brothers. This type of thing happens wherever the terrorists go.
>
> In the heat of battle I can understand a man being placed against the wall and shot, but the systematic plaza type of executions I cannot understand. In León, for example, this type of situation is gathering momentum. . . . They use cruel methods. In battle, they are like the Red Chinese, and use human wave attacks. In Costa Rica, we have information that in the southern pockets they are using speed pills to feed these people. They put them up in a screaming line and then say GO! Then they are shot down like dogs.[17]

As I listened to these charges, I wondered if El Chiguín had forgotten the abuses of the EEBI. Most of the cases he was citing were old ones. I had the feeling that he had entered the conversation on cue. At one point he almost apologized: "I don't want to be calling the kettle black."[18]

"The system which has been imposed on these people [in rebel-occupied cities] is not quite like Wall Street," he continued. "People who have been our enemies before, are now coming out of the cities saying, 'Thank God for you.' "[19]

There was no point in arguing. I told him that I had heard about the Sandinistas' food distribution program in León. The session was over. O'Donnell and I bid our goodbyes.

That night Somoza called to invite me to lunch on Saturday to "discuss my proposal." I suggested we meet the next day. Somoza said he had information that Torrijos, Pérez, and Carazo were meeting with the Sandinistas in Costa Rica to "plan another invasion of Nicaragua."[20] When I assured him they were working toward a peaceful transition and seeking guarantees against reprisals, he seemed relieved.

Given my concern that the situation was quickly deteriorating, I asked the State Department if I could be authorized "to get Somoza's agreement to leave Sunday, or Monday at the latest. I realize that our position is to lay this decision on his lap," I argued in a 'Flash' message, "but we run the risk of having events overtake us if we do not act soon."[21]

The next morning I received a cabled letter from Secretary Vance to be delivered to President Somoza:

> The polarization and violence we feared has reached a point that calls for the most courageous and far-reaching response. It is absolutely clear that the situation cannot be resolved militarily in a satisfactory manner. . . . The only chance that remains to achieve an enduring and democratic solution is to establish a transition process that follows the precepts of the OAS resolution. . . . With each day that passes, our capacity to influence the situation and the transition diminishes. A continuation of the status quo beyond the next day or two will radicalize the situation even further, and is likely to result in the renewal of the offensive. . . . I therefore urge you to arrange your departure without delay. We will receive you in the U.S., as Ambassador Pezzullo has indicated. Your continued delay will only prolong the conflict and bloodshed and compromise our ability to try to achieve a moderate outcome.[22]

Managua was rife with rumors. Many still didn't believe it possible that their dictator would give up power. "Every American ambassador since the departure of Turner Shelton in 1975 has told us that Somoza would be leaving, and we just don't believe it this time," remarked one Nicaraguan businessman to Bernard Diederich of the *Washington Star.*[23]

But Somoza's military situation was increasingly precarious. "The battle appears to be won," said Lt. Col. James McCoy, the embassy's defense attaché, to our assembled staff. "The Guard no

longer has the capacity to launch an offensive to recapture cities."
Despite five days of heavy fighting on the outskirts of Masaya and
heavy air attacks with incendiary bombs and napalm, Somoza's
forces had been repulsed. "The Sandinistas now have the option
of organizing a major offensive to push northward or trying to
capture the southern capitol of Rivas. In my opinion they'll try for
a military victory and converge on Managua."[24]

We knew that the Guardia's stocks were running low. "They've
got enough for three weeks' fighting," said McCoy. "They're especially low on mortar and .50-caliber machine-gun ammunition."[25]
Somoza's only source of resupply had been clandestine DC-6
flights to Honduras, Guatemala, and El Salvador. Although he
had been able to bolster his depleted air force with six T-28 train-
ers fitted with rocket launchers purchased through arms dealers
in the States, Somoza was getting desperate.

"Men we have," Somoza told reporters, "But ammunition is lacking. We are trying to buy ammunition on the open market. Or
maybe we will make another decision. We could turn the table
around and become guerrillas."[26]

On the morning of the thirteenth, Somoza secretly boarded his
white and blue executive jet and flew to Guatemala City. To the
leaders of the Central American Defense Council (CONDECA),
he proposed that Guatemala, El Salvador, and Honduras send
troops to disarm the Sandinistas, once a cease-fire was in effect.
This would extinguish the "international communist threat." Even
the hardened anticommunist military officers considered his request bizarre. Somoza was incensed. After he left, Guatemala's
Gen. Lucas García called him "a dinosaur."[27]

In Washington, Congressman John Murphy, speaking for Somoza, claimed that the meeting "was not the first in the past two
weeks" and that his friend Somoza was "trying to get those countries to exercise their responsibility" under a Central American
mutual defense treaty.[28] Apparently on Murphy's advice, Somoza
then placed a call to President Carter at the White House. Deputy
Secretary of State Christopher took the call. Through Christopher, Somoza requested a meeting with the president to "explain
the reality of the situation."[29] Christopher assured him that the
president understood and he should talk with me instead.

When I met with Somoza on the evening of the thirteenth, he
explained why he had done this. "I don't want you to think I'm
going around you."[30] I assured him that I understood and then

read the message from Secretary of State Vance. He listened attentively. He was still concerned that we were offering no guarantees to the Liberal party and the National Guard. I told Somoza that we and other OAS member governments had been engaged in a major effort to assure that a pluralistic government would follow his and that a cease-fire and commitment to avoid reprisals would permit institutions like the Guardia Nacional to survive. Neither the United States nor any other authority could provide guarantees. The survivability of political entities like his Liberal party would depend on their ability to adapt.

"I would leave if I were selfish," Somoza told reporters that evening. "But remember I've been with these people for thirty-three years and they have helped me make this country what it is and I have helped them. I don't want to leave them without protection."[31]

At a Special Coordinating Committee meeting of the NSC the same day, Brzezinski sounded as though the United States had been defeated. According to Pastor, he spoke of "the baton being passed from the United States to Cuba." "It fills me with unease," he said. "We must lean harder on the Latin Americans to recognize that their security is involved."[32] Brzezinski believed that the Guardia would collapse without outside support. President Carter refused to offer support without the concurrence of our Latin allies, who had no interest in aiding the Guard.

The Special Coordinating Committee produced a list of potential Guard commanders which they asked me to propose to Somoza when I met with him on July 14. Finally forsaking their efforts to change the size and composition of the junta, the SCC instructed Bowdler to press for assurances that the transition would be as smooth and bloodless as possible.

Also, on the afternoon of the thirteenth, Humberto Ortega issued a call to all Sandinista forces to stand in place, in anticipation of a negotiated settlement. Although the rebels were within fifteen miles of their last target, Managua, the FSLN Directorate understood that it could only be taken with heavy casualties. The Guardia had been beaten back on all fronts, but their armor and elite troops were still concentrated in the capital in defense of Somoza. Humberto Ortega later admitted that "the armed movement of the vanguard never had the weapons needed to defeat the enemy."[33]

Meanwhile, in San José, Ambassador Bowdler was hoping to concentrate on eliciting guarantees from the junta to offer safe haven for those Nicaraguans who might feel endangered by the transition of power. But a meeting called for the morning of July 13 had to be canceled because he once again felt sick. Junta spokesman Father Miguel D'Escoto immediately went to the press, complaining, "Our patience has been used up." And contending that the junta had no desire to continue talks unless "the United States has something important to say," Violeta Chamorro backed him up, saying that Bowdler's attempts to negotiate with the junta were "completely finished."[34]

Chamorro and other junta members met instead with former Venezuelan President Carlos Andrés Pérez, General Omar Torrijos, and Costa Rican President Rodrigo Carazo. D'Escoto told reporters that the foreign ministers of the Andean Pact countries planned to meet in Venezuela on Sunday to break relations with Somoza and recognize the junta as Nicaragua's legitimate government.

Once again D'Escoto denounced the United States' reluctance to pressure Somoza to leave until a U.S.-approved political settlement was reached. "Our people are being massacred," D'Escoto said, "while the United States talks around in circles. They are trying to make us believe they can make Somoza's resignation effective in a matter of hours. We think it's criminal and we hope for their sake their policy will change."[35]

While Father D'Escoto was voicing his frustration, the first two chartered U.S. DC-8s landed in Managua laden with badly needed food. The final hour of the Somoza regime was drawing near and everyone's nerves were on edge.

15

Dictators ride to and fro upon tigers which they dare not dismount.
And the tigers are getting hungry. —Winston Churchill

Saturday, July 14, proved to be a turning point in Nicaraguan history. When I met with Somoza in the early afternoon, he announced that he would be leaving early Tuesday morning, July 17. Monday was ruled out because of a scheduled visit by Venezuela's Foreign Minister Zambrano. Despite reports that he was drinking heavily, Somoza remained sharp.

He announced to Tom O'Donnell and me that he had selected Liberal Congressman Francisco Urcuyo as interim president. He had chosen him, he said, because "Urcuyo is a good sound man. He's from Rivas and his niece is married to Pedro Joaquín Chamorro Barios [the slain newspaper editor's son]. He's a medical doctor trained in Mexico, he's been back there a number of times, and he should be acceptable to Mexico and the rest of the Latin American community."[1]

With that decision out of the way, we moved to the new commander of the Guardia. "The officer who fills that position will be the principal instrument in assuring the survivability of the

190

Guardia," I said. "His role will be enhanced if he has credibility among other Guard officers, the international community, and the junta."[2] I told him that Washington felt that Col. Inocente Mojica was such an officer. Somoza frowned.

"He's retired," he retorted. "And I don't know if he's known well enough by the active officers to command their support and respect." Somoza suggested General Humberto Sanchez, former head of the air force. We knew Sanchez had a reputation for being "one of the fastest guys with a buck" and told this to Somoza. His reply: "Sanchez is a very good negotiator, but maybe he has a sweet tooth."[3]

We discussed other officers—Col. Enrique Bermúdez, military attaché to Washington, Colonel Miguel Blessing, and Colonel Guerrero. Somoza doubted whether Colonel Bermúdez could muster much support within the Guardia because he had been out of the country so long. I told Somoza that Blessing and Guerrero were unacceptable to the junta in San José. He suggested Lt. Col. Alberto Moreno. Defense attaché McCoy, who knew him, felt that Moreno lacked prestige.

Later that afternoon at a second session, Somoza introduced Urcuyo. The sixty-five-year-old president of the lower house of Congress seemed like a little mouse. Somoza said to me, "Now, Mr. Ambassador, I want you to go over the whole scenario." And as Tom O'Donnell remembers, "We went over our whole what, where, when."[4]

Urcuyo didn't ask a question; he didn't say a thing except "Sí, jefe; sí, jefe."

"I remember that very clearly," says O'Donnell. "He kept referring to Somoza as 'jefe.'"[5]

The plan I described called for Somoza to tender his resignation to Congress on the night of Monday, July 16. Urcuyo would then be elected interim president and immediately name a new commander of the Guardia Nacional, an individual previously approved by both the junta and Somoza. Urcuyo would invite Archbishop Obando y Bravo, Ismael Reyes, the head of the Inter-American Human Rights Commission, Andean ambassadors, representatives of the junta, and the FSLN command to meet with him in Managua early the next day. Urcuyo would escort the delegates to the nearby Camino Real Hotel, where the combined national and international press corps would be waiting. The archbishop would speak first and call for a cease-fire and a stand-down of forces. To avoid reprisals, he would offer sanctuary in churches throughout the country for anyone who felt in danger. This was all to be broadcast live on national television and radio.

As interim president, Urcuyo would accept the call for peace. He would invite Humberto Ortega, as military commander of the FSLN, to meet with the new Guardia commander to work out details of the cease-fire and to begin discussing the merger of their forces into a new Nicaraguan army. To save the nation, Urcuyo would announce that he was prepared to step down and turn power over to the FSLN junta. He and his advisers would then meet with the junta to work out the modalities of transferring authority to the new Government of National Reconstruction. The transfer was to take no more than seventy-two hours.

After we went over all the points step by step, I turned to Urcuyo and said, "This may be a little difficult for you to absorb, Congressman, so Tom O'Donnell here will be available to go over the scenario again in detail, at your convenience."[6] Urcuyo invited Tom to meet him at the Intercontinental Hotel the next morning.

Luis Pallais remembers getting a call from Urcuyo asking if he could sit in on the meeting with Tom O'Donnell. Pallais replied, " 'Hold on, Chico, let me talk to the president.' Somoza said to Pallais, 'Don't you do it. Let him take care of this himself.' "[7]

Tom O'Donnell went to the Intercontinental on the morning of the fifteenth accompanied by embassy officer Mayer Nudell to help with the translating. "We had written talking points translated into Spanish," O'Donnell remembers.[8]

> We checked at the desk of the Intercontinental Hotel. Urcuyo was in one of the smallest rooms. It had one bed and one chair. He insisted on giving me the chair. He was very polite and deferential, sort of bowing and ushering me in. He was by himself. I sat on the chair, he and Mayer Nudell sat on the bed.
> And we went over it. Urcuyo just kept bowing and scraping. Though he seemed somewhat intimidated, everything was 'Sí, señor; sí, señor.' He was just there to serve.[9]

This time Urcuyo did make one suggestion: "Maybe it would be better if I made the proposal for the cease-fire and the archbishop endorsed me." O'Donnell told him that the idea would be taken into consideration, " 'but for the time being we'll go with this scenario.' And I left it with him. And that's the only comment that he made."[10]

When O'Donnell returned to the embassy, I asked if he thought Urcuyo would be prepared. He said that Urcuyo was all alone without a staff. We considered whether or not the embassy should get involved in helping Urcuyo and decided that it should remain the responsibility of Nicaraguans on both sides to work out the details of the transfer.

Meanwhile, in San José, Ambassador Bowdler was telling the junta that Somoza was leaving within seventy-two hours and that power would be transferred to them through an interim president. Junta members were ecstatic. They were still congratulating each other when they met the press in the living room of Sergio Ramírez's house.

The junta's foreign minister, Father Miguel D'Escoto, said that Bowdler told them, "You are the government of Nicaragua." Sergio Ramírez added: "There is no point of disagreement between us."[11] According to D'Escoto, Bowdler had expressed satisfaction with two documents produced by the junta. One was another letter to the OAS in which the group invited observers to monitor its pledge to honor the civil rights of its enemies and to allow those who wanted to leave the country to do so. The second came in response to a request from Bowdler for "explicit explanations" of how these guarantees would be carried out.

Among them, said D'Escoto, were ways in which the safety of members of the Guardia would be assured and locations where people intending to leave Nicaragua could take refuge. "The Government of National Reconstruction is going to heed all the people who fear any reprisals against them," said Ramírez. "They are going to have the opportunity to go to safe places in Nicaragua. These safe places are going to function under the authority of the Catholic Church."[12]

"We are going to call the bishops," Ramírez explained, "to cooperate with us in establishing these places in which all the members of the Somocista party and all members of the National Guard can go before leaving the country." Asked about the idea of adding new members to the junta, Ramírez answered, "Bowdler never brought it up."[13]

Apparently the idea was still alive in some minds. Alfonso Robelo and other COSEP leaders had traveled to Venezuela in early

July to seek the help of the new Venezuelan president Luis Herrera Campins. On the fourteenth, Herrera Campins invited Archbishop Obando y Bravo, Ismael Reyes, the national coordinator of the Permanent Commission for Human Rights, José Esteban González, and others to Caracas.

Jaime Chamorro, brother of the slain *La Prensa* editor, was one of the Social Democrats who received an invitation to the meeting. He was told that they were going to discuss the enlargement of the junta. Chamorro called his sister-in-law, Doña Violeta, in San José. She advised him not to go, because Somoza would be leaving in a day or two.[14]

Archbishop Obando y Bravo, Rafael Cordova Rivas, and others were at Las Mercedes Airport from 11 A.M. to 6 P.M. on the afternoon of July 15 waiting for the plane from Venezuela. The archbishop noticed truckloads of effects being loaded into a DC-6. When he asked whose they were, he was told they were the personal belongings of the Somozas.[15]

That afternoon I received a call from Bill Bowdler in San José telling me that two representatives of the junta—Noel Rivas and Edmundo Jarquín—would be calling on me in Managua to help facilitate the transfer of power. Within an hour they telephoned. O'Donnell and I welcomed them at the embassy at 5:20 P.M. Edmundo Jarquín and I had met before after I lobbied Somoza for Jarquín's release from prison.

Jarquín and Rivas expressed the junta's desire to make the transition in eight hours. We told them that was impossible. Seventy-two hours was what had been agreed upon. We reviewed the scenario and suggested that other arrangements for the transfer be made directly with Urcuyo. They concurred.

O'Donnell telephoned Urcuyo in the presence of Jarquín and Rivas. Urcuyo suggested that the meeting be put off until Somoza left town. He said he would see Jarquín and Rivas at 9 A.M. on the seventeenth. They exchanged phone numbers where they could be reached.

On the morning of the sixteenth, O'Donnell and I drove to "La Curvita." We carried a list of six National Guard officers that I had instructed the CIA station chief to put together the night before. Since we were running out of time and no acceptable candidates were coming from Washington, I decided to take the initiative by submitting the names of capable Guard leaders untainted by Somoza.

As the first order of business, I presented the list to Somoza. El Chiguín was by his side. After looking it over, Somoza raised his head. "Where did you get this?" he asked. "These are all good people. You know your onions."[16] He and his son left the room to consult. They took fifteen or twenty minutes to choose Col. Federico Mejia, who was currently serving as executive officer of the police department. An engineer by training, Mejia had attended the Brazilian military school and married a Brazilian. That's all we knew.

Then we made final arrangements for the arrival of Somoza's party in the United States. Somoza and his entourage were to land at Homestead Air Force Base near Miami on the morning of July 17 in several personal planes and the presidential jet. Three cars and three buses would meet them at the airport. Somoza asked if they could carry Uzi submachine guns for their protection. We said no. He then amended his request to pistols and hunting rifles. I told him I'd check.

He informed us that he expected a lien to be slapped on the presidential jet when it landed at Homestead. Apparently he had been evacuating his wounded officers to a Miami hospital and had run up a bill of several hundred thousand dollars which hadn't been paid. "He had absolutely no shame in telling us this," O'Donnell remembered.[17]

In the car as we drove back to the embassy, we heard Radio Nacional reporting the retirement of all Guardia officers with more than thirty years of service and announcing the new appointments. The retirement, which included more than 100 generals and colonels, would "benefit the Guardia, and the ones who are fighting will be those who will run things in the future," said a government spokesman.[18]

Events were moving quickly. We assumed that Bowdler in San José and policy makers in Washington were keeping up. Back at the Chancery, I immediately called Bowdler in San José. I told him that Somoza had agreed to Lieutenant Colonel Mejia, who seemed like a solid character, unsullied by either Tachito or his son. I asked Bowdler to get approval from the junta. He quickly called back with the junta's okay.

Everything seemed to be falling into place. I had been reporting to Washington either by flash cable or scramble phone every detail of my negotiations with Somoza. I assumed that other interested parties in San José, Panama, and Venezuela were being kept informed. Apparently they weren't.

When Archbishop Obando y Bravo finally arrived in Caracas on the morning of July 16, he received word that President Luis Herrera Campins wanted to see him and the other Nicaraguan visitors immediately. In his presidential office, Campins informed the group that Somoza was resigning that night. "He reiterated his desire for peace for our country," remembered the archbishop, "and kindly offered us a plane so that we could return to Costa Rica . . . to make the necessary contacts with the new junta and Frente Sandinista."[19] The archbishop and his party didn't arrive in San José until 2 A.M. on the seventeenth.

Washington was even more confused. At a Special Coordinating Meeting of the NSC on July 16 chaired by Brzezinski, most of those in attendance were not aware that Somoza was resigning that night. According to Bob Pastor, "The meeting actually discussed for the fourth consecutive time Col. Mojica, the Nicaraguan Attaché in Guatemala, as a possible head of the Guard."[20]

That afternoon, a green camper was seen making repeated trips from the bunker to the airport. One of those trips transported the disinterred bodies of Tachito's father and brother, Luis. Among the last effects to leave the bunker were five green and red parrots.

"The people of Nicaragua are not throwing me out," Somoza told reporters. "The ones throwing me out are the people who are giving arms and ammunition to a few mercenaries and the few dumbbells who are fighting around Nicaragua."[21]

Following an emotional farewell with his favorite officer, Major Emilio Salazar (Comandante Bravo) at the Intercontinental Hotel, El Chiguín drove the short distance to the bunker. The sky was dark and threatening. Waiting for him in the conference room was the surviving general staff of the Guardia Nacional. Faces were grim and tired. They came with bloody uniforms and wounds from the front.

El Chiguín had tears in his eyes and could barely speak. "We've negotiated a deal with the gringos. The Guardia will pass to younger hands. We're going. The United States has promised that within forty-eight hours a division of U.S. Marines will come to support the Guard in stopping communism. Keep up the fight, men. . . . If the gringos don't come through, we'll strike back. I'll be in Miami. I won't abandon you. There in Miami I'll be visiting the wounded. My heart is with you."[22] Of course, we had made no such promise of U.S. troops. Chiguín started writing checks drawn on the Bank of Miami. Five thousands dollars each for closest officers and friends. Between El Chiguín and his father, witnesses estimated that $3–4 million was spent that night.[23]

Maj. Pablo Emilio Salazar, his black beret at a jaunty angle, was stopped by reporters as he walked down the street in front of the bunker. "The National Guard will stand firm and continue fighting to maintain democracy even without Somoza," he said.

"Will you join the new army?" *Time* correspondent Bernard Diederich asked.

"I would have to wait and see if it were going to be democratic first."[24] Night had fallen on the bunker. An elderly sentry used a flashlight to guide visitors to the sidewalk.

At the embassy we were busy making arrangements for the transfer to begin the next morning at 8 A.M. Statements had to be prepared; security at the airport and the Camino Real Hotel had to monitored. If all went according to plan, the forty-year-old Somoza dynasty would end that evening when Somoza resigned and ceded presidential authority to Francisco Urcuyo. Then Somoza would leave for exile in the United States, Urcuyo would join with the archbishop of Managua in a call for a cease-fire and stand-down of forces, and Urcuyo would turn over executive authority to the new Government of National Reconstruction, which promised a pluralistic government for the people of Nicaragua.

I was at the "Casa Grande" residence when the phone rang. It was around 8 P.M. "You're going to have a shoot-out at the airport," said Somoza. "You're going to provoke a confrontation. There's no way you can prevent a bloodbath."

"What are you talking about?" I asked.

"You can't have people from the Sandinista forces on that plane. They get off at the airport and the National Guard troops, well, that will be just like waving a red flag in front of them. They're going to react. There's no way to prevent them from firing."

Annoyed, I asked: "Why didn't you bring this up before?"

"The alternative would be to have them meet somewhere else," Somoza suggested.

"Where?"

"Have the military men meet separately. Maybe somewhere near the border."

I considered his suggestion for a minute before answering, "Your point is well taken. Let me raise this with San José."[25]

I immediately got in touch with Bowdler, who said he would talk to the FSLN *comandantes*. Within a half hour he called back. They understood the problem and were prepared to meet earlier in the morning in Costa Rica. Bowdler suggested the resort town of Puntarenas on the Pacific coast and offered to dispatch our attaché plane to pick up the new Guardia commander, Colonel Mejia, at seven the next morning.

"You can assure him that there will be no problem with security," Bowdler added, "we'll have people from the embassy to meet him."[26]

I called the bunker, but couldn't get through to Somoza. After repeated attempts I was connected with Mejia. It was the first time we had spoken. I congratulated him on his new position and told him about the conversations I had just had with Bowdler and Somoza.

"What security will I have?" he asked.

I assured him that I would send our military attaché Lieutenant Colonel McCoy to accompany him on the flight. "It's a U.S. plane, and you will be flying under the protection of the United States." Before I hung up, I urged him to please be at the airport promptly at seven. "Everything hinges on this meeting."[27] He seemed to agree. I quickly called McCoy and told him what had happened. "Stay close to Mejia, and be alert to any problems. If anything goes wrong, give me a call."[28]

It was maybe 9:30 or 10:00 P.M. I decided to try to catch a few hours' sleep. Who knew if I'd be able to get any in the next couple of days?

16

Cowards die many times before their deaths;
The valiant never taste of death but once.
—William Shakespeare

It was almost midnight, but in the artificial light of the Salon Rubén Dario of the Intercontinental Hotel it could have been any hour. The thick shag carpet was the color of blood. Approximately seventy-five congressmen from the Liberal and Conservative parties had been milling around for hours. All were wearing *guayaberas.* Many had slipped back to their rooms for a couple of drinks from the looted stocks peddled in the hotel lobby that afternoon. They were anxious to do their duty and return to their families. Many had already made arrangements to leave the country.

By 1 A.M. on July 17, 1979, when Francisco Urcuyo was finally ushered in from the service elevator, many of the congressmen were drunk. He was the only one wearing a suit and tie. The tall, rotund Alceoa Tabalda Solis, political secretary of the National Liberal party, read Somoza's resignation. "Having consulted the governments which are interested in the pacification of the country, I have decided to accept the resolution of the OAS, and by this means, I resign the presidency to which I was popularly elected. My resignation is irrevocable. I have fought against communism, and I believe that when the truth is known, history will say I was right."[1]

There was scattered applause, cries of disbelief, and many tears. Alberto Rener Valle, president of the Senate, nominated Francisco Urcuyo to succeed Somoza. At this point most Nicaraguans regarded Urcuyo as an affable, extroverted man from Rivas who wrote poetry in his spare time. His best known poem was a tribute to a man he admired—Pedro Joaquín Chamorro.

Once Urcuyo was unanimously elected, Luis Pallais placed the blue and white presidential sash around his neck. The whole session lasted about half an hour. Most congressmen rushed to their rooms to grab their bags and flee to safety. A few diehards, overcome with liquor and emotion, accompanied Urcuyo out of the hotel shouting that they would stay and fight communism. Confused journalists asked if that meant that Urcuyo was not prepared to quickly relinquish power to the FSLN junta. He answered gruffly that he hadn't even had a chance to form his cabinet. As a believer in pluralism, he would invite various democratic groups to help him heal the wounds and bring peace. He said the whole process might take three months!

A light drizzle fell as Somoza stood waiting for his helicopter on the driveway in front of the bunker. He was wearing a gray suit with a blue tie and gold pin. Despite the air of defeat that hung over everything, he was trying to look dignified. According to Urcuyo, Somoza's last words to him before boarding the helicopter were: "Chico, don't forget that you have to negotiate and negotiate with Pezzullo until the junta disappears from his mind. Don't forget that this junta is a communist menace and Pezzullo needs to understand this. He's wrong."[2]

As Somoza's blue and white Hughes helicopter lifted off, the pilot switched on the landing lights, illuminating the bunker and "La Curvita," and quickly switched them off. "As I took one last look at the lights of Managua," remembered Somoza, "tears started rolling down my cheeks." In front of the Intercontinental, congressmen and military aides scurried into cars and jeeps. The moon peaked through the clouds as the thirty-two-car convoy slipped away to join Somoza at Las Mercedes Airport.

I had just drifted off to sleep when the phone rang. I looked at the clock; it was 2:30 A.M. Lieutenant Colonel McCoy was on the line. "Something's going wrong here, Mr. Ambassador. I'm at the airport. I called the command and Mejia says he can't go."

"What?"

"Mejia says he's acting on instructions from the president," McCoy continued.

"The president?" I asked, trying to rouse myself.

"Yes. The president told Mejia he can't leave Nicaraguan territory."

"Well, I don't understand," I felt my heart pumping faster. "This whole flight to Costa Rica began because of Somoza. This was his idea. Why the hell is he putting on new conditions? At the eleventh hour! This is supposed to begin at seven."

"I don't know," answered McCoy, "you'd better talk to the president."[3]

I hung up the phone and thought to myself: "Who is the president?" I began calling. The only number I had was for the bunker. I was getting the runaround. I would be switched from one extension to another and then the line would go dead. I kept demanding to talk to the president. Finally someone said, "The president is coming on the line."

It was Urcuyo. His voice was different. He sounded extremely impressed with his self-importance. Addressing him as "Mr. President," I congratulated him. I explained the call from Somoza and the subsequent calls to Bowdler and General Mejia. There was no response. I reviewed the whole scenario. Finally, he answered: "I'm meeting with my commanders at ten o'clock."

Responding as calmly as I could, I asked: "What does that have to do with what we have already put in place? There's a plane arriving from Costa Rica at seven to fly General Mejia to a crucial meeting with the Sandinista commander."

"I know nothing about that," he answered sharply. "I'm meeting with my commanders at ten."

"Mr. President, you seem to be forgetting a whole series of things we agreed to."

"I know nothing about these things," he answered.

"You certainly do understand these things. There's no question you understand. You sat there with President Somoza as I went through them. I'll repeat them to you now."

"I don't want to hear this," he said, emphatically.

"Well, you're going to because I'm going to repeat it."

"I won't listen."

"Furthermore, Tom O'Donnell went to your hotel room and went over the whole scenario again. There's no way in the world that you can tell me that you don't know what this is about!"

"I've got a country to run," he answered, signaling that he had heard enough, "I'm meeting with my commanders at ten o'clock."

"You're committing a tremendous blunder. You're going to be responsible for an awful lot of bloodletting."

"You're being insulting to me!"

"I don't mean to be insulting," I replied, "I'm just trying to be very clear about the consequences of this action on your part."[4]

He obviously didn't want to talk about it. I hung up. It was four o'clock in the morning. I tried to get Mejia on the phone. It was impossible.

Meanwhile, at Las Mercedes Airport, Somoza was pacing back and forth nervously waiting for his son El Chiguín. The engines of his blue and white jet had been running since 2:30. Pablo Rener, Luis Pallais, Julio Quintana, and Luis Valle were already aboard. He placed several calls to the bunker and spoke to Urcuyo. "Where's my son?"

At one point, a Guardia soldier approached the former dictator and asked him if he could spare a few dollars for him and his family. Somoza panicked. Afraid that the soldier would shoot him on the spot, he reached into his pocket and handed the Guardia soldier everything he had. The surprised soldier walked off with several thousand dollars.

When El Chiguín finally arrived at the airport at 6:30 A.M., he and his father exchanged angry words. "I was sharp with him and marched him over to the aircraft in which he was to fly," Somoza remembered. "I still thought he might decide to stay in Nicaragua. So I gave orders to the pilot to taxi out for take-off and my plane would follow."[5] Somoza boarded his refueled jet, and the convoy of five planes took off for Homestead Air Force Base in Florida. From Homestead, Somoza, his son, and aides were driven to Somoza's estate on Sunset Island on Miami Beach. His family's domination of Nicaragua was finally over.

Archbishop Obando y Bravo was trying to sleep off a cold in his hotel room in San José when he awoke. An aide, Monsignor Bismarck Carballo, had just returned from a reception at the Venezuelan embassy attended by Violeta Chamorro and other members of the junta. The archbishop listened in disbelief as Monsignor Carballo informed him for the first time of his role in the transfer plan. "The plan couldn't have been more simple and logical for the junta and Washington," he remembers thinking, "but it didn't take into account that certain protagonists might decide, for one motive or another, to take matters into their own hands."[6]

After tuning in Radio Reloj, the archbishop heard more surprising news—instead of dissolving the constitution and turning power over to the junta, Urcuyo had decided to serve out his term until 1981. He immediately called Ambassador Bowdler, who responded: "Monsignor, this can't be. . . . What you heard might have been a joke, or a rumor that was picked up by the media."[7] A few hours later, Bowdler called back. It was true.

In the zig-zag trenches of the Southern Front, July 16 had been a day electric with rumors and expectations. Rain fell all afternoon on the green hills, and with nightfall came a torrential downpour. The next morning there was news. It came with the firing of rifles along the hills. "The dictator has fled!"

"The morning was an intense high," wrote Alejandro Murguía, "insane jubilation mixed with a heavy sadness, a weariness that kept bringing everybody down."[8]

The day began with exuberant celebrations in all the FSLN-controlled towns—Jinotepe, Masaya, Diriamba, León, Matagalpa, San Marcos, Estelí, and others. In one of the last government-held cities, Granada, eight units of the Sandinistas' Rolando Orozco battalion attacked simultaneously. Entering the city in high-speed cars and trucks, they fought street by street with the Guardia, slowly forcing them back into the fort of La Polvora.

According to Comandante Carlos Nuñez, this Conservative party capital on the shores of Lake Nicaragua "had not distinguished itself in the war, or before, by its bellicose spirit." But the *compas* were able to call on the combat experience gained from weeks of hard fighting, "that is to say, opening frontal attacks, advancing through houses, breaking breaches in walls, evading the fire of tanks and mortars, advancing, advancing, advancing."[9]

From the "Casa Grande" overlooking Managua, I called Washington to report that Urcuyo had thrown a monkey wrench into the plan. I then contacted Bowdler in San José. He said the plane bearing Humberto Ortega and the other Sandinistas had already left for Puntarenas. He was worried.

"This thing is coming apart, Bill. I don't know why yet, but clearly the signals have changed."[10]

Lieutenant Colonel McCoy was at Las Mercedes Airport when the attaché plane arrived from Costa Rica at 7 A.M. I persisted in trying to get Mejia on the phone. Finally, after much effort, he came on. Just minutes before, he had been promoted to general by order of the new president. I told the new Guardia commander that the plane and our military attaché were waiting for him at the airport. He said he couldn't go anywhere, under orders from President Urcuyo.

"This is an utter disaster," I told General Mejia. "You don't realize what's happening, but your president is undercutting an agreement that was carefully worked out."

"I'm sorry, Mr. Ambassador, but I'm under orders from my president," Mejia responded.[11]

I called Vaky in Washington. "We've got to consider some action of our own, Pete; otherwise it's going to look like we're party to some dirty game."

"Larry, what do you have in mind?"

"I think we've got to condemn the actions of Urcuyo and divorce ourselves from this immediately."

"We want you to go back to Urcuyo," Pete answered. "Maybe he doesn't understand."

"He understands perfectly," I insisted.

"We'd like you to go back and explain things and see if you can turn him around."[12]

I tried telephoning President Urcuyo, but couldn't get through. So O'Donnell and I drove to the bunker. It had been emptied. Everything of value—rugs, pictures, mementos—was gone. An aide ushered us in to see General Mejia. Our military attaché was already there. General Mejia and I shook hands for the first time.

My first impression was that Mejia seemed like a decent professional—one who had suddenly been elevated from lieutenant colonel to commander of the Guard and was somewhat overwhelmed by the pace of events. I felt it was important that he understand everything that had transpired. Starting from the beginning of my talks with Somoza, I quickly related the events leading to the formulation of the transfer plan. I could tell from his face that he hadn't heard any of this before.

When I finished, he said, "Let's go up and see the president."

We drove the last 500 meters up to "La Curvita." The atmosphere there was dramatically different. The house was teeming with well-wishers and hangers-on. Urcuyo was a changed man. "Mr. Ambassador, come in," he said in a grand, theatrical manner.

He escorted us to a room down the hall from the living room where I had met with Somoza. The curtains were open to a sun-splashed patio and pool. We sat facing one another. General Mejia sat on his right; O'Donnell was on my left.

I began in as calm a voice as I could muster. "Let me go over the agreement that was reached with President Somoza. . ."

As I started to explain in detail events that were supposed to take place that very morning, Urcuyo interrupted. "I'll have nothing to do with those communists," he said, referring to members of the FSLN junta.[13] He denied that he had ever agreed to the transfer plan.

I was stunned. "You are a transitional president," I stated emphatically, "not Somoza's successor. The circumstances that led to your appointment were extraordinary, to say the least. You were briefed fully on the scenario agreed to by Somoza, the United States government, and the Junta of National Reconstruction in San José."

Urcuyo continued to deny his knowledge of such an agreement. "I will not turn power over to the communist junta," he reiterated.

"History will hold you responsible for the destruction of the Guardia Nacional," I warned. "It can't hold. It's going to collapse."[14] I wanted General Mejia to hear this, so that he might realize he was being used. Mejia sat there stone-faced, taking it all in, but not reacting.

Jolted by my prediction that the Guardia would collapse, Urcuyo defended his position as a responsible one and fully within his authority as constitutional president of Nicaragua. "Pezzullo maintained that I was acting against the peace of Nicaragua," Urcuyo wrote of this interchange in his book *Solos*, "and that I would be culpable for the bloodbath and terror that would result from my not turning over the presidency to the Junta of Reconstruction. I argued energetically that the United States and the Frente Sandinista would be responsible if the fighting intensified. The Sandinistas couldn't continue fighting without the help of Carter and his allies."[15]

"It was an incredible performance by Urcuyo," remembered Tom O'Donnell. "It was like he had never seen us before. Mejia was sitting there wondering whom to believe. We didn't know what to make of him."[16]

After an hour of fruitless verbal dueling, O'Donnell and I left. I immediately called the State Department. "This is a complete washout," I reported to Vaky. "Urcuyo is adamant that he and Somoza never agreed to the transition plan. I assume he's acting on Somoza's instructions. I can't believe he has taken this on himself. He's a sycophant, not a man of independent will. Somoza had us. His only concern was getting out of here alive. He wants to punish this country. He's punishing the Guardia. That's the only explanation. The only way for us to preserve our position is for me to pull out with most of the embassy. I'll make a statement at the airport."[17]

Pete Vaky said, "Larry, I'll have to talk to a few people and get back to you."

"I would suggest that you order a couple of C-130s from Panama right now, so we can move this thing."

"Larry, I'll be back to you," Vaky repeated.

Following our meeting, Urcuyo and Mejia crossed the street to the Intercontinental Hotel, where President Urcuyo delivered his inaugural address as a weary General Mejia and the new general staff of the Guardia looked on.

> As Supreme Commander of the Armed Forces I order an immediate cease-fire. As president of the Republic I call on all irregular forces to lay down their arms, not before or to anyone, but on the altar of the country.
>
> The time has come to bandage the wounds inflicted by the communist terrorists and apply balm to the wounds of war. Together we must work to rebuild our republic from the ashes. We must forget the past, in the name of the present, with our eyes fixed on the future.[18]

The government-run *Novedades* newspaper of July 17 carried a front-page photograph of Urcuyo wearing the blue and white presidential sash. The caption under the picture read: "The new President Urcuyo will complete the constitutional term of ex-president Somoza Debayle until May 1981."[19]

In San José, the junta was enraged. "If Urcuyo remains," said spokesman Manuel Espinoza, "he will be responsible for a blood-bath. . . . He is playing with the blood of Nicaraguans. If he is captured he will pay for these crimes."[20]

The day had begun with jubilation for Nicaraguan exiles and their supporters in San José as the city's fire sirens began to wail at 2:30 A.M. when the news broke that Somoza had resigned. Cars wove through downtown streets with lights flashing and horns

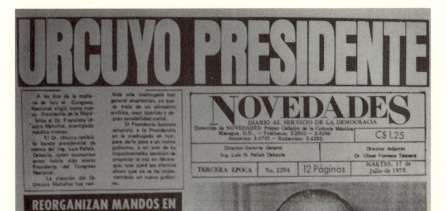

The front page of the government-owned *Novedades* of July 17, 1979, shows President Francisco Urcuyo Maliano wearing the presidential sash.

beating out festive tattoos. Taciturn junta member Sergio Ramírez received the news at the Venezuelan embassy and then drove home to greet well-wishers and his wife. "I'm listening to the radio here with Tulita," he told reporters minutes later. "It's a great moment for me and my people."[21]

Later in the day, after it was clear that the Urcuyo had broken the agreement, Alfonso Robelo informed Bowdler that the junta still planned to fly to Managua. At 3 P.M. Archbishop Obando y Bravo was at San José airport when he saw a huge red carpet rolled out. A full-dress military band waited at the airport for the junta's triumphant send-off. It never happened. Urcuyo refused to give their plane permission to land. Nor would he give permission to Archbishop Obando y Bravo, who was told that he could never return to Nicaragua. In the early afternoon, the junta met and decided to delay their travel plans by a day.

Red Cross President Ismael Reyes hitched a ride on a Red Cross food flight that arrived in Managua at 7 A.M. At Las Mercedes airport he saw Guardias trying to commandeer incoming flights and wounded men ripping medical supplies out of boxes. "It's the end," he thought.[22]

To the widow and daughter of retired Guardia General Emilio Marenco, the seventeenth was like their worst nightmare. They awoke to the news that Somoza had fled. "He'll be back," Señora Marenco kept saying. The maid and chauffeur had disappeared. She called friends until she found one who was willing to drive them to Las Mercedes airport. "The city was weird," remembered her daughter, "nobody knew what was going to happen."[23]

Arriving at the airport with their tickets and official passports, they found the terminal packed. "It was a scene like you can't imagine," said the daughter. "Suddenly two Red Cross planes landed and we saw the EEBI (the Elite Infantry Battalion) running toward the plane, overpowering it. A woman screamed: 'They're going to bomb the airport!' And all these people ran outside. I lost my Mom."[24]

The deposed dictator, meanwhile, was meeting reporters on the sun-drenched rear porch of his Miami Beach mansion. "I am prepared, my friends, for the eventualities that politics give you," he said as four State Department security men looked on. "If it is a lifetime in exile, I will wipe floors if I must."[25] With an estimated wealth of from $100 million to $1 billion and the owner of extensive businesses throughout South Florida, he seemed unlikely to meet this fate.

In Washington, Vaky consulted with Acting Secretary of State Christopher and called me back. "Larry, Christopher feels you should make another attempt to convince Urcuyo."

It was not what I wanted to hear. "Look, Pete, this is absurd. Time's a-wasting! We're losing ground here, man! We're not saying anything in the face of what is clearly a double-cross. The people in San José must think we're crazy. If we don't act now, we're going to lose every ounce of our credibility. People are going to think we're party to this."[26]

Vaky said that Christopher was going to talk to Somoza in Miami to try to get Somoza to turn Urcuyo around. I said, "Fine, I'll go in and see Urcuyo again."

It was around 5 P.M. by the time Tom O'Donnell and I returned to "La Curvita." In the interim, Urcuyo had met with the new Estado Mayor (chiefs of staff) of the Guardia. "All of them were preoccupied by the fact that the help that had been promised to General Somoza had not arrived," wrote Urcuyo. "At the same time, after hearing the proposals of Pezzullo, they started to seem like another trick by the North American government."[27]

President Urcuyo received sixteen calls from Somoza that day, telling him to hold on, that help would be coming. He also called on his skills as a medical doctor to cure the hangovers of his brothers Henry and Alfredo.

Between receiving friends, political cronies, and family members who came to offer their congratulations, Urcuyo called his private secretary Alberto Torres to form his cabinet. When he asked to meet with Congress, Torres informed him that only four Liberal deputies remained in the country.

At our second meeting on July 17, President Urcuyo was accompanied by General Mejia and a young man who had been appointed foreign minister, Harry Bodan. I began with as many courtesies as I could muster and tried to remain calm. I told them I had talked to Washington and received my instructions. Washington felt they might be confused about the agreement. "What has happened is obviously a mistake, so now it's time to take steps to rectify the situation."

Urcuyo would have none of it. "I'm the president of Nicaragua. I don't take orders from anyone! I will never turn over power to a bunch of communists! I have never heard of these plans."

"You certainly did, Mr. President!" I stopped short of calling him a liar. "The consequences of following the course you have taken are grave," I continued. "Secretary Warren Christopher is in contact with ex-President Somoza to remind him again of the terms of the agreement. They were explicit. All involved in the Nicaraguan government of Anastasio Somoza, including you as his selected successor, the United States government, and the Junta of National Reconstruction knew exactly what had been worked out."[28]

Urcuyo broke in again. "I know nothing about these agreements!"[29]

The situation was absurd. I made one last attempt to appeal to General Mejia: "The Guardia Nacional will collapse; there is no possibility of a negotiated settlement with the junta; retribution will be heaped on the people caught in the middle."[30]

Taking my leave, I informed Urcuyo that I would be reporting our conversations to my superiors in Washington, who were unable to comprehend his actions. He said that he was acting within the authority of his constitutional position.

As O'Donnell and I headed back to the Chancery, we agreed that the second meeting had been even more contentious than the first. The arrogance and stupidity of Urcuyo were hard for either of us fathom. Once again, General Mejia had not uttered a word.

It looked bad.

17

My country, my people, and I were betrayed.
    —Anastasio (Tachito) Somoza Debayle

Sandinista military strategist Humberto Ortega was taking no chances. On the morning of July 17, he ordered all units—north, south, east, and west—to prepare to converge on Managua. Gustavo Gutiérrez volunteered for one of the special sabotage teams that were being smuggled into the city. Hiding in the back of a poultry truck, he traveled to an abandoned chewing gum factory on the outskirts of Managua.

Overcome with nostalgia, just before night fell on the seventeenth he set out to visit his father. With a borrowed .38 hidden under his sport shirt, he kept an eye out for Guardia patrols. Compared to Masaya, Managua was eerily calm. Through the darkness Gustavo could make out his house. In the light of a lone street lamp, he could see the shutters were shut. He wondered if his father was home. He had so much to tell. A dog was barking in the pink stucco house next door. Suddenly, a dark silhouette stepped out of the shadows. "Pare, hijo de puta!" (Halt, you son-of-a-bitch!) Before Gustavo could open his mouth, the boy fired. Two shots entered Gustavo's chest.

Gustavo's father was lying in bed when he heard the shots. He sat up, put down the book he was reading, and peeked through the shutters. Five men were looking down at a body sprawled on the ground. A dark trail of blood reflected the light of the street lamp. A neighbor turned and pointed at the Gutiérrez house. That's when Manolo decided to go down.

At first he didn't recognize the angelic face in the pool of blood. It was the way his neighbors were staring that made him take a closer look, past the long hair and growth of whiskers. "Oh, God!!!" It hit him all at once. His body shook uncontrollably, and he screamed in the night: "Porqué?"[1]

At the "Casa Grande" I was calling Vaky in Washington to report on my second meeting with Urcuyo. "It's a total wash-out, Pete. This man is not going to give in."

"All right, Larry, I'll notify Panama to get two C-130s ready and we'll see how we play this thing. Wait until you hear from me."[2]

Just before I went to bed, I received a call from the Casino, the Guardia Nacional officer's club adjacent to the bunker. It was a Lt. Col. Alberto Smith. I had heard his name before and remembered that he had a good reputation. His English was good, but he had clearly had a few drinks.

"I'm sitting here with some of my buddies," he said, "and we just want you to know that you're going to be responsible for me and these others being put against a wall and shot."

"That's nonsense," I answered. "If you get shot, you can thank your former president."

There was a nasty edge to his voice: "What do you mean?"

"If you're sober enough, I'll explain. Are you sober enough to understand?" I asked.

"Yes."

I went over the negotiations with Somoza and the junta in San José. It was a poignant moment. Lieutenant Colonel Smith had spent his whole career in the Guardia, and clearly the life he had been leading was over. He listened without uttering a word. Then the line went dead.[3]

At one o'clock in the morning on July 18, President Urcuyo was abruptly awakened by a telephone call. It was General Mejía calling from the bunker. "He wanted me, as Supreme Commander of the Armed Forces, to meet immediately with him and the Estado

Mayor," Urcuyo remembered. Urcuyo went down to the bunker accompanied by Foreign Minister Bodan and Mejia's brother, Dr. Luis Mejia González.

"At the meeting they told me that all the major cities, including Puerto Somoza, the principal route of resupply, were in the hands of the Sandinistas," wrote Urcuyo later. "Only the departments of Rivas, Chinandega, and the city of Managua were under the complete control of the army. They also informed me that the Sandinistas had begun to surround the capital of the republic and that they didn't have shells for the 105 mm. artillery, or the armored units, or gasoline for transportation. I asked if it was possible to concentrate all forces in defense of the capital. They told me they would study my suggestion and give me a reply."[4]

Earlier in the day, General Mejia had watched Guardia units from Jinotepe and Matagalpa enter the city. "They carried their wounded . . . and their weapons and looked incredibly tired," he said, "but they shouted that they had come to support the troops that were defending the capital. They thought that in Managua they would find sufficient ammunition, and that once Managua was under control and the army regrouped, we could retake the positions that we had abandoned."[5]

At the fishing village of San Juan del Sur on the Pacific coast, just north of the battlegrounds around Rivas, Guardia Lieutenant Briceno woke to find that his men had disappeared during the night. He found their Galils, M-16s, and uniforms scattered on the floor of the little barracks and on the dirt street outside. He quickly made up his mind to hijack a boat and sail up the coast to El Salvador. With the barracks empty, barefoot boys from the town drifted in to claim souvenirs.

Alfonso Robelo, Sergio Ramírez, and Violeta Chamorro of the Junta of Reconstruction had spent the night meeting with Ambassador Bowdler, President Carazo, and the foreign ministers of Bolivia, Colombia, the Dominican Republic, Ecuador, Peru, Panama, and Venezuela. President Carazo, incensed by the Urcuyo gambit, urged the junta members to return to Nicaragua as soon as possible. "I will make two planes available to you, and I don't want you to spend another night in Costa Rica."[6] Daniel Ortega was already in León, the provisional rebel capital.

In a tense two-hour session at the home of Sergio Ramírez, the junta asked the Costa Rican government to permit Venezuelan

Carlos Nuñez, Sergio Ramírez, Father Ernesto Cardenal, and Omar Cabezas at a rally in León shortly after the revolution. Credit: Piers Cavendish Camera Press, London 34433-2 (48) Globe Photos, Inc. 1993

and Panamanian fighter planes to escort them. President Carazo refused. It was then concluded that the safest route was to go forty miles to sea, then approach Godoy Airport in León over the Poneloya beach resort area. At first the plan was for forty-five people to travel in two DC-3s, but it was decided that they might attract too much attention.

At 11 P.M. on July 17, the three junta members left Ramírez's house in two cars. Approaching the airport entrance, Costa Rican Vice President José Miguel Alfaro, who was driving the lead car, noticed an occupied jeep with its lights off waiting along the side of the road. Alfaro drove through the entrance and accelerated. The jeep pulled onto the highway and followed. Alfaro sped to the terminal with the jeep in pursuit. Running out of patience, he stopped the car and confronted the occupants of the jeep. They turned out to be a reporter and photographer from a local newspaper.

Ramírez in a sweater, Alfonso Robelo in a windbreaker, and Violeta Chamorro in fatigues stood on the windy airstrip as pilots waited for storm clouds to pass over the mountains. "We recognize you as the Government of Nicaragua," announced Costa Rican Vice President Alfaro.[7]

At 12:11 A.M., the first Piper Navajo took off with Ramírez and Robelo. "We are leaving behind a long night, and day has come," Ramárez said as he boarded. "We are now to fight a very long fight and it is the reconstruction of our ravished country."[8] Doña Violeta followed in the next Navajo.

Poet Ernesto Cardenal, who had just been named the junta's minister of culture, was on the Ramírez-Robelo plane. He described the flight in "Lights":

> The top-secret flight at night.
> We might have been shot down. The night calm and clear.
> The sky teeming, swarming with stars. The Milky Way so
> bright behind the thick pane of the window,
>   a sparkling white mass in the black night with its
> millions of evolutionary and revolutionary changes.
> We were going over the water to avoid Somoza's air force,
>   but close to the coast.
> The plane was flying low, flying slowly.
> First the lights of Rivas, taken and retaken by Sandinistas,
>   now almost in Sandinista hands.
> Then other lights: Granada, in the hands of the Guardia
>   (it would be attacked that night).
> Masaya, completely liberated. So many fell there.
> Farther out a bright glow: Managua. Site of so many battles.
> (The bunker.) Still the stronghold of the Guardia.
> Diriamba, liberated. Jinotepe, fighting it out. So much
>   heroism glitters in those lights. Montelimar—the pilot
>   shows us——: the tyrants estate near the sea. Puerto
> Somoza, next to it.
> The Milky Way above, and the lights of Nicaragua's
>   revolution.
> Out there, in the north, I think I see Sandino's campfire.
>   ("That light is Sandino.")
> The stars above us, and the smallness of this land but also
>   its importance, these tiny lights of men. I think:
>   everything is light.
> The planet comes from the sun. It is light turned solid.
> The plane's electricity is light. Its metal is light.
>   The warmth of life comes from the sun.
>   "Let there be light."

There is also darkness.
There are strange reflections—I don't know where they
  come from—on the clear surface of the windows.
A red glow: the tail lights of the plane.
And the reflections on the calm sea: they must be stars.
I look at the light of my cigarette—it also comes from the
  sun,
                    from a star.
And the outline of a great ship. The U.S. aircraft carrier
  sent to patrol the Pacific Coast?
A big light on our right startles us. A jet attacking?
No. The moon coming out, a half moon, so peaceful, lit
  by the sun.
            The danger of flying on such a clear night.
And suddenly the radio. Jumbled words filling the small
  plane.
The Guardia? The pilot says: "It's our side."
            They're on our wavelength.
Now we're close to León, the liberated territory.
A burning reddish-orange light, like the red-hot tip of a
  cigar: Corinto: the powerful lights of docks flickering on
  the sea.
And now at last the beach of Poneloya, and the plane coming
  in to land, the string of foam along the coast gleaming in
  the moonlight.
            The plane coming down. A smell of insecticide.
And Sergio tells me: "The smell of Nicaragua!"
It's the most dangerous moment, enemy aircraft
            may be waiting for us over this airport.
And the airport lights at last.
We've landed. From out of the dark come olive green-clad
  comrades
                                to greet us with hugs.
We feel their warm bodies, they also come from the sun,
  that also are light.
            This revolution is fighting the darkness.
It was daybreak on July 18th. And the beginning
            of what was about to come.[9]

Three hours later, when the two planes returned, their pilots reported that their mission had been successful. The Junta of Reconstruction was in the Sandinista-held city of León.

Tom O'Donnell remembers me waking him at about 5:30 in the morning. "Tom, I'm getting out of here," I told him. I had made up my mind. We had to make a break with the Urcuyo government to dramatize our disapproval of his actions.

We had breakfast; on the way to the embassy, I went over what we had to do. "We'll keep about five people here, Tom; the minimum. Notify the others to pack their bags and meet me at the airport."[10] The marine gunnery sergeant was driving with security officer Jerry Wilson riding shotgun. We figured we had about forty people to evacuate and that we would all probably fit on one plane.

Meanwhile, from his house in Miami Beach, Somoza was being interviewed on television. "Urcuyo must have some reason," he told the *Today* show. "I don't know what it is. But he must have some reason for wanting at least some protection for these people. We've had so many people shot summarily in Nicaragua that people are afraid. We've had over 300 people shot without trials. And this is a situation where Mr. Urcuyo, I surmise, is taking his own protection for the people—which is something which I wanted to do, but the United States suggested that I leave as soon as possible to avoid further bloodshed."[11]

When asked about what steps could be taken now to end the war, Somoza answered: "I think the United States should live up to what it said should be done, and that is an orderly transition with due guarantees."[12]

"Wasn't that all part of the agreement that you and President Urcuyo broke?" asked the interviewer.

"None of that was negotiated with me," said Somoza with a straight face, "with Ambassador Pezzullo. He said he would take care of [the transition] later and it did not materialize."

To another reporter, he had the temerity to say: "Right now I think the junta's best bet is to make a deal with the Liberals; otherwise they won't be able to rule, because the Liberals will go to war unless they get enough agreement to go to an election."[13]

As he held forth, Somoza received a phone call from Deputy Secretary Warren Christopher at the State Department. Christopher informed Somoza that his "solemn commitment" to the arrangements for the transfer of power was part of package that included U.S. willingness to allow Somoza to take refuge in the

United States. He "strongly urged Somoza to use his influence to get the situation back on the rails," said a State Department spokesman.[14]

Luis Pallais was in the room when Somoza took the call. "Let's get the hell out of here," said the ex-dictator, hanging up the phone. "Those sons-of-bitches will come after me."[15] One of his friends in Congress, Rep. George Hansen, went to the press to complain that Somoza had been "threatened to be kicked out of the United States" if he didn't cooperate with the transfer of power.[16]

Somoza got on the phone to Urcuyo in Managua. "Chico, I'm lost," he said. "I'm a prisoner of the State Department. Deputy Secretary Warren Christopher just called me to say that if you didn't hand over power to the Junta of National Reconstruction, they were going to give me to the Sandinistas. Without a doubt, you can forget about any aid from the United States."[17] Somoza immediately began making arrangements to leave for the Bahamas.

At the embassy in Managua, we were receiving reports that the Nicaraguan Air Force had flown C-46s, C-47s, DC-6s, and three helicopters to Honduras. I was reviewing a departure statement I had prepared for the press when the phone rang. It was Pete Vaky. "Larry, we think you should press Urcuyo one more time."

I lost my temper. "What the fuck is the matter with you people?" There was a pause on the other end. I learned later that Deputy Secretary Christopher was listening on another line. Then, Vaky came on again. "Okay, go out and make your statement and then go to the airport. A C-130 will be waiting."[18]

At the front entrance of the embassy chancery, about thirty reporters had gathered with cameras. "I'm being recalled," I said, "because of our unhappiness with the actions being taken by the Urcuyo government which are a breach of the understanding that we reached with Somoza and Urcuyo before the transfer took place."

"What was the understanding?" asked one reporter.

"The understanding was that he would be a very short-term president and that he would turn over power to the government of National Reconstruction."[19]

Leaving the press with copies of my departure statement, I headed for the airport. The rest of the embassy staff, except for the five who were staying with O'Donnell, were already on board the C-130. Security Officer Jerry Wilson and I walked up the rear ramp of the military transport and the ramp closed behind us.

The airport was in chaos, the atmosphere extremely tense. Four Guardia Nacional jeeps surrounded our C-130. Their .50-caliber machine guns were aimed at the plane. I was looking out at the jeeps when Jerry Wilson came over with a bullet-proof vest for me. "Jerry, this isn't going to stop a .50-caliber bullet."

"Just put it on, please," he insisted.[20]

Since the airplane was stifling hot, I laid the vest on my chest. The pilot was waiting for clearance from the tower. Suddenly the engines roared and we took off.

Once we had reached our cruising altitude, I went forward to thank the crew. The pilot was young man from the Tennessee National Guard. "That was pretty hairy," he said with a sigh of relief. He and the rest of the crew were on their two-week tour of duty in Panama. Their plane was named *Nashville*. "I didn't wait for clearance. Man, I didn't feel like waiting there a minute longer."[21]

I later learned that our plane was the last to take off from Las Mercedes Airport. A British Air Force relief flight that landed minutes afterwards was rushed by Guardia soldiers. The pilot, seeing that his plane was being overpowered, immediately took off again. Soldiers were hanging onto the landing gear. The plane climbed several hundred feet before they fell.

At noon Tom O'Donnell—who became chargé d'affaires upon my departure—and Mayer Nudell went to the bunker to deliver the full State Department statement and inform Urcuyo that the U.S. ambassador had left. They were met by General Mejia and his legal adviser, Col. Felix Sánchez. They both looked as though they hadn't slept in the last two days. "Mejia said that he realized at last that he had been deceived by Urcuyo and Somoza," remembered O'Donnell. "He said that Urcuyo had been taken care of; that he was in isolation. He said he was ready now to do what he could to implement the transition."[22]

O'Donnell had the impression that Colonel Sánchez was the one who had convinced Mejia that he had been duped. "They were almost like equals," O'Donnell recalled.

"I've not been able to set up a meeting with Humberto Ortega," said Mejia. "Can you help us?"[23]

Chargé O'Donnell explained that the United States had been badly burned by Somoza's betrayal and that it would be difficult to get the junta to go along. The hour was late, he said, and, given developments of the past twenty-four hours, it might be too late. Several times Mejia and Sánchez expressed their desire to preserve "what was left" of the Guardia.

When O'Donnell suggested that they arrange the prompt return of Archbishop Obando y Bravo to lend moral support to a call for a cease-fire, both Mejia and Sánchez agreed. "I'll do what I can," he said as he left.[24]

It took another hour or so for General Mejia to get in touch with Humberto Ortega at the Sandinista Central Command in Palo Alto, Costa Rica. Mejia proposed to negotiate a cease-fire and reactivate the transition plan that had been worked out with the Junta of National Reconstruction and Somoza. Ortega would have none of it. "We're not negotiating anything," he said, "We're simply giving you the opportunity to surrender before the bloody battle to take Managua, which the Guardia Nacional will surely lose."[25]

Mejia already knew that the Estado Mayor of the Guardia would not agree to surrender. "In order to avoid problems on either side," he offered, "let's make a cease-fire."

"We don't need to make a cease-fire," countered Humberto Ortega, "for the simple reason that the battle is on our side. We're simply giving the remainder of your troops, who have frankly been defeated, the option of a bloodless exit."[26]

"We're still proceeding according to the plan that was worked out by the U.S. ambassador and which the junta agreed to," Mejia countered.

"That was broken the moment that Urcuyo Maliano took the action he did."[27]

When Mejia continued to argue, Ortega spelled out the situation in blunt terms. "If you think that you're strong and you can triumph there in Managua, I respect your opinion. . . . We'll find out who's right on the battlefield."[28]

Mejia said he had to consult the Estado Mayor and would be back in touch around 7 P.M. At three in the afternoon, Urcuyo asked Secretary of Information and Press Humberto Sánchez Uriza to interrupt his inventory of government funds and place a call to President Videla of Argentina. President Videla didn't want to get involved. Urcuyo called President Lucas García of Guatemala. "My country is lost," said Urcuyo; "I entreat you to send some air force planes to remove me and my functionaries."

Tomás Borge (center) with Junta Foreign Minister Miguel D'Escoto (far left). Credit: Agencia de Comunicación Internacional, Managua

"I can guarantee one plane," replied the Guatemalan leader. "I'll call back at five to confirm if I can send more."[29]

The government inventory turned up a mere 18,000 cordobas, which Urcuyo instructed Sánchez to convert into dollars so that he could take them into exile.

While Managua was still gripped with fear, the residents of León were in a triumphant mood with the arrival of the junta. Lucía Gutiérrez was one of the *compas* chosen to escort Tomás Borge through the city. He stopped and addressed a crowd. "We want unconditional surrender from the stupid puppet and an end to the war. It will mean the total destruction of the National Guard."[30]

At 2 P.M., reporters were invited to the city's bullet-scarred main square for a news conference with the junta. "A smooth-talking Sandinista in his early thirties met us and guided us . . . a few blocks away to the University of Nicaragua," wrote *Miami Herald* reporter Guy Gugliotta.

The junta arrived with Sandinista suddenness and no fanfare. Violeta de Chamorro, Alfonso Robelo and Sergio Ramírez . . .

were on hand, as was Daniel Ortega. . . . It fell to [Tomás] Borge to present the junta, a task he performed with delicate expertise and great emotional effectiveness. As the world's ranking Sandinista, Borge's role was important, almost priestly. He laid hands on each member as he introduced them. Here they are, he seemed to say. I give them my blessing. It was the first time the government had met together in Nicaragua and the significance of the occasion could be found in the tears of some of the local Sandinista leaders.[31]

At 2 P.M. the besieged Guardia *cuartel* of La Polvora in Granada raised a white flag. "I want to talk to your *comandante,*" screamed its newly appointed commander, Colonel Ruiz, as he held his hands over his head. When FSLN comandante Monica Baltodano strode forward in olive fatigues, Colonel Ruiz's face turned red. "I refuse to surrender to a woman," he shouted.[32] Such were the indignities of defeat.

Guardia Corp. Efren Mondragón, a photographer with the Central Archives of the First Battalion of Managua, went to Las Mercedes Airport to try to leave the country. "It was insanity," he recalled. "It seemed like the end of the world. I saw that amid the lunacy some Guardia units were forming a convoy to travel up the Pan American Highway. They were yelling, 'Let's go! Let's get out of here!' "[33] Soldiers commandeered trucks, jeeps, and Israeli-made personnel carriers. "At the airport, I found a car, a Citroen, with the keys inside," said Corporal Mondragón. "I got in and said, 'I'll follow this convoy and see what happens.' "[34]

To the northeast, in the department of Matagalpa, the Sandinistas learned that a convoy of eighty vehicles with 2,200 Guardias was about to pass through Sebaco on the way to Honduras. Paulo Palencia was part of the Frente's Matagalpa column. "We set up a roadblock between Sebaco and Dario," he remembered.

> We overturned buses; we used logs, furniture. We used anything we could find to stop the trucks. When the convoy arrived it stopped by the roadblock and their commander requested a meeting with us. Our leader was a young man named Justo. Justo walked forward to meet with them as they had requested. Then they opened fire and killed Justo and many other *compañeros.* Then the battle began. We lost many men and women.

> Many innocent people were killed. But we won. We killed many
> of the fascists and the others surrendered. Then we turned those
> very same vehicles around and we marched to Managua. It was
> the saddest day of my life, and the happiest.[35]

Corporal Mondragón managed to escape. But that night in the
darkness and rain, as he tried to make his way to the village of
Cinco Piños, he was captured and taken to Estelí. Forty-two days
later, he was freed.

Archbishop Obando y Bravo spent the morning of the eighteenth the same as he had the seventeenth—waiting at the airport
in San José. He had spoken to President Carazo first thing in the
morning, and Carazo had promised to reserve his private jet for
the archbishop's use. "After a day of insistent calls to the control
tower in Managua," the archbishop recalled, "we finally were authorized, at 5:30 in the afternoon, to land at Las Mercedes."[36] Accompanying him were Monsignor Bismarck Cabello, an aide, and
a nun.

At around seven, the archbishop's plane finally touched ground
in Managua and was immediately surrounded by military vehicles
overflowing with armed soldiers. It was a dramatic demonstration
of how radically things had changed in three days. To Archbishop
Obando y Bravo, "The Guardia Nacional, with their crumpled
combat fatigues and tired faces, were a grim reminder of the terrible combat of the last several weeks."[37]

The archbishop and his entourage were ordered into a Chero-
kee jeep and driven to the nearby Nicaraguan Air Force headquarters. An officer asked them to sit. "Sirs, we are officers who
have always complied to the constitutional law of our country," he
said. "We don't believe that because we have worn this uniform we
deserve to go to jail or die. Therefore we beseech you to help prevent more loss of blood."[38]

Next a wounded captain spoke: "We were informed that Dr. Urcuyo would be allowed to leave the country as soon as you landed.
We have orders to take you to the bunker where the Estado Mayor
is waiting to see you."[39]

The archbishop was separated from his colleagues and driven to
a military helicopter. He passed President Urcuyo, who was stepping out of a limousine wearing the presidential sash. As the archbishop looked on, Urcuyo got back into the car and sped back to

the city. It turned out the president of thirty-six hours had forgotten his medical diploma. Four frantic hours later, with his diploma in hand, Urcuyo flew to Guatemala.

The helicopter was "an enormous cavern without doors or lights," remembered the archbishop. It was a few yards off the tarmac when Guardia soldiers started spraying it with machine guns. The copilot jumped out. The wounded captain, who had accompanied the archbishop, grabbed a megaphone and in a strong voice barked: "This helicopter holds Monsignor Obando who has been called by the Estado Mayor. The Estado Mayor requires his presence in the bunker. Hold your fire! Nobody is trying to escape!"[40]

Allowed to take flight, the helicopter cruised over Lake Managua before landing at the Basic Infantry Training School across from the bunker. Three hundred armed soldiers came running toward the chopper. "I thought it was the last moment of my life," said the archbishop.

Seeing him, the soldiers broke into cheers. "Hey, it's the Monsignor! We're happy to see you here to take power. What's the news?" Totally surprised by their reaction, the archbishop responded: "No, I don't have any news; only what you've heard. I've been summoned by the Estado Mayor and I'm on my way to the bunker."[41]

Arriving at the bunker, he was shown into a conference room, where he was introduced to General Mejia and other officers, some of whom had just returned from schools abroad. "The situation in the bunker was of total disorder and confusion," the archbishop remembered, "none of the officers there knew what was going on."[42]

General Mejia, seated at the head of the table, rose and offered his place to the archbishop. "Excuse me, Monsignor, but this place belongs to you, as the one who will be in power."

"You're mistaken," responded Archbishop Obando y Bravo. "It's the job of laymen to manage secular affairs like the governing of a nation."

Chaos broke out, as all the officers at the table spoke at once. General Mejia, overcome by anxiety, was unable to keep control. The archbishop saw one officer lower his face into his hands and repeat over and over: "I'm going to shoot myself. I don't think it will hurt much."

Another declared loudly: "I'm going to take my family to Honduras. I'll use a jeep and a machine gun to clear the way if necessary." A third officer turned to the archbishop and asked: "Monsignor, would you do something so that they respect our lives and those of our families?"[43]

The archbishop telephoned President Carazo of Costa Rica, who pledged to do what he could. At the same time, General Mejia was taking another call from his counterpart in the FSLN, Humberto Ortega. "Remember, time is against you," said Ortega. "At this moment our forces are advancing on Managua."[44] Over the radios in the background, the archbishop could hear military units of the Guardia informing their commanders that combat around Managua was growing more intense.

Humberto Ortega asked Mejia to go on national television and radio to order his men to return to the barracks and lay down their arms.

"Who is going to guarantee that nothing happens to the troops?" asked Mejia.

"That's easy," responded Ortega, "once they lay down their arms, authorities of the Junta of National Reconstruction and the Red Cross will make sure that absolutely nothing happens to them."

"Wouldn't it be more believable if you and I met and issued the order together in an official manner so that all the world could see the good faith?"

"Look," answered Ortega, "you know that we have more of a right to have doubts, in the sense that our people have suffered directly because of the Guardia Nacional."

"The people have suffered on all sides," countered Mejia.

"It's simple; if we don't hear the call from you, we can't guarantee anything."[45]

Ortega made the same offer to the archbishop: "Advise the Guardia to raise white flags, turn in their arms, and their safety will be guaranteed." But the Estado Mayor was asking the archbishop to serve as a mediator between themselves and the Sandinistas. They wanted the archbishop to accompany them the next morning to Costa Rica to work out the terms of surrender.

When Humberto Ortega called back at 2 A.M., he repeated that the Frente Sandinista had no intention of negotiating. "Either issue the order to your troops to surrender, or fight." He was particularly displeased that the Guardia was shelling advancing rebel forces from Fort Coyotepe overlooking Masaya. Ortega demanded that General Mejia order them to stop; otherwise, "The forces that we seize in Coyotepe will be shot immediately."[46]

On a conciliatory note, Ortega was still offering Mejia and other parts of the Guardia "that hadn't been compromised" a place in the new army. Mejia, who was growing increasingly agitated, didn't seem to know what to do.

As the archbishop was being escorted across the street to spend the night at the Intercontinental Hotel, his heart grew heavy. Fighting had already erupted in and around Managua. He found the rooms in the hotel in complete disorder.

18

In Nicaragua it will always be the 19th of July.
—Graffiti sprayed on the walls of Managua

At six in the morning on July 19, Archbishop Obando y Bravo was awakened by someone pounding on his door. The reporter on the other side was as surprised as the archbishop.

"Monsignor, aren't you afraid that you'll be killed here in this hotel?"

"Friend, we're always in the hands of God," answered Archbishop Obando y Bravo.

The journalist told the archbishop that the bunker was deserted. A Guardia colonel, Ernesto Matamoros, joined them in the hall. "Excellency, they have left me alone."[1]

The archbishop was summoned to the lobby where two exhausted Guardia soldiers asked to turn in the their arms. "At this early hour of the morning, the situation turned into a scene of great madness," recalled the archbishop.[2] Slowly the hotel lobby filled with soldiers shedding their uniforms and throwing them in the corners. One soldier rushed in from the fighting, unbuckled the radio from his back, tossed it into a corner and fled.

Colonel Matamoros suggested that the archbishop go to the Hospital Militar to ensure the wounded soldiers were protected.

Driving through the streets of Managua at 7 A.M. "we were confronted with scenes from Dante," the archbishop remembered.

> Military vehicles were driving wildly through the empty city streets. Guardia Nacional soldiers had gathered in the doorways of the Military Hospital, and were throwing their uniforms and military gear onto a huge bonfire. Their faces spoke of fear and shame, of defeat and exile, of standards and uniforms reduced to a thick column of black smoke. . . . The same people who days earlier swore they would kill me, looked at me today with eyes that begged for mercy.[3]

Among the many unforgettable impressions the archbishop received that morning was that of a wounded sublieutenant rising from his bed to confront Colonel Matamoros. "You glorious cadets of West Point have run and left us. I want you to know that I have one patrol fighting at the gates of the hospital and another fighting in the western barrios, and even though I'm wounded I'm going to get out of bed and fight alongside my soldiers."

Strongly, but with sympathy, Colonel Matamoros answered: "Soldier, in war sometimes you win and sometimes you lose. Today is our turn to lose."[4] He then instructed the sublieutenant to order his soldiers to lay down their arms.

By eleven, the sounds of battle grew closer to the doors of the hospital. The archbishop emerged on the front steps to confront the rag-tag group of attackers. "Brothers, if you don't silence your arms, you'll be breaking the agreement whereby churches, the Red Cross and hospitals are to be respected."

"Monseñor, this is a military hospital," one of the Sandinistas answered, "and the agreements reached don't apply."[5] Comandante Tomás Borge was summoned; not until he arrived, escorted by a group of Sandinistas, did the rebels agreed to honor the sanctity of the hospital.

At about this time, the lobby of the Intercontinental Hotel was being invaded by barefoot urchins, the oldest about eight years old. With great effort they lifted the discarded Guardia weapons and staggered out into the parking lot to try them out. For a few seconds bullets flew everywhere. Then the kids began running for the bunker. It was deserted. At the nearby EEBI compound, they managed to kick-start a few abandoned motorcycles, but quickly fell off.

Newsmen who followed the *muchachos* explored the ten window-less rooms of the bunker for the first time. They found Somoza's office knee-deep in shredded paper. On the huge presidential desk were photographs taken during the two-month rebellion. The drawers were empty. On the dining room table stood a large bottle of tabasco sauce; on Somoza's unmade bed lay his army fatigues.

Manolo Gutiérrez rose early on the nineteenth and loaded the body of his son Gustavo in the back seat of his Toyota Cressida. Oblivious to the chaos around him, he drove quietly to the family plot in a shaded churchyard off the Highway Sur. With gunfire in the background, he dug a grave and lay his son's body on the fresh earth. "I'm sorry," he said. "You paid for our sins." With tears burning his cheeks, he covered his son's body and drove home.

U.S. Chargé O'Donnell woke on the morning of the nineteenth to the news that Mejia and the Estado Mayor had left earlier that morning on the last Guardia flight. Mejia's last act had been to turn his authority over to Lieutenant Colonel Largaespada of the traffic police. Sometime before noon, the national radio began broadcasting separate orders from Largaespada and Humberto Ortega to cease firing. Largaespada told remaining Guardia Nacional units to lay down their arms and fly white flags. The Frente Sandinista would guarantee the life and welfare of those who complied.

During the night of the eighteenth, prisoners held in the Guardia fortress El Coyotepe overlooking Masaya noticed strange goings-on. At 7 P.M. they were ordered to unload trucks carrying tank and artillery rounds and an immense quantity of ammunition. Then at one o'clock in the morning they were awakened to reload the trucks. This time the prisoners were told that the Guardia was leaving "because the Yanquis are coming to take charge of Coyotepe. Those Sandinista sons-of-bitches will see! The Yanquis will kick them out of Masaya like pieces of mule dung." At five in the morning, the Guardia started to leave. "It was an interminable line of trucks and cars," remembered one prisoner. "After having being threatened with death at any moment, we were suddenly free! And frankly we didn't know what to do."[6]

On the morning of the nineteenth, junta member Moises Hassan was marching to Granada with reinforcements. "I met William Ramírez on the road," recalled Hassan. "He told me to prepare to go to Managua. Joaquín Cuadra and Oswaldo Lacayo had already

taken the barracks of La Polvora and from that point were organizing a simultaneous march from Granada, Masaya, and Carazo.
We put together the forces from the south and southeast and
formed a long column of trucks, machine guns, and groups of
armed men and started very slowly toward Managua."[7]

Edén Pastora, on the Southern Front, was hoping to finally
break through Guardia lines. For fifty-two days he and his 2,000
men had been bottled up on a narrow strip of land between Lake
Nicaragua and the Pacific Ocean trading artillery assaults and
firefights with elite government troops. Daybreak on the nineteenth
found Pastora directing artillery fire on Hill 50. Empty boxes
were strewn everywhere. The young artillerymen were barely
awake. His aide Pichardo had his binoculars trained on Hill 50.

"Nothing," said Pichardo. "I don't see any signs. We fire and
there's no answer."

"What?"

"They're gone, *comandante*. They've given up the position."[8]

Pastora got on the radio and tried to find out what was going
on. The situation was confusing. Fighting raged in Managua. The
junta was preparing to arrive there tomorrow. He had the artillery, which might be needed.

"Let's go for Managua!" Pastora told his troops.

His exhausted, ragged troops sang songs of revolution and love
as they drove up the highway. At the side of the road by the lake
was the military school of Cibolca, a modern two-story red brick
barracks surrounded by coconut palms. In the front was a massive
obstacle course. It was the site where the Guardia had trained with
shouts of "Kill the people!"

Pastora's troops rushed through the gate that had been blasted
off its hinges and fanned out through the building's empty hall-
ways and wings. Shots echoed through suspected hiding places.
But there was no resistance. There were no Guardias anywhere.
All they found were deserted barracks and dining halls turned up-
side down. Out behind the barracks was a half-burned mound of
green uniforms and helmets piled near a large outdoor training
complex with an olympic-sized swimming pool. The whitecaps of
the lake slapped the concrete edge of the complex. Hundreds of
green frogs had fallen into the half-empty pool with no way of getting out.

Forty kilometers up the road in Masaya, a group of rebels had
captured the brutal police commander, Alberto Gutiérrez, known

as "Macho Negro," as he was trying to escape to Managua. A huge crowd of townspeople and rebels gathered as the tall, heavy-set man was escorted with his hands tied in front of him to the Plaza Pedro Joaquín Chamorro in the barrio of Monimbo. "I haven't done harm to anyone," he shouted to his inquisitors. "I'm a friend of the workers and peasants."[9]

Townspeople demanded the maximum punishment for the notorious torturer. Women and mothers tried to break through the security guard to strike him. "The despots and assassins tremble because the time has come to balance accounts before the people," said Comandante Carlos Nuñez.

"*Comandante,* I have a wife and children. Condemn me to thirty years in prison, but don't shoot me," pleaded Macho Negro.

"In the name of the Revolution, the Frente Sandinista and the People, we condemn you to the firing squad," announced the improvised Sandinista tribunal.[10] Macho Negro stood erect against the wall and took his punishment.

Meanwhile, in Miami, Somoza, El Chiguín, and seventeen aides and bodyguards boarded a 108-foot yacht. "The United States is making me responsible for an act I had no control over," said the deposed dictator.[11] Then, picking up a gold-colored megaphone, he directed the yacht to the Bahamas.

Around noon, Moises Hassan's troops started entering Managua. "It was unforgettable," remembered Hassan, "the jubilation of the people gathered along the road, overflowing with enthusiasm."[12]

María Cano, a housewife in Managua, was waiting for her three sons to return. "It was eleven in the morning. . . . The radio kept repeating that the Guards were laying down their guns, that they were leaving. I could feel it everywhere—victory. It was eleven o'clock, and I hadn't even made the coffee or breakfast or anything. Then some kids ran in shouting, 'Doña María! Henry's coming!' " I hadn't seen or heard from him in days and days, and there he was, marching down the other side of the street. I was crazy with happiness, blowing him kisses in the air. Half an hour later Javier, the second one turned up, riding a jeep painted PATRIA LIBRE O MORIR. I cried out to him, too.

But there was still one missing—my youngest. I went inside, wringing my hands and thinking, 'My baby's missing! They've killed my little boy!' Everyone from the neighborhood had appeared, all but my little one. I went outside again and watched and waited. Someone said they saw Enrique coming, riding a tank, others said, no, it wasn't him. I was afraid it wasn't the truth. Then suddenly I saw him. He was coming. I ran over, held him. touched him, embraced him. It seemed impossible that he had come!"[13]

At 2 P.M., U.S. Chargé O'Donnell got a call from the United States ambassador to Costa Rica, Marvin Weisman, informing him that Ambassador Bowdler had left for the airport and would be arriving soon. "Why is he coming to Managua?" O'Donnell asked.[14]

"He didn't say. But some of the negotiators are coming down and I think he has some junta members with him."

"Does he want me to meet him at the airport?"

"He didn't say," answered Weisman.

O'Donnell had ordered the embassy staff to lie low and had even debated whether it was prudent to raise the flag. By ten in the morning, trucks teeming with Sandinista fighters had started passing by the gates of the embassy on their way into Managua. "Whenever they cheered," O'Donnell remembered, "we cheered back." He called Washington. "I got this strange message from San José. Bowdler is coming. Should I meet him at the airport?"

O'Donnell was told to do what he thought was right. "I told the gunnery sergeant that we were going," O'Donnell recalled, "and he recommended that we take along the major from the air force evacuation team to ride shotgun. He also thought we should fly the flag."

It was a fifteen-minute ride through the city. "The first few miles were okay," O'Donnell remembered.

> All of a sudden there were roadblocks and these kids were out there with black and red headbands and automatic rifles. The gunnery, who is bilingual, went out to explain that we were on an urgent mission. He said it in this very authoritative voice and the kids waved us on. We got into the center of town and people were celebrating. In front of the police station, preadolescent kids were passing out guns and ammunition and were trying to figure out how to get the clips into the rifles. These kids were firing into the air, and pickup trucks were passing by with victory banners and people firing. The closer we got to the airport, the more noise and gunfire. I was beginning to get a little nervous and wondering if this really was a good idea.

The airport was closed. There were several hundred kids milling around holding up their new trophies. The gunnery drove around to the VIP area and was stopped by a youth in a red and

Humberto Ortega, Tom O'Donnell, and Ambassador Pezzullo at the U.S. ambassador's residence in 1980. Credit: Agencia de Comunicación Internacional, Managua.

black bandana. "Nobody gets in," said the *muchacho*. He looked at the U.S. flags flying on the front fender of the car and added: "No flag here except the Sandinista flag. Take that off!" O'Donnell continued his story:

> The gunnery sergeant got out and started fooling around with the flag. And he tells the kid, "This is terrible. If we can't get in, we'll have to use our car radio to tell the airplane to turn around and cancel the arrival of the junta."
>
> The kid says, "Wait a minute." He comes back several minutes later with the officer who is running the airport. The officer escorts us into the VIP lounge and gives us a cup of coffee. He wants to know what we know, which is that Bowdler is on the plane with a couple of junta members.
>
> We wait. The plane is supposed to arrive any minute, but apparently the Mexican government, which owned the plane, was asking everyone in San José to sign elaborate release forms before they allowed the plane to leave. They didn't want responsibility if something went wrong. So the plane didn't take off until about 6 P.M.

Hanging from the walls of the VIP lounge were huge portraits of Somoza and his wife, Hope. The gunnery sergeant decided that he wanted them and organized a group of Sandinistas to try to pry them off. They were attached so firmly that they couldn't be moved. Finally a couple of tablecloths were found and hung over the portraits. In O'Donnell's words,

> I was getting more and more nervous. Everybody was asking, "Where's the junta?" Red Cross officials arrived at the airport and, seeing that a group of air force personnel were being held at gunpoint by the *muchachos,* escorted the prisoners into the duty-free section and locked them in for their own protection.
>
> Meanwhile, various Sandinistas and street kids had gone up into the tower and arrested the men manning it because they were wearing uniforms. The Chilean Red Cross official in charge had to go up to the tower and say: "You can't do that. You guys don't know how to run a tower." The *muchachos* obeyed.

Since the airport wasn't equipped to handle a night landing, everybody was getting nervous. Dusk was falling. "An old DC-3 landed at around six with a group of reporters," said O'Donnell.

> Everyone thought it was the junta and started firing in the air. The *muchachos* were everywhere—on the roof, on the balconies. And they didn't know what they were shooting at. If there had been a foxhole, I would have jumped in it. The Chilean Red Cross official said, "It's friendly fire." And I said: 'You can get killed by friendly fire.' "

The plane finally landed at 6:30 P.M. Off came Bowdler, FSLN Foreign Minister D'Escoto, and other representatives of the junta, the Sandinistas, and the governments of Mexico, the OAS, the Andean nations, and Dominican Foreign Minister Jiménez. There were no junta members on the plane. "Bowdler was exhausted," O'Donnell remembered. "He was just out of the hospital and he wasn't looking good."

Bowdler thought that there would be a brief airport ceremony to swear in the junta and he would return to San José the same night. But the junta was in León. The airport tower was trying to get through to them. Suddenly a voice came over the radio: "This is Tomás Borge. There won't be any swearing in ceremony today because I can't get to Managua. It will be tomorrow."

The U.S. chargé tried to communicate with the embassy, but his car radio was out of range. Curfew had fallen; it wasn't safe to travel. So the Red Cross bused everyone to the nearby Camino Real Hotel. "They prepared a wonderful meal for us," O'Donnell remembered.

> A Nicaraguan business leader who later was elected to the new Chamber of Deputies, sat down at my table with a big jug of California wine. He started telling us what a wonderful day it was; the only one like it in his experience was in 1961 when Fidel Castro's troops entered Havana. He had been attending the Catholic University in Havana at the time. But this was going to be different, everything would turn out all right.

The only junta member in Managua was Moises Hassan. "The night of the nineteenth I was at the entrance of the Intercontinental Hotel watching the rain," he remembered. "I was told that I was to go to the airport for a flight to León."[15]

Edén Pastora and his 2,000 men and artillery were traveling slowly in trucks up the Highway Sur. Pastora sat in the first truck acknowledging the cheers from the crowds. Dressed in fatigues covered with dirt, several weeks' growth of beard, and hair down to his shoulders, he was the picture of the guerrilla hero.

By the early hours of the twentieth, his force had advanced as far as Masaya, twelve miles from the capital, into an area called Piedras Quemadas. There his aides debated whether they should stay where they were and ask the other *comandantes* to negotiate, or join the celebration. Though he was the most popular Sandinista, Pastora had been given neither a place on the national directorate of the FSLN nor a prominent position in the new government. He had only been offered vice minister of the interior under Tomás Borge. After listening to his advisers, Pastora decided that it was time for conciliation. His country had suffered enough.[16]

When chief Sandinista military strategist Humberto Ortega arrived in Managua on the afternoon of the nineteenth, he called on the commander of the Internal Front, Joaquín Cuadra, and the two of them drove up together to take command of the bunker.

Pastora reached the bunker with his bodyguards on the morning of the twentieth to find the *comandantes* discussing how to disarm him. Humberto Ortega was busy taking control of the army, while Tomás Borge with the help of Cuban advisers was creating the Sandinista security apparatus. The FSLN commanders decided to house Pastora at Mrs. Hope Somoza's old house, "El Retiro," on the outskirts of town. His forces, meanwhile, were divided and integrated into the new army.

Chargé O'Donnell shared a room at the Camino Real Hotel with Bowdler. He continued his narrative:

> I got up at daybreak—say, 5:30—got hold of the gunnery and the major and headed to the "Casa Grande." The city was deserted and quiet. The radio was already broadcasting that the swearing in would take place in the national palace in downtown Managua at noon. I showered, shaved, and returned to the Camino Real Hotel to pick up Bowdler. He was already awake. Adolfo Calero was there greeting everyone, telling them it was a wonderful day for Nicaragua. So was Archbishop Obando y Bravo and quite a few foreign dignitaries.
>
> They organized everyone into a convoy. Most of the OAS party traveled in a small bus. Bowdler and I followed in the Ford Granada. Behind us was the archbishop in his car with Spanish Ambassador Pedro Echevarría. We had to drive about eight miles into town. The closer we got, the more and more people we saw. Bowdler said he had been in Havana in '61 and the feeling was very much the same. People were extremely happy, flashing us victory signs.
>
> When we got to within a hundred yards of the national palace, the crowd was too densely packed for us to go on. We got out of the car and formed a snake-line, holding hands, and sort of squeezed our way into the building. I wasn't sure we were going to make it. Bowdler was cheered all the way through. He was recognized as a hero and it seemed to brighten him up a lot.
>
> We had left the flag on the car, and the gunnery sergeant said, "We've seen the last of that flag." But when we came back two and a half hours later, the car and flag were untouched. At the car when we returned were a group of women waiting to thank Bowdler for bringing peace to Nicaragua. They were very humble women and wanted him to know that just across the street behind the Rubén Dario Theater is where Somoza used to shoot the young boys and students that the Guardia Nacional picked up. Bowdler was very touched.[17]

There were people everywhere, covering the dome and ruins of the national cathedral across the street. In the sweltering heat, approximately 100,000 had gathered. An announcer asked people to refrain from firing in the air out of respect for the distinguished foreign visitors. For the most part, they obeyed.

Along with Chargé O'Donnell and Ambassador Bowdler were the foreign ministers of the Dominican Republic and Panama, two Costa Rican vice presidents, and Mexico's Ambassador Andrés Rosenthal.

"It was a weird scene," remembered O'Donnell. "There was Alfonso Robelo, whom I had known as a businessman. He now had a revolutionary beard. The *comandantes* and their troops came in trucks, buses, and tractors. It was like a meeting of warlords from all different parts of Europe gathering together for the first time after the Crusades. Each had his own phalanx of guards who looked suspiciously at the other guy's guards."[18]

As the ceremony was about to begin in the national palace, Edén Pastora appeared at the back door. It was locked and nobody could find the key. It took him about half an hour to make his way through the crowd to the front door.

Inside the national palace, the members of the Junta of Reconstruction were sworn in by Archbishop Obando y Bravo. The *comandantes* watched in their fatigues. "What did we feel at this moment?" wrote Comandante Carlos Nuñez. "A mixture of joy and sadness; sadness for our fallen comrades who couldn't march at our side singing the hymns of victory."[19]

"Frankly, my head was spinning," remembers Violeta Chamorro. "I was crying because I could only think of Pedro, because I was thinking that we were going to find democracy. I asked God, our Lord, for things to turn out the way Pedro envisioned them. I asked him, 'Enlighten me, enlighten me, so that everything may turn out for the better.' "[20]

"I felt overwhelmed facing the prospect of responding to the expectations of the people," said junta member Moises Hassan. "I remember as we were coming to Managua, crowds lined the road—tens of thousands of people were greeting and cheering our advancing columns. I remember at that moment being fully aware of the enormous responsibility we were taking on."[21]

"Everyone treated Bowdler like a prince," O'Donnell remembered, except for Daniel Ortega. When it was his turn to speak, he made a long rambling diatribe about United States imperialism. It was a theme we came to know well—like Ravel's "Bolero"—starting in 1855 with William Walker. Afterwards, when Bowdler went over to congratulate Daniel, he started again. "We want friendship with the U.S., but it has to be on the basis of mutual respect," etcetera. Bowdler stood there and took it. He had his picture taken with everybody, especially Comandante Cero, Edén Pastora. Bowdler felt, and I think properly so, that the U.S. had to be seen as participating in this historic event.[22]

After the swearing in, the various junta members, *comandantes,* and the archbishop took turns stepping out onto the balcony to greet the huge crowd gathered in the plaza. "It was a strange crowd," said O'Donnell. "Because at the front with big banners was 'Los Montañeros Presente.' The internationalists were already there. On a scale of one to ten, Pastora received the biggest ovation—say, a ten—followed by the archbishop with an eight and a half; Doña Violeta got an eight; Borge a five; Wheelock, the Ortegas, and the others just a smattering of applause; they were clearly not well known."[23]

Manolo Gutiérrez was there. He had dressed quietly that morning and allowed himself to be swept up in the crowd and enthusiasm that carried him downtown. The great outpouring of love, happiness, and goodwill was a consolation. "This is what Gustavo died for," he repeated to himself. "They're cheering him." In a yellow school bus that entered the plaza, he saw the face of his daughter, Lucía. She was dressed in olive fatigues and wore a black beret with a big red star in the middle. He pushed his way through the crowd and embraced her. It seemed everything was possible.

For most Nicaraguans, July 20 seemed like a new beginning. But they would be haunted by the ghosts of the past.

19

Tyrants do not die, they are killed. —Seneca

Fourteen months after he fled Nicaragua, on September 17, 1980, Anastasio Somoza Debayle's white Mercedes was hit by a rocket 500 meters from his Spanish-style mansion in Asunción, Paraguay. Somoza, his Nicaraguan driver, and an American business associate were instantly killed. His mistress, Dinorah Sampson, who had been living with him in exile, ran toward his mangled body screaming, "I want to see him! I want to see him!"[1] She had to be taken away in an ambulance.

A squad of six people with ties to the Argentine Montañeros were arrested two days later and charged with the crime. Meanwhile, crowds sang and danced throughout Nicaragua. "He who kills by the sword, dies by the sword," said poet (and colleague of Pedro Joaquín Chamorro) Pablo Antonio Cuadra.[2]

Somoza's eldest son, Anastasio (El Chiguín) Somoza Portcarrero, lives in Miami, where he manages the Somoza family businesses. He has forsworn all involvement in Nicaraguan politics.

Dr. Francisco Urcuyo returned to Nicaragua at the end of 1991 after twelve years of exile in Guatemala, Mexico, and Miami. In his book *Solos*, recounting his last forty-three days in Managua, he

239

refers to himself as "the Constitutional president of Nicaragua." It's been reported that he still wears the presidential sash in public.

Viron (Pete) Vaky left the foreign service in 1980. Since then he has taught at Georgetown University.

On January 21, 1981, when the Reagan administration took office, Bill Bowdler, then serving as assistant secretary for American republic affairs, was ordered to pack up and leave. After a long career of distinguished service, he submitted his resignation. He lives quietly in retirement in southern Virginia and doesn't like to talk about this period.

After leaving the National Security Council, Bob Pastor became professor of political science at Emory University in Atlanta. He is currently the director of the Latin American and Caribbean Program at Emory's Carter Center. He has written extensively about the fall of Somoza. His book, *Condemned to Repetition,* deals with U.S. policy toward Nicaragua during the Carter and Reagan administrations.

Alfonso Robelo quit the Junta of National Reconstruction on April 20, 1980. "To continue there," he said at the time, "would just have been to lend my presence to the appearance of pluralism. The FSLN has violated its trust and broken the political unity of Nicaragua."[3] In June 1982 he formed a political-military alliance (ARDE) with Edén Pastora to overthrow the Sandinistas. In March 1985 he was named (along with Arturo Cruz and Adolfo Calero) to the leadership of UNO (Unidad Nicaraguense Opositora), the political arm of the contras. Violeta Chamorro, the widow of Pedro Joaquín Chamorro, resigned from the junta on April 19, 1980. She ran against Daniel Ortega for the presidency of Nicaragua in 1990 under a broad coalition of opposition parties. On February 25, 1990, she stunned the world by winning with 55 percent of the vote.

Moises Hassan served on the junta until March 1981 when he was named minister of construction. In May 1983 he became vice minister of the interior and in 1986 was elected mayor of Managua. He was removed from his post on April 1988 after he announced that he was quitting the Frente Sandinista. "Too many groups within the Sandinista Front have become isolated," he warned; "cut off from the daily lives of normal people. You begin to believe everything is the way that you would like it to be."[4] He is now an outspoken critic of the Sandinistas who, he maintains, corrupted and violated their committment to bring about fundamental democratic change.

Daniel Ortega was elected president of Nicaragua on November 4, 1984. In an effort to show the world that Nicaragua was a true democracy, he ran for reelection on February 25, 1990, and lost to Violeta Chamorro. He remains general secretary of the Sandinista party.

His brother, Humberto Ortega, was named Commander of the Revolution and minister of defense in January 1980. In an effort to heal the country, Violeta Chamorro allowed him to retain his post when she assumed the presidency in 1990.

Edén Pastora (Comandante Cero) broke with the Sandinista leadership in April 1982 and in June of that year formed a political-military alliance (ARDE) with Alfonso Robelo to oppose the Sandinista regime that he saw abusing power in Nicaragua. Operating near the Costa Rican border, he resisted efforts by the U.S. Central Intelligence Agency to merge his army with the FDN— the CIA-backed contras operating out of Honduras. He was nearly killed by a bomb smuggled into his headquarters near the Costa Rican border on May 30, 1984. He has at various times accused the CIA and Sandinistas of trying to assassinate him.

Archbishop Obando y Bravo became an outspoken critic of the Sandinistas and their people's church, Iglesia Popular. In June 1985 he was elevated to cardinal by Pope John Paul II. He was named to head a commission to monitor Nicaragua's compliance with the Arias peace plan in August 1987.

On July 31, 1981, General Omar Torrijos's private plane crashed in bad weather. General Manuel Noriega, his chief of intelligence, took his place as military strongman of Panama.

I returned to Managua on July 28, 1979, with a planeload of food and medical supplies. At a press conference the same day in Washington, President Carter said that the United States had "a good relationship" with the new Nicaraguan Government and hoped to improve it.[5] To my surprise, instead of being met at the airport by a representative from the foreign ministry, I was welcomed by Minister of the Interior Tomás Borge, who escorted me all the way into my office at the U.S. Embassy.

Two years later, with the Reagan administration clearly intent on a radical change in policy, I engineered a transfer to the University of Georgia as a diplomat-in-residence. One year later, I retired from the Foreign Service after twenty-eight years of service. Since 1984 I have been executive director of Catholic Relief Services.

Epilogue

Life is only understood backwards, but it must be lived forward.
—Kierkegaard

This book has described how the Somoza regime crumbled and fell ignominiously on July 17, 1979. The last torchbearer Anastasio (Tachito) Somoza Debayle had all but ceased to govern after the assassination of *La Prensa* editor Pedro Joaquín Chamorro nineteen months earlier. He spurned an opportunity later that year to negotiate a face-saving transition of power. By May 1979, he stood isolated in the hemisphere and faced a national insurrection.

The seeds of the dynasty's collapse were sown less than a decade before when Tachito fulfilled his brother Luis's prophecy by usurping presidential power for a second term. A complicitous administration in Washington did not react and may even have given him the green light. Unfortunately, insensitivity to the political and social demands of the citizens of Third World countries was very much in character. Wasn't the Nixon administration unmoved when a military clique in El Salvador stole an election from Napoleon Duarte in 1972? Didn't administration officials ignore

242

the protestations of the Latin American Bureau in the State Department two years later when the military in Guatemala seated its own presidential candidate through election fraud? Seemingly a slave to the status quo, the Nixon administration also stood transfixed when Ferdinand Marcos declared martial law in the Philippines in 1974, ushering in a period of political repression that eventually brought about Marcos's political demise.

While the Somoza dynasty shared many similarities with other authoritarian regimes, it was unique in one particular: a close relationship with the United States was critical to its survival. The founder of the dynasty, Anastasio Somoza García, set the pattern of courting U.S. officials, a practice his sons embraced as an article of faith and followed assiduously. Tachito, who graduated from West Point, cultivated his schoolmates and U.S. Military Academy alumni to help develop a wide circle of influential American friends. These efforts produced, among other benefits, "associates" who advocated the interests of the Somoza clan at the highest levels of the U.S. government. One would be hard pressed to identify another country, especially one so small and strategically insignificant as Nicaragua, that was so well wired into Washington.

To be sure, it was not a one-way street. The Somozas served U.S. interests on many occasions, as significant as providing a training and launching base for the abortive Bay of Pigs operation in Cuba, or as mundane as passing messages or gaining support from Latin countries on issues of interest to the United States. In the process of doing our bidding, the Somozas gained cachet. Tachito, in particular, was a notorious name-dropper. Nothing pleased him more than to boast to his Latin American colleagues that he had friends in high places in Washington and could get his way with the gringos.

It was a lopsided relationship that benefited the Somozas disproportionately. This was recognized and disparaged by scores of officers in the State Department. But Nicaragua was such a small blip on our international radar scope that it never commanded enough attention to prompt serious policy review. Inertia kept this unhealthy relationship afloat until the bottom dropped out in the late 1970s.

Whether he truly believed it or not, Tachito Somoza was vociferous in accusing his "enemies" in the Carter administration of precipitating his collapse. Pedro Joaquín Chamorro was more astute. He recognized that the Somoza dynasty could not withstand open criticism from the United States. It weakened an essential strut of its power base. In being laid bare as a repressive ruler no different from other despots in Central and South America, Somoza was demystified. This gave his erstwhile flaccid opposition the impetus to coalesce and join an increasingly restless Nicaraguan people to form an irresistible force for change.

Decades of corruption and brutishness had taken their toll in eroding whatever base of support the Somozas had built. Tachito's illegal second term, the flagrant corruption pervading Managua's earthquake reconstruction, the brutal Guardia search-and-destroy campaigns in the northern highlands of the mid-1970s, Tachito's near fatal heart attack in 1977, the atrocities committed by the Guardia in putting down the uprisings in Monimbo, Matagalpa, and Estelí in 1978, and Somoza's duplicity during the OAS mediation were the actions of a regime that had become a rogue elephant.

Confronting the crumbling of the Somoza dynasty was a task thrust upon the Carter administration. History dictated the timing. Rather than holding its nose and swallowing, the Carter administration misread reality during the critical OAS mediation and later in 1979 tarried behind events until the eleventh hour.

What was the reality that escaped Carter's advisers? Simply put, it was the view held in Nicaragua, certainly in Latin America and most probably throughout the world, that the Somoza regime was our ward and that the United States, and only the United States, had the power to bring it to heel. This was the legacy of allowing the Somozas to define our bilateral relationship. The United States became hostage to Somoza's self-serving image.

Arguably, we could have persuaded Somoza to resign during the OAS mediation of 1978–79. His cousin Luis Pallais makes a plausible case that Somoza was seriously thinking of leaving and only needed inducement from the United States to bite the bullet. Even he acknowledges, however, that such a move would have required direct intervention by President Carter. Given the fact that President Carter and his principal advisers, including Zbig Brzezinski and Cyrus Vance, were convinced that the United States should not intervene directly in the affairs of other nations—certainly not to the extent of asking a sitting president to resign—there was never a chance, despite the valiant efforts of Pete Vaky, that this nation would take a forceful stand. But the fact remains: a historic opportunity was missed. The transitional option designed by the FAO (Broad Opposition Front) during the OAS mediation—the last best chance for a peaceful and moderate solution—was not forced on Somoza. Tachito foolishly slammed shut that window of opportunity. He thought he could weather the storm and complete his term as president. He, too, would have been spared an ignominious defeat had we pushed harder.

The collapse of the OAS mediation brought down the moderate opposition with it. The only remaining option was armed conflict and the FSLN. Ironically, the FLSN had feared that the mediation would succeed. Its failure made them the vanguard of the quickly expanding violent opposition.

During the gathering of the thunderhead—between January and May 1979—as the FSLN and its supporters armed for battle, the United States stood on the sidelines, ill informed and confused. We brought ourselves to the crux of the crisis again in mid-June by focusing on the same bottom line that we had turned our backs on seven months earlier: the United States alone had the power to induce Somoza to step down.

Once again, however, we blanched because of the NSC's fear of a vacuum of power in Nicaragua. Several plans were devised to plug the dikes around an imperiled Nicaraguan political culture. The first, the Executive Committee scheme, was impossible to implement. Characteristically, the United States was trying to turn back the clock. Our effort to expand the FSLN junta was more pernicious. It conjured up illusions without substance and wasted time and lives. Hadn't Arturo Cruz told us a month earlier that the FSLN commanders, not the junta, would wield power? Since we feared this was true, we pretended not to hear Cruz's words.

Everything we set out to accomplish in late June 1979 turned on one pivotal event—the resignation of Somoza. His earlier obdurateness had subliminally conditioned Washington into believing he would be equally stubborn in June 1979. But the massive popular insurrection and the vote in the OAS, which Somoza saw as pitting "300 million people in the hemisphere" against him, had taken their toll. When I found at our first meeting (on June 28) that Tachito was willing to call it quits, I recommended to Washington that we act quickly—by setting an early date for his departure. But Washington hesitated. In my judgment, that was an error. The one event over which we could have exercised some control was put on hold as history unfolded around us. Had we seized the initiative, we could have dictated the pace of events and earned the political capital that comes with leadership, while at the same time pushing less controllable and potentially complicating currents to the periphery. Our hesitation also sent the wrong signals to Somoza, to the junta in San José, to Nicaraguans of all stripes—especially members of the Guardia Nacional—and to our hemispheric neighbors.

Washington, to paraphrase Lincoln, was beset with the "slows." The reaction of the Carter administration was not unique. Change, especially radical change, is difficult for any U.S. administration, especially when the alternative becomes festooned with all the ideological trappings of a communist revolution. Ever since the "fall of China" in 1949, administration after administration has been haunted by the specter of losing a country to communism on its watch. We paid a tragic price in Vietnam because of this syndrome. The Carter administration was understandably concerned about being faulted for "losing" Nicaragua.

Somoza's behavior, especially his double-dealing at the end, though thoroughly reprehensible, was true to character. His principal motivation was survival. He feared that a member of his precious Guardia would do him in. The plan we proposed made sense to us, but Somoza saw it as a prescription for his extermination. We should have been forewarned when he accused me of setting him up for assassination when he learned that U.S. military attaché McCoy was talking directly to officers of the Guardia. He wanted to close that channel down. And he succeeded by alerting his "associate," Congressman John Murphy, who lost no time in registering alarm with officials in Washington.

With the Guardia nicely cordoned off, Somoza was free to act out the charade of agreeing to our plan while secretly pursuing his own agenda. That included telling the Guardia that he had worked out a deal with his friends in Washington to bring in U.S. military support once he had left the country. That's exactly what his son El Chiguín told the assembled Guardia commanders on the night of July 16. There was no reason for them to question Somoza, who already had convinced them that he could get his way with the gringos; he had friends in high places.

Thus, Somoza destroyed the Guardia to save his own skin. As soon as it became clear that they had been duped, the Guardia deserted en masse. General Mejia came to realize the truth thirty-six hours too late. His plaintive plea to Humberto Ortega on the evening of July 18 that he was prepared to implement the U.S. plan was pure irony. His troops had disappeared. The FSLN, as Humberto had rightly asserted, had no reason to negotiate. It was all over.

One is prompted to ask why the Guardia permitted one man, albeit once its most loyal benefactor, to determine its fate. Where was the survival instinct one finds in other Latin American military institutions that drives them to topple one of their own when a leader jeopardizes their survival, as the El Salvadoran military did in unseating President (General) Romero in October 1979, only four months later? The evidence suggests that the Guardia Nacional was unique—more a praetorian guard than an army. It had been nurtured and eventually neutered by the Somozas. When faced with a moment of truth, it had no will of its own.

This brings into question whether the Guardia could have fulfilled the role envisioned in the United States' plan. On paper, a professional military force with control of the nation's capital, its major airport, and its principal seaports would be in a commanding position, especially if it enjoyed the legitimacy stemming from a negotiated international agreement. But the Guardia Nacional's collapse after Somoza's departure is strong evidence that it had been so conditioned by the Somozas, who prevented the emergence of any rivals to power, that it couldn't survive on its own. The Guardia was not defeated on the field of battle, as some Sandinistas would have one believe; it fell apart.

According to veteran Sandinista Oscar René Vargas: "The Sandinista Front thought it was going to have a piece of the power and no more. We assumed we were going to have to negotiate with the Guardia. But when the Guardia fell apart, we found ourselves in complete command. It was a better situation than we had imagined in our wildest dreams."[1]

Urcuyo, who chose to believe Somoza's version of reality, was left behind in an untenable situation along with the Guardia. It was his own stupidity that caused him to dismiss the discussions he had with me and Tom O'Donnell and to trust instead Somoza's promise that he would get his friends in Washington to save Nicaragua from the communist beasts. The disintegration of the negotiated transitional plan caused much unneeded suffering. For instance, 7,000 people, including thousands of Guardia soldiers, were rounded up and imprisoned instead of receiving sanctuary from the Red Cross and Catholic churches.

There is a natural temptation to draw lessons from the events of history. In diplomacy as in comedy, timing is almost everything. The right move at the right time, with emphasis on the latter, is crucial. This probably isn't appreciated by academic "model" makers and "balance-of-power" enthusiasts, precisely because it calls on intuition rather than scientific formulas.

Intuition is an invaluable tool in diplomacy, as in life. Rarely if ever are decision makers overinformed. Even with the best of intelligence, there are gaps and blind spots. The conventional wisdom is to wait and see. Sometimes it is the wisest path. But wait and see was costly in Nicaragua. Pete Vaky's intuitive judgment in 1978 that we would sacrifice the moderate opposition and encourage the violent vanguard if we didn't strongly urge Somoza to resign was right on target. It wasn't heeded by the political leaders of the Carter administration, who in the main were distracted by other crises and, importantly, by their pristine commitment to the principle of nonintervention.

They were not alone. We missed a series of opportunities: in 1973 after the Managua earthquake, in 1974 when Somoza ran for his constitutionally illegal second term, in 1977 when he suffered his heart attack, during the OAS mediation of 1978, and finally in late June 1979 when Tachito told me he was prepared to resign.

Further limiting U.S. effectiveness has been the common practice of commissioning a substantial percentage of political appointees to head our diplomatic missions. Aside from the David Bruces, Averill Harrimans, Ellsworth Bunkers, and others of their stature whose contributions are widely regarded, how can one defend sending political friends and widget manufacturers abroad to represent a superpower with worldwide interests and responsibilities? One could argue that the sorry state of U.S.-Nicaraguan relations was a direct result of this spoils system.

There exists a popular misconception—in part fed by the Central Intelligence Agency—that diplomatic and military intelligence is some special treasure trove collected covertly and analyzed in secret. The fact is, that with the exception of sensitive matters of security and information regarding individuals in high places and their confidential views and activities, most of what makes up the intelligence regarding a foreign country is publicly obtainable. The difficulty, or the artistry, lies in digesting the mass of information, putting it into a fluent, cultural context, and arriving at judgments that benefit both countries. This difficult task demands a diplomatic service that understands history and is acutely sensitive to the culture of each society. The opportunities missed in Nicaragua were, in some cases, seen and reported on by officers in the field or in Washington, who then urged (as in the case of Pete Vaky) that appropriate actions be taken.

The current trend of turning our chanceries into what appear from the outside to be maximum security prisons is a sad metaphor for the state of the U.S. diplomatic service. How can our diplomats get to know a society if they don't get out and mingle with the people? To paraphrase Robert Frost, when you wall others out, you wall yourself in.

As we look back from the vantage point of the present, several things are clear. First, we should never allow another country to set the tone and substance of a bilateral relationship. Second, we should never underrate U.S. power and prestige abroad. Had we been honest and forceful with Somoza earlier, much of the pain of June/-July 1979 could have been spared.

Alexis de Tocqueville probably would have pointed to the openness of our democratic system as the culprit. I disagree. If anything, there was not enough public scrutiny of our Nicaragua policy. More intensive questioning as to what was going on in Nicaragua might have forced an earlier review and change of policy. The cold war offered a pretext to support a strong, anticommunist regime in Central America. But close examination would have revealed how little we received in return from the self-serving Somozas. But there was very little interest in Nicaragua either within a succession of U.S. administrations or among the public at large. Given such inertia, the intense self-interest of Somoza became the woof and warp of our bilateral relationship.

Ultimately, our children will judge our choices. These were not particularly noble or wise during the final days of the Somoza dynasty. But we had our moments. We convinced a dictator to hasten his final exit, thereby ending a bloody civil war. The emphasis we placed on protecting the innocent did limit reprisals. And our insistence on a transition to democracy compelled the Sandinista leaders to honor their commitments by calling for general elections in 1984. Lamentably, our leaders in Washington at the time were so obsessed with overthrowing the Sandinista government by violent means that they missed an opportunity to hold the Sandinistas to their word and to ensure a fair election. But the Nicaraguan people finally found their voice in 1990 and elected opposition candidate Violeta de Chamorro president of the country.

Appendix
Notes
Index

Appendix

Chronology of the Nicaraguan Revolution 1933–July 1979

1933

February 2—Augusto César Sandino signs peace pact with President Juan Sacasa following the withdrawal of U.S. Marines from Nicaragua.

1934

February 21—Sandino is assassinated by the National Guard (GN) headed by Anastasio Somoza García.

1936

June 6—GN Chief Director Anastasio Somoza García deposes President Sacasa. Somoza is elected president in September and establishes the National Liberal party (PLN) as his political machine.

1948

February 2—PLN candidate Leonardo Arguello wins fixed election with Somoza's backing.
May—Arguello is overthrown by Somoza after less than a month in office.

1950

February—Somoza is elected to a third term.

1954

April—Costa Rican–based rebellion by Guard officers, Emiliano Chamorro, and several young Conservatives, including Pedro Joaquín Chamorro and Ernesto Cardenal, fails.

1956

September 21—Somoza García is assassinated by Rigoberto López Pérez, a young dissident Liberal. Sons Luis and Anastasio Somoza Debayle assume the presidency and GN directorship, and conduct massive arrest of dissidents.

1957

February 2—Luis Somoza is elected president.

1958

July—Students at National University (UNAN) demonstrate against a visit by Milton Eisenhower.
September 15–October 18—Sandino veteran Ramón Raudales begins a guerrilla campaign with less than forty men in Nueva Segovia.

1959

January 1—Fidel Castro and the Movimiento 26 de Julio topple the Batista regime in Cuba.
February—Dr. Enrique Lacayo Farfan and P. J. Chamorro build 112-man force in Costa Rica to overthrow the Somozas. Chamorro seeks Cuban aid, but is rejected by Castro for being too bourgeois.
May 29—Conservative general strike fails after 300 business, labor, and political leaders are arrested.
May 31—P. J. Chamorro-led Conservative invasion force lands in Chontales. Clashes with GN and retreats into Darien mountains.
June 14—P. J. Chamorro surrenders with surviving insurgents. Luis Somoza pardons rebels in December.
June 27—Honduran army surrounds Cuban-backed Rigoberto López Pérez column at El Chaparral. Carlos Fonseca is wounded and flees to Cuba.
July 23—Student demonstrations in León are violently suppressed by GN. Marks the beginning of campus radicalism.
November—Sandino Revolutionary Front (FRS) is founded by Alejandro and Harold Martínez; includes Edén Pastora. Conducts raids along Honduran border.

1960

April—FRS attacks GN post at Las Trojas; disbands by year's end.
May–September—Leftist Nicaraguan Patriotic Youth (JPN) and other student groups stage demonstrations in León and Managua.
July—Carlos Fonseca is deported to Guatemala.
July 23–25—Major student riots in Managua.
November—Luis Somoza welcomes U.S. Alliance for Progress as part of a strategy to reform the regime through economic development.

1961

April—Bay of Pigs invasion force departs from training bases in Puerto Cabezas, Nicaragua.

July 23—The Sandinista National Liberation Front (FSLN) is founded by Carlos Fonseca, Tomás Borge, and Silvio Mayorga in Tegucigalpa, Honduras. First called the National Liberation Front, the movement added "Sandinista" to its title in 1962 at Fonseca's insistence.

1962

May—Fonseca organizes the Revolutionary Student Front (FER) as the FSLN's campus arm.

July—Jorge Navarro begins organizing FSLN's urban network. Fonseca and Sandino veteran Colonel Santos López plan a guerrilla campaign in Rio Coco border region.

September—A sixty-man FSLN camp is established on Rio Patuca in Honduras.

1963

February 2—Somoza's candidate, René Schick, is elected president. Conservatives boycott the election. Schick further liberalizes the regime.

March 3—In first FSLN armed action, Jorge Navarro leads takeover of Radio Mundial for a propaganda broadcast.

May 30—Navarro directs the first FSLN bank robbery at a Banco de América branch in Managua.

June–October—FSLN guerrillas led by Santos López, Tomás Borge, and Modesto Duarte occupy Raiti and Walaquistan on the Rio Coco. Attacks on GN outposts fail, with heavy losses. Surviving guerrillas retreat to Honduras and are arrested.

1964

June—FSLN is involved in Nicaragua's first legal strike.

June 20—Fonseca and Victor Tirado of the FSLN are arrested.

December—FSLN militants Daniel Ortega, Selim Schible, and Edmundo Pérez are arrested. Father Ernesto Cardenal founds the Solentiname lay community.

1965

January—Fonseca is exiled to Guatemala where he meets FAR guerrilla leader Luis Turcios Lima.

1966

January—FSLN delegate Carlos Reyna attends the First Tricontinental Conference in Havana.

April—Fonseca returns to Nicaragua; starts planning a new guerrilla campaign.

July–October—Oscar Turcios leads an FSLN contingent to fight with the Guatemalan FAR as training for a return to guerrilla warfare in Nicaragua.

September—FSLN finances the guerrilla war with robberies of La Criolla supermarket and the Banco National El Calvario branch. The rural front in Matagalpa is reinforced with urban cadres.

November—National Opposition Union (UNO) is formed by the Traditional Conservatives and Liberals not aligned with the Somozas. FSLN issues a manifesto rejecting the approaching elections and calling for armed struggle.

1967

January 20—FSLN commandos rob San Sebastián bank.

January 22—UNO stages 60,000-person rally in Managua. Aguero calls for GN to desert the government. Over 200 are killed when troops fire on the crowd.

February 6—Anastasio "Tachito" Somoza Debayle is elected president.

April—Luis Somoza dies of a heart attack, leaving Tachito free to militarize the regime.

May 1—FSLN sets off bombs and robs banks as Somoza takes office.

May—Pancasán guerrilla *foco* is organized into three columns: under Carlos Fonseca (HQ group), Tomás Borge (logistical line to Matagalpa), and Silvio Mayorga (mountain raiding column). Skirmishes with GN.

August 27—GN ambushes the Silvio Mayorga column at Pancasán, killing twenty of thirty-five combatants, including Silvio Mayorga. FSLN retreats to the cities; many flee to Cuba.

November 4—FSLN-DN member Casimiro Sotelo and three others are killed in Managua. Gladys Baez is captured.

November 18—FSLN urban leader Daniel Ortega is imprisoned. Borge flees to Cuba with the collapse of the urban resistance. FSLN cadres Julio Buitrago and Ricardo Morales Aviles try to rebuild the urban underground.

1968

FSLN exiles in Costa Rica led by Carlos Fonseca meet to reassess the Cuban-inspired *foco* strategy and to lay the foundation for the adoption of the Asian concept of "prolonged popular war" (GPP). After the Latin American Bishops Conference in Medellín, seven "liberation theology" priests call for an end to torture, political imprisonment, and the unjust economic order.

September 18—Buitrago-led robbery of the Buenos Aires branch of Banco de America marks the first major FSLN action after Pancasán.

December—Ricardo Morales, Lenin Cerna, and other militants of the Buitrago commando unit are captured.

1969

National Directorate is reorganized with Fonseca as secretary-general. Collective leadership is emphasized. Fonseca consolidates Sandinista ideology, program, and internal structure. FSLN resumes political work in the mountains of Matagalpa.

July 15—Dramatic, televised GN assaults on Managua safe houses in Las Delicias del Volga and Santo Domingo barrios result in the deaths of Juilio Buitrago and three other Sandinistas.

September 1—Carlos Fonseca is jailed by Costa Rican authorities for bank robbery.

November 4—Juan José Quezada and Pedro Arauz Palacios of FSLN hijack a Lanica airliner to Cuba. Leonel Rugama leads robbery of BANIC branch in León.

December—Revolutionary Student Front (FER) under Edgar Munguía and Bayardo Arce assumes leadership of the National University student government (CUUN) and steps up mobilization of students behind the FSLN.

December 20—Rugama leads robbery of Fabrica Santa Cecilia offices.

December 23—Germán Pomares leads FSLN commandos in attack on Alejuela jail in Costa Rica. Raid fails to free Fonseca. Humberto Ortega is wounded and captured.

1970

Miguel Obando y Bravo becomes archbishop of Managua and maintains critical distance from the Somoza regime.

January 7—Rugama leads robbery of El Boer branch in Managua.

January 15—GN raid on Managua safe house kills Leonel Rugama and two others.

February—GN discovers the Pablo Ubeda column organized from Zinica peasants by FSLN cadres Enrique Lorente, José Benito Escobar, and Victor Tirado. As part of GPP strategy, FSLN goes deeper underground "to accumulate forces in silence," while relying on intermediate organizations for support.

March—GN conducts mop-up operations of suspected FSLN sympathizers in Wamblan, Kilambe, Hacienda El Carmen, Hacienda La Gloria, and El Cua.

September 6—Patricio Arguello of FSLN is killed while attempting to hijack an El Al airliner over France with Leyla Khaled of the PLO.

September 9—Juan José Quezada aids PLO hijacking of a British BOAC plane to Jordan in an effort to free Khaled. Occupation and hunger strike in the national cathedral by students and Central American University rector, Father Fernando Cardenal, protests political repression.

October 21—Carlos Aguero leads hijacking of Costa Rican plane and holds four United Fruit officials hostage to gain release and transfer to Cuba of Fonseca, Humberto Ortega, and others.

November—Somoza negotiates power-sharing arrangement with the Fernando Aguero faction of the Conservative party. The Kupia Kumi Pact of March 28, 1971, gives Conservative seats in Congress and on an executive Triumvirate. P. J. Chamorro forms Conservative National Action (ANC) after being expelled from the Traditional Conservative party (PCT) by Aguero for opposing the deal.

December—José Benito Escobar and sixteen other FSLN cadres are captured, leaving Turcios as the only free DN member in Nicaragua.

1971

Leading Sandinistas Henry Ruiz, Tomás Borge, Victor Tirado, Edén Pastora, José Valdivia, and Pedro Arauz, return to Nicaragua. Most go into the northern mountains to revitalize the GPP. Turcios and Arauz concentrate on urban organizing in León. The Frente numbers fifty to seventy legal members and ten to fifteen clandestine militants.

January—Major demonstrations are staged by university students.

April—Doris Tijerino, Germán Pomares, and other FSLN militants are released after occupation of churches and schools by students.

May 19—Archbishop Obando y Bravo and other church officials condemn the violence of the regime.

August—In accordance with the Liberal-Conservative Pact, Congress dissolves itself pending the election of a constituent assembly.

1972

Father Uriel Molina, Luis Carrión, Joaquín Cuadra, and other young Catholic radicals form the Christian Revolutionary Movement (MCR) to raise political consciousness in the university and the urban barrios.

February 3—UNAN students march from León to Managua.

February 6—Constituent elections produce agreed 60–40 Liberal-Conservative split in Congress.

May—Three-man junta of two Liberals and one Conservative (Fernando Aguero) assumes executive power. Somoza retains control of the GN.

December 23—A massive earthquake kills 18,000 people and destroys central Managua. Somoza declares an emergency and assumes dictatorial powers, diverting international relief in his effort to control the nation's economy. Large-scale business alienation results.

1973

FSLN urban groups step up recruitment efforts among refugees displaced by the earthquake. MCR joins the FSLN as an intermediate organization.

January—Five Protestant relief agencies form the Evangelical Committee for Development Assistance (CEPAD), a vehicle for church-based social activism.

April—Construction workers strike over wages. FER students attempt to radicalize the strike.

August—2,000 textile workers strike for higher wages.

September—Subtiva Indians take over land in Chinandega. Bus fare increases inspire urban protests.

September 17—The GN kills FSLN-DN members Oscar Turcios and Ricardo Morales at their Nandaime, Granada, safe house.

September 18—Juan José Quezada and Jonathan González are gunned down near Nandaime by GN, convincing those who support the prolonged war strategy (GPP) of the futility of urban operations.

1974

FSLN decides to escalate the GPP beyond political recruitment and agitation to include guerrilla group operations. Bayardo Arce is assigned to build an underground supply line from León to the Jinotepe mountains. UNAN student protests in support of political prisoners are dispersed by the GN.

March—Private enterprise assembly (COSIP) protests Somoza's candidacy for president.

May—FSLN moves its major student cadres into the mountains.

June—Group of Twenty-seven, led by P. J. Chamorro, calls for an election boycott.

August 6—The Bishops' Conference questions the morality of the Liberal-Conservative pact.

September 1—Somoza is elected to a second term, with a 40 percent abstention rate.

November—Democratic Union of Liberation (UDEL) is formed by P. J. Chamorro, uniting Christian Democrats, trade unionists, and Socialists (PSN).

December 27—A FSLN commando unit led by Eduardo Contreras and Germán Pomares seizes the Managua home of José María Castillo Quant during a party, killing Castillo but failing to capture U.S. Ambassador Turner Shelton. Somoza declares martial law. Following mediation by Archbishop Obando y Bravo, Somoza agrees to release fourteen prisoners, pay $6 million, raise the minimum wage, broadcast a 12,000-word FSLN communique, and arrange the commandos' flight to Cuba on December 30.

1975

Guerrilla war in the eastern mountains escalates. GN repression inflicts great suffering on the peasantry and attracts world attention, cutting the GPP off from its urban base.

March 21—Guerrillas enter Rio Blanco, Boaco. GN counters by turning Rio Blanco into a major counterinsurgency base.
September—Carlos Fonseca returns to Nicaragua and joins the guerrillas.
October—The GPP-dominated National Directorate (DN) expels the Jaime Wheelock urban faction for their criticism of the rural guerrilla strategy. Wheelock, Luis Carrión, and Carlos Roberto Huembes form the Tendencia Proletaria (TP), which concentrates on organizing urban workers and educating barrio dwellers along orthodox Marxist lines.

1976

February—Tomás Borge of the DN is captured in Managua.
November 8—Secretary-general of FSLN Carlos Fonseca is killed by the GN in the Zinica area of Jinotega.
December—Somoza suffers first heart attack.

1977

Counterinsurgency effort of GN forces the GPP guerrillas to abandon the northern highlands and the eastern mountains and retreat to the isolated frontier of the Atlantic coast. An estimated 2,000 campesinos are killed in the 1975–77 guerrilla war. With many GPP leaders in prison or underground, exiled Sandinistas in Costa Rica led by the Ortega brothers exert new leadership. The Tercerista or insurrectional tendency (TI) calls the GPP strategy of protracted rural warfare outdated and adopts a strategy of urban-based insurrection uniting all opposition forces.

January 1977

January 20—Jimmy Carter becomes president of the United States.

March 1977

March 4—State Department issues first public U.S. criticism of Somoza's human rights record.
March 28—Rep. Ed Koch (D-N.Y.) calls on Congress to halt all aid to the Somoza regime.

May 1977

May 4—TI political-military platform outlines a commitment to Marxism-Leninism and Humberto Ortega's strategy for the rapid overthrow of Somoza through a popular front alliance.

June 1977

Eight prominent Nicaraguans (later known as the "Group of Twelve") recruited by Sergio Ramírez, a Nicaraguan writer and secret FSLN militant meet with Humberto Ortega in Costa Rica. Ortega asks them to be part of a broad-based provisional government to rule Nicaragua after a successful insurrection.

June 23—Somoza allies, Reps. John Murphy (R-N.Y.) and Charles Wilson (D-Tex.), succeed in restoring $3.1 million in U.S. military aid to Nicaragua. The Carter administration suspends military credits and economic aid to Nicaragua in a test of the new human rights policy.

July 1977

July 25—Somoza suffers second heart attack and is flown to Miami to recover.

August 1977

Humberto Ortega recruits Edén Pastora and Fernando Chamorro, two longtime anti-Somoza activists with social democratic reputations.
August 15—Amnesty International releases critical report on the government, condemning torture and murder of campesinos and political prisoners.
August 24—Citing election fraud, corruption, human rights abuses, and harassment of non-Somocista businessmen, UDEL condemns the government.

September 1977

September 7—Somoza returns from Miami and dismisses Cornelio Hueck and Gen. José Alegrett of GN for conspiring.
September 19—Martial law and press censorship are lifted in an effort to appease the Carter administration.
September 23—New U.S. Ambassador Maurice Solaun introduces the U.S. policy of human rights advocacy and political neutrality.

October 1977

October 5—President Carter restores military aid to Somoza.
October 10—Sergio Ramírez and the Group of Twelve prepare a provisional government in Costa Rica.
October 12–13—Squadrons of the FSLN-TI's Carlos Fonseca Northern Front (FNCF) ambush GN patrols at Finca San Fabian near Ocotal, Nueva Segovia, and kill fifteen guardsmen with no losses to themselves. The thirty-two-man column includes Daniel Ortega, Germán Pomares, Victor Tirado, Joaquín Cuadra, Francisco Rivera, and Dora María Tellez.
October 13—Twenty-five combatants of the TI's Benjamin Zeledon Southern Front (FSBZ) launch an assault from the Solentiname Islands on the fifty-man GN post at San Carlos. Another FSBZ squadron takes Cardenas in the Rivas department.
October 14—Realizing that the Tercerista offensive would not succeed, the Twelve issue a document (later published in *La Prensa*) calling for the resignation of Somoza and the inclusion of the FSLN in a provisional government.

October 17—Fourteen-man TI squadron launches unsuccessful attack on the GN barracks in Masaya, while three others ambush a 150-man GN reinforcement column.

October 23—Archbishop Obando and Nicaraguan Development Institute (INDE) president Alfonso Robelo form a National Dialogue committee, with the backing of UDEL and the Superior Council of Private Initiative (COSIP). Somoza refuses to negotiate.

October 25—Three TI squads take the village of San Fernando.

November—GN sacks the Solentiname community in retaliation for the attack on San Carlos.

November 11—Father Ernesto Cardenal becomes an FSLN militant, motivated by his commitment to the Gospel. Somoza lifts price and currency controls for the first time in thirty years.

December—Ambassador Solaun arranges dialogue between Somoza and the opposition, with high hopes for change.

December 27—The FSLN-DN (Tercerista) rejects the national dialogue; calls for a popular insurrection based on a moderate thirteen-point program.

1978
January 1978

January 9—Bishop's Conference pastoral letter denounces state terror and concentration of wealth.

January 10—Editor of *La Prensa* and UDEL opposition leader Pedro Joaquín Chamorro is gunned down on the streets of Managua. The public blames Somoza and violence erupts.

January 11–12—Rioters in Managua set fire to Somoza-owned buildings; 30,000 attend Chamorro's funeral.

January 23—The UDEL, now led by Rafael Cordova Rivas, calls a general strike to demand an investigation into Chamorro's death and Somoza's resignation. Business associations, congressional Conservatives, and trade union federations endorse the strike.

January 24—Factories close, but many small businesses stay open. 50 percent closure is achieved in Managua, 80 percent in most provincial cities. Demonstrations become daily occurrences.

January 28—GN, under the state of emergency, attacks public gatherings in Managua.

January 30—GN attacks UNAN-Managua students and tear-gasses 200 upper-class women at Managua UN office. Central Bank and ESSO oil refinery workers join the strike.

January 31—Venezuelan unions embargo oil exports to Nicaragua. Killings continue as the GN breaks up demonstrations.

February 1978

February 2—Strike begins to break.

February 2–3—Camilo Ortega leads a 330-person TI unit in an attack on the La Polvora barracks in Granada. Pastora and Father Gaspar García Laviana lead a forty-person column in an unsuccessful assault on the Rivas GN post, after taking the Peñas Blancas border post. Battles break out between GN patrols and Carlos Fonseca Northern Front guerrillas, led by Pomares, Tirado, and Daniel Ortega, in Santa Clara and El Rosario areas of Nueva Segovia. FSLN attacks Jalapa.

February 4—FSLN destroys cotton warehouses in the port of Corinto and ambushes a patrol of the First Armored Battalion near Managua.

February 5—Municipal elections are boycotted by most voters. Dialogue talks are canceled.

February 9—Archbishop Obando publishes a letter in *La Prensa* stating that armed resistance is acceptable as a last resort.

February 20–28—GN tear-gasses a crowd gathered in the Monimbo Indian barrio of Masaya to hear a mass in memory of Chamorro. The riot turns into insurrection as the residents resist the GN. FSLN militants Camilo Ortega, Arnoldo Quant, and Moises Ribera are killed on February 26 as they try to slip through GN lines to establish FSLN leadership of spontaneous revolt. Assaults on February 26–28 by 600 troops under Major Somoza with air and armor support retake the barrio. Up to 200 civilians die in the fighting and clean-up operations.

February 26—40,000 attend pro-Somoza rally in Managua.

February 27—Fighting breaks out between the GN and rioters in Diriamba.

February 27—GN storms the UNAN campus, killing three students.

February 28—GN attacks armed barricades and students in the Subtiava Indian barrio of León.

March 1978

Nicaraguan Democratic Movement (MDN), with 3,000 members, is founded by Alfonso Robelo made up largely of businessmen and commercial farmers. TI sends its forty members into the northern cities to prepare for insurrection.

March 1—One-day strike is called by UDEL; it is sporadically observed.

March 2—Riots break out in León and Jinotepe.

March 8—Kidnapping and murder of Gen. Reynaldo Pérez Vega is engineered by FSLN militant Nora Astorga.

March 28—Renewed protests break out in Monimbo.

April 1978

April 3—FSLN robs a BANAMER branch bank in Managua.

April 6—60,000 students in sixty schools begin a strike that ends in early May when Somoza agrees to improve conditions for political prisoners.

April 20—GN forcefully ends the hunger strike of forty students at a Masaya school. Three Managua factory workers are killed when the GN fires on a demonstration.

May 1978

FAO (Broad Opposition Front) formed by UDEL, MDN, Socialist party (PSN), and other political and labor groups. Alfonso Robelo is named leader.
May 16—U.S. Congressman Charles Wilson gets $12.5 million in development aid approved for Nicaragua after threatening to hold up the Panama Canal treaties. President Carter refuses to release $5.3 million in military credits.
May 25—3,000 riot in Estelí.

June 1978

FSLN-Insurrectional (Terceristas) issue a twenty-five-point program. Three FSLN tendencies agree to coordinate tactics, but little progress is actually made toward reunification.
June 1—Sandinistas rob a Managua bank.
June 17—Somoza government drops legal charges against the Twelve.
June 20—Somoza invites the Inter-American Human Rights Commission to inspect Nicaragua.
June 29—Student strike to free political prisoners begins.

July 1978

Major business and sales tax increases are imposed to meet the government credit crisis. Sandinista raids near the Costa Rican border provokes the recall of Nicaragua's ambassador to Costa Rica.
July 5—A crowd of 30,000 greets ten members of the Twelve as they arrive at the Managua airport. Declaring themselves Sandinistas, they join the FAO and tour the country promoting a national unity government.
July 9—Several civilians are killed in rioting in Jinotepe.
July 15—DN-GPP member José Benito Escobar is gunned down in Estelí.
July 17—United People's Movement (MPU) formed by twenty-two student, labor, and political organizations representing the TP and GPP as well as the Socialist (PSN) and Communist (PCdeN) parties. Under the leadership of Moises Hassan, the MPU serves as FSLN's urban mobilization arm (PCdeN).
July 19—The FAO calls a one-day strike to protest GN repression of pro-Twelve demonstrations. GN clashes with protesters in Estelí and Monimbo.
July 20—Fernando ("El Negro") Chamorro fires two rockets at Somoza's Managua bunker from the Intercontinental Hotel, but misses; he is captured and imprisoned.

July 25—Bishop's Conference calls for Somoza's resignation. Its declaration is endorsed by the FAO and Alfredo Pellas, head of the BANAMER business group.

August 1978

August 1—Somoza releases to the press a June 30 letter to him from President Carter praising improvements in human rights.

August 11—Somoza purges GN regional chiefs for using "excessive force," in an effort to blunt public criticism and head off coup attempts.

August 21—FAO publishes a sixteen-point plan for a transitional government and free elections. Prepares for a general strike.

August 22–24—FSLN commandos under Edén Pastora, Hugo Torres, and Dora María Tellez capture the National Congress to gain release of Tomás Borge and fifty-eight other prisoners, $500,000, and passage to Panama.

August 25—FAO begins an open-ended general strike which hampers the government's tax collection efforts. Urban riots sweep the country.

August 27–September 2—Rioting associated with the general strike develops into a spontaneous insurrection in Matagalpa by 200–500 armed *muchachos* and a few GPP militants. Aerial bombardment and infantry assaults by 400 elite EEBI reinforcements under Major Somoza begin on August 29. Red Cross estimates that eighty civilians are killed and 400 wounded in the fighting, bombardment, and mop-up operations. GN regains control of the city by September 3.

August 28—Somoza arrests Lt. Col. Bernardino Larios and several other GN officers for plotting a coup.

August 29—Somoza revokes the Chamber of Commerce charter and threatens to confiscate the assets of striking firms.

September 1978

September 3—200 FAO and business leaders are arrested for refusing to abandon the strike. A government spokesman accuses the U.S. State Department Human Rights Bureau of Marxism.

September 4—The White House National Security Council holds its first meeting on Nicaragua; it recommends support for Costa Rican mediation.

September 9—150 Terceristas launch coordinated attacks on GN posts in Managua, Masaya, León, Chinandega, and Estelí. Large numbers of civilians armed with hunting rifles and machetes join the revolt, besieging GN garrisons in the latter four cities. TP and GPP cadres decide to join in the revolt despite reservations. GN garrisons hold, while elite troops backed by tanks and airplanes retake the cities one at a time.

September 10—GN police station in Masaya's Monimbo barrio is overrun by 300 armed rebels.

September 11—GN's General Somoza armored battalion begins counter-attack on Masaya, backed by helicopters and armored cars.

September 12—150-person FSLN–Southern Front (FSBZ) column armed with heavy weapons is repulsed by 300 GN defenders at Peñas Blancas and Sapoa on the Costa Rican border. Fighting breaks out in Diriamba.

September 13—Somoza declares martial law. GN retakes Masaya, with over 300 civilian casualties. President Carazo of Costa Rica expropriates Somoza's holdings in Costa Rica.

September 14—FAO nominates Alfonso Robelo, Rafael Cordova Rivas, and Sergio Ramírez (representing the Twelve and indirectly the Terceristas) to participate in mediations. GN troops try to force Managua businesses to open.

September 15—Venezuela signs a defense pact with Costa Rica, marking the beginning of a major weapons shipments to the FSLN from Venezuela.

September 16—GN retakes León after three days of street fighting.

September 17—FSBZ led by Pastora and Daniel Ortega takes Peñas Blancas, but retreats after a GN counterattack. Estelí is surrounded by 1,200 Guard troops and subjected to heavy bombardment.

September 18—Rigoberto López Pérez Western Front (FORL) units led by Blas Real withdraw from Chinandega. At El Sauce, León GN units ambush FSLN guerrillas retreating to Chinandega and Estelí.

September 19—U.S. Embassy proposes a mediated solution to the crisis.

September 20—The September insurrection ends when the GN retakes Estelí, which is sealed off as mop-up operations continue. Red Cross estimates that 1,500–5,000 die in the September uprising, with Estelí hardest hit. The FSLN gains thousands of recruits.

September 22—The United States warns Torrijos about using his bombers to support the FSLN.

September 23—OAS resolution endorses mediation.

September 25—FAO general strike ends.

September 30—Somoza agrees to mediation with FAO, but says he will serve out his term until May 1981 and run for reelection. Attacks Venezuela, Panama, Costa Rica, and Cuba for supporting the FSLN.

October 1978

MPU begins organizing Civil Defense Committees (CDCs) to build a resource and organizational base for future urban uprisings. FSLN guerrillas reorganize and train. GN recruiting drive brings its strength up to 14,000.

October 3–12—OAS Human Rights Commission inspects Nicaragua.

October 4—The Ortega brothers declare that the TI would reject any mediation designed to achieve "Somocismo sin Somoza." Quietly allows S. Ramírez to negotiate for the FSLN.

October 5—FAO accepts U.S. mediation offer to negotiate Somoza's resignation. Refuses face-to-face talks with the regime.

October 6—Mediation team, comprised of William Bowdler, Adm. Ramón Emilio Jiménez (the Dominican Republic's foreign minister), and Alfredo Obiols Gómez (Guatemala), arrives in Managua.

October 25—Ramírez and six other members of the Twelve announce their withdrawal from the mediation effort and the FAO. FSLN resumes military harassment of the regime, with a strength of about 2,500.

November 1978

November 1—Blas Real Espinales, leader of the Chinandega revolt, and several others are killed.

November 14—Carter decides to propose negotiating terms for free plebiscite.

November 17—The Inter-American Commission on Human Rights report, strongly condemns abuses of the regime.

November 21—FAO outlines terms and conditions for direct talks. Costa Rica severs diplomatic relations with Nicaragua after four members of its Civil Guard are killed in border fighting with the GN.

December 1978

December 4—FSLN announces in Mexico City that negotiations between the TI, TP, and GPP have resulted in an agreement to unite in the future. Fidel Castro has exerted strong pressure to unify as a condition of Cuban aid. Luis Pallais flies to Washington on a secret mission; presents three questions about Somoza's departure: (1) Could Somoza and his entourage get asylum in the US? (2) Would the United States extradite him? (3) Would his assets be secure from seizure?

December 9—FSLN communique is issued in Havana. Father Gaspar García and four members of a FSBZ squad are killed in combat in Cardenas. Sporadic skirmishes continue on the Costa Rican border.

December 10—Under U.S. pressure, the remaining members of the FAO agree to direct talks with Somoza representatives.

December 15—UN General Assembly Resolution 33/76 condemns repression by the Nicaraguan government and its violation of Costa Rican territory.

December 20—Mediation team presents detailed plebiscite proposal; Bowdler delivers ultimatum to Somoza.

December 21—Lt. Gen. Dennis McAuliffe of the U.S. Southern Command in Panama tries to talk Somoza into resigning.

1979
January 1979

January 9—Luis Medrano Flores, leader of the moderate CUS trade union federation, Nicaragua's third largest labor group, is gunned down on the streets of Managua.

January 11—The Mediation team returns to Managua with a proposal for an internationally supervised plebiscite. Both Somoza's PLN and FAO express reservations. Washington threatens to reassess relations with Somoza unless a plan acceptable to the FAO can be negotiated.

January 19—Guerrillas engage GN near Hacienda El Descanso, Estelí. The FAO calls the mediation "closed."

February 1979

FSLN column briefly occupies Yali, Jinotega.

February 1—3,000 in the Managua baseball stadium celebrate the formation of the National Patriotic Front (FPN) from the MPU and the Twelve.

February 8—Washington terminates all military agreements with Nicaragua, places a moratorium on future economic aid, recalls the Peace Corps, and reduces U.S. Embassy staff by half.

February 14—FSLN attacks the customs house in Peñas Blancas.

February 21—FSLN simultaneously assaults GN in Diriamba, Granada, León, Masaya, and Managua barrios. Campaign of economic sabotage is launched to cut export revenues.

March 1979

Three Conservative factions unite to form the Democratic Conservative party (PCD), with Fernando Aguero, Rafael Cordova Rivas, Clement Guido, and Adolfo Calero as executive council.

March 7—A nine-man combined National Directorate (FSLN-DNC) is named, with three representatives from each tendency. Military units begin to integrate. Costa Rica's Radio Sandino improves military and propaganda coordination. Significant military aid begins to flow from Cuba.

March 12—Luis Herrera Campins becomes president of Venezuela and suspends the material support provided the FSLN by former President Carlos Andrés Pérez.

March 26—Germán Pomares and eighty guerrillas of the FNCF Oscar Turcios column briefly occupy El Jicaro, Nueva Segovia, and attack the GN post as part of a FNCF strategy to draw GN troops into the northern highlands. Pomares withdraws to the mountains of El Chipote.

March 30—FSLN units attack San Carlos and San Juan del Norte on the Rio San Juan and the towns of Rivas, Tola, and Potosí.

April 1979

The 140-man Jacinto Hernández column under Oscar Benavides and Ivan Montenegro crosses the Rio San Juan from Costa Rica to open a new front in southern Jelaya and draw GN forces away from the southern border. Ambassador Pezzullo, serving in Uruguay, accepts transfer to Nicaragua to deal with the crisis.

April 7—Units of the FSLN occupy El Sauce and attack Condega and Ducualo, north of Estelí. FAN retaliates with air strikes. Guerrillas shoot down two planes.

April 8—Central Bank announces a 43 percent devaluation of the cordova in an effort to secure an IMF loan. This reflects the rapidly deteriorating economic situation marked by surging inflation, high unemployment, and capital flight.

April 8–13—Francisco Rivera leads the 200-person Filemon Rivera column into Estelí, forcing the GN garrison to retreat to its barracks. Many civilians join the battle. Rivera holds the city, which comes under FAN bombardment and 1,000-man GN counterattack.

April 10—FSLN guerrillas hit Yali; Turcios column attacks Wiwili to take pressure off Estelí.

April 13—Diversionary attacks outside Estelí enable Rivera to slip through GN lines and escape with over 100 new recruits, while GN mop-up operations commence.

April 16—GN attacks a León safe house, killing Edgar Lang and five other FORL-FSLN leaders.

April 29—100 guerrillas battle the GN for six hours in León.

April 30—In an effort to head off a May Day strike, the government arrests forty FAO political and labor leaders, including Alfonso Robelo and Rafael Cordova Rivas. The United States protests the arrests.

May 1979

May 1—Strikes and demonstrations go on despite arrests.

May 7—National student strike begins.

May 8—GN discovers the Jacinto Hernández column at Cano El Chacalin, Zelaya. Up to 1,000 GN troops are airlifted into the Nueva Guinea area of Zelaya and San Juan and surround the Jacinto Hernández column at Hacienda El Tori Bayo, Rio San Juan. Suffering heavy casualties, the Sandinistas break through GN lines and flee to the west.

May 10—GN barracks in Matagalpa are attacked by eighty guerrillas.

May 14—IMF approves loan of $66 million to Nicaragua over U.S. objections.

May 15—GN posts in Wiwili and Masaya are attacked.

May 16—Costa Rica assures the United States it is not trafficking in arms, while arranging for direct Cuban flights that deliver over 30,000 pounds of arms in twenty-one flights between late May and July 19. State Department's Conference of Chiefs of Missions convenes in Costa Rica, discusses whether or not Somoza could be convinced to step down when he finishes his term in 1981.

May 17—Surviving members of FSLN's Jacinto Hernández column are wiped out at Paso de Las Yeguas, Rio San Juan.

May 19–22—Pomares's 500-strong Turcios column (FNCF) prematurely attacks the city of Jinotega. Outgunned by the GN, Pomares withdraws on May 22 and dies on May 24 of wounds. Javier Carrión assumes command.

May 20—After meeting with Castro and President Rodrigo Carazo of Costa Rica, Mexico's president severs diplomatic relations with the Somoza government.

May 21—Fighting breaks out in Rivas.

May 28—The final offensive begins, with over 100 guerrillas of the Pablo Ubeda Northeastern Front (FNPU) seizing the northern Zelaya mining towns of Rosita and Bonanza. The Sandinistas withdraw to the mountains with 250 new recruits.

May 29—Edén Pastora leads a 350-man column of the FSBZ across the Costa Rican border to seize the area around El Naranjo on the Pacific coast. GN airlifts troops to El Ostinal to stem this southern front attack. For the next eleven days, artillery pins down the Sandinistas dug in on Colina 155, west of El Naranjo. Uprising begins in Rivas.

June 1979

June 2—FORL units attack Chinandega and El Viejo in conjunction with 500 civilian recruits. Repulsed by the GN garrison, they retreat to El Chonco and Tonala bases.

June 3—180 cadres of the FORL directed by Dora María Tellez and field commanders Leopoldo Rivas and Leticia Herrera mobilize the León militia forces and attack the 600-man GN garrison. Fighting continues until 9 July.

June 4—A joint FAO-FSLN coordinated general strike closes down factories and businesses throughout the country. OAS meeting rejects a Nicaraguan resolution invoking the Rio Treaty against Costa Rica for allowing the FSLN to invade Nicaragua. El Godoy airport in León falls to rebels.

June 5—The Oscar Turcios column (FNCF) under Javier Carrión enters Matagalpa, links with GPP cadres and civilian recruits, and begins a month of street fighting for control of the city. Other guerrilla columns, including elements of the Santos López brigade under Bayardo Arce, join the Sandinista attack on Matagalpa. Fighting erupts in the Carazo cities of Jinotepe and Diriamba. General Torrijos of Panama pledges not to interfere in Nicaragua's affairs.

June 7—FNCF attacks Ocotal, Nueva Segovia.

June 9—The FNCF under Francisco Rivera enters Estelí and mobilizes a popular insurrection that puts the GN garrison under siege. Pressured by EEBI troops under Pablo Emilio Salazar (Commander Bravo), the 600–800 man FSBZ force at El Naranjo withdraws to Costa Rica to regroup. 500 EEBI troops are sent north to reinforce Managua. The Eastern Front (FORH) under Luis Carrión opens its offensive with an attack on Presillitas, Zelaya. GN reinforcements turn back the attack.

June 9–27—Fighting breaks out in the eastern and western barrios of Managua, directed by the Internal Front (FI) under Carlos Nuñez, Joaquín Cuadra, and William Ramírez. The GN and some 300 FSLN regulars and 1,200 militia members battle for control of the barrios.

June 10—San Rafael del Norte, Jinotega, is occupied by elements of the Santos López brigade FNCF) moving northwest from La Concordia.

June 11—Sierra 13 police station in eastern Managua is overrun by the FI. FSLN control is strongest in eastern barrios; access to Las Mercedes airport is cut. GN destroys *La Prensa*. Aerial bombardment of Managua by the FAN begins.

June 12—The GN concentrates counterattack on Managua's eastern barrios. Carter approves the U.S. National Security Council (NSC) plan to link Somoza's departure with peace force and transitional government.

June 13—GN counterattack on FNCF positions in Matagalpa is repulsed.

June 14—The Jorge Sinforoso Bravo column (FNCF) liberates Condega, then heads south to join the battle for Estelí.

June 15—FSBZ, with 1,000–1,500 men and newly arrived artillery, attacks from Costa Rica and takes Peñas Blancas by surprise. Positional trench warfare develops along the lakeside Pan-American Highway, tying down large numbers of GN troops. Beginning of Carter-Brezhnev summit in Vienna.

June 16—Sapoa falls to the FSBZ. The FSLN announces the creation of the Government of National Reconstruction (JGRN). Its executive junta consists of D. Ortega, Moises Hassan, Violeta Chamorro, Robelo, and S. Ramírez. The countries of the Andean Group grant belligerent status to the opposition forces.

June 17—The "21" Jail in León falls to the FORL.

June 18—Continuing guerrilla action in the Rivas area supports the Southern Front campaign. *New York Times* reporter Alan Riding interviews Sandinistas in Managua barrios. One hundred U.S. congressmen and five senators sign a letter supporting Somoza. Ambassador Pezzullo meets with Foreign Minister Pallais in Washington.

June 19—The Central Command barracks in León falls and the GN retreats to Fort Acosasco. First Armored "Somoza" Battalion spearheads a major assault on Managua's eastern barrios. Ammunition for the FI is running low. Defense of the western barrios begins to fall. FSLN junta in San José broadcasts its Plan de Gobierno. NSC meeting in Washington (with Pezzullo in attendance) outlines peace plan.

June 20—ABC news reporter Bill Stewart is executed at a GN checkpoint in Managua. Film of the incident is broadcast on U.S. television, increasing American hostility to Somoza. An administrative junta is set up in León. The FORH column attacks Santo Tomás, Chotales, while turning back GN reinforcements from Nueva Guinea. GN abandons Santo Tomás, La Gateada, and Rama.

June 21—The OAS Consultation of Ministers rejects a proposal by U.S. Secretary of State Cyrus Vance that Somoza be replaced with a national reconciliation government supported by an OAS peace-keeping force. Panama breaks relations with the Somoza government and recognizes the new junta. FSLN plane tries to bomb Somoza's bunker.

June 22—The FORL overruns the GN command post in Chichigalpa. Sandinistas liberate Diriamba. Brzezinski makes a case for U.S. intervention at a breakfast meeting; Vance and Brown are opposed. Carter rules out unilateral intervention.

June 23—The OAS approves Venezuelan resolution supporting opposition forces and early free elections. Eastern barrios of Managua suffer heavy helicopter bombardment. NCS meeting (with Pezzullo in attendance) reviews events and sees the military situation as a standoff. Carter makes state visits to Korea and Japan and attends the Tokyo summit.

June 24—GN garrison falls at Masaya. Col. Fermin Meneses Galla withdraws his troops to the hilltop fortress of Coyotepe and continues to shell the city. FAO endorses the junta. FORL units from Chichigalpa take the San Antonio sugar mill. Recommendation by Special Coordinating Committee (SCC) of the NSC is cabled to Carter in Tokyo, who refuses to unconditionally support a post-Somoza GN. He approves proposal to designate new GN commander and to form an Executive Committee, or ExCom (of "wise men") to head the transitional government.

June 25—Carter returns to Washington; SCC meeting (Pezzullo in attendance) recommends a two-pronged strategy: influence the junta while trying to establish an ExCom. CIA update is given.

June 26—Brazil breaks relations with Somoza. FSBZ is bogged down in the Peñas Blancas area. Rivas barracks put under siege. Pezzullo flies to Panama, meets with Torrijos.

June 27—Ambassador Pezzullo arrives in Managua and has first meeting with Somoza in his bunker, attended by U.S. Congressman Murphy and Pallais. COSEP endorses the junta. Ambassador W. Bowdler and A. Moss meet with the junta in San José. Retreat from Managua: at night the FI evacuates the eastern barrios of Managua and retreats with 6,000 people to the liberated city of Masaya; completed on June 29.

June 28—Pezzullo has second meeting with Somoza, attended by Malcolm Barnebey and Lieutenant Colonel McCoy. The Nicaraguan Congress is called into session—most living at the Hotel Intercontinental. Pezzullo meets with Archbishop Obando and cables Washington that "wise man" scheme is a nonstarter. Mini-SCC meeting decides not to abandon "wise man" idea. The *New York Times* discloses a four-point U.S. plan.

June 29—After a third meeting with Somoza, Pezzullo holds press conference and meets with Ismael Reyes. Arturo Cruz talks to State's director of Central American affairs and rejects "wise man" idea. At a mini-SCC meeting, Vaky says the United States should look for a way to stop the fighting; the "wise man" idea is nonviable. Pezzullo issues visas to Somoza and his entourage.

June 30—Achuapa, León, is liberated by elements of the FNCF. Pezzullo cables Washington that GN can be reconstituted and "wise man" idea is extremely problematic. Vaky tries to convince Pastor to abandon the idea. Robelo and Alfredo César draft a moderate social democratic "Program of the Government of National Reconstruction," which (to their surprise) the FSLN accepts. McCoy meets with GN colonels to discuss post-Somoza GN. They are shocked and report immediately to El Chiguín.

July 1979

July 1—Pezzullo flies to Washington with Bowdler to report on progress of talks.

July 2—GN withdraws from Matagalpa to Cerro Calvario. SCC meeting with Pezzullo, Bowdler, Moss, and others. Pezzullo lays to rest the ExCom "wise man" idea. Brzezinski presents four points, which include expanding the junta. Pezzullo is impressed by Carter and how he is not being served by his staff.

July 3—300 combatants from the Internal Front leave Masaya for Diriamba. FNCF units from Estelí take the road junction to Sebaco, key to control of the northern meseta. Pezzullo, Moss, and Bowdler stop for the night in Guatemala. Bowdler and Pezzullo meet with Col. Inocente Mojica, possible future GN commander. Carter meets secretly with Torrijos, who agrees to talk to the junta about expanding.

July 4—Pezzullo returns to Managua and holds fourth meeting with Somoza. Carter receives birthday greetings from Somoza and Sevilla-Sacasa.

July 5—Internal Front troops attack Jinotepe and San Marcos from Diriamba.

July 6—Sandinistas gain control of Carazo with the fall of Jinotepe, San Marcos, and Masatepe. GN defenders retreat to Granada. Road communications are cut between Managua and GN units on the Southern Front. Somoza tells Karen De Young of the *Washington Post* that he is going to leave.

July 7—The Fortin de Acosasco in León falls to Leticia Herrera of the FORL. After emerging from the Cordillera Chontalena, the FORH ambushes and defeats a GN force on the Rio Apompua and occupies La Palma the following day. Pezzullo cables Washington with an assessment of positions on the ground.

July 9—With surrender of the last GN stronghold, León is declared free. Tititapa, west of Managua, is liberated. At a SCC meeting, no progress is reported in the expansion of the junta.

July 10—GN fails to retake Sebaco junction west of Matagalpa. Tomás Borge and Daniel Ortega arrive in León. Congressmen Hansen (R-Idaho) and McDonald (D-Ga.) make a one-day trip to Nicaragua to bolster Somoza and criticize the press. The junta tells Bowdler in Costa Rica that they expect power to be transferred directly to them. Vaky tells Pastor that he doesn't think the Guard will hold. At a SCC meeting,

Brzezinski voices frustration; he decides to ask Torrijos, Pérez, and Carazco to pressure the junta to expand. Miguel D'Escoto holds a news conference.

July 11—Junta plan for a cease-fire is announced. Somoza makes a speech on television. Bowdler presents SCC ultimatum to junta in Puntarenas, Costa Rica.

July 12—Junta sends a letter to the OAS general secretary asking for OAS support. Bowdler meets again with the junta in San José.

July 13—Somoza flies to Guatemala to enlist military support and fails. U.S. airlifts food to Managua. SCC meeting comes up with five recommendations. Somoza calls President Carter to request an audience in Washington; Pastor takes the call.

July 14—Twelve members of the junta's cabinet are announced. Tomás Borge is the only FSLN commander among them. Pezzullo meets with Somoza and sets the timetable for Somoza's departure. Bowdler meets with the junta in San José to review the plan.

July 15—Pezzullo meets with Somoza, who picks Francisco Urcuyo to succeed him. Pezzullo and O'Donnell brief Urcuyo in Somoza's presence.

July 16—The besieged GN garrison of Estelí falls. Pezzullo meets with Somoza, who picks Colonel Mejia to head the new GN. O'Donnell briefs Urcuyo at the Intercontinental Hotel. GN officers with more than thirty years' experience are retired. Somoza meets with his field officers, says that he's being forced to leave and that the United States will give them aid once he's out of the country. Somoza gives Urcuyo last-minute instructions to continue negotiating with Pezzullo. SCC members are out of touch with events in Managua and San José. Pezzullo calls Mejia, who knows nothing about the transition plan.

July 17—Somoza sends resignation to Congress at 1 A.M. and flies to Miami. Once named president by Congress, Urcuyo violates the understanding on transfer of power by announcing plans to serve out Somoza's term until 1981. When Pezzullo wakes Urcuyo to talk to him, Urcuyo denies knowledge of the plan. Pezzullo calls Vaky, who asks him to try again. The SCC meets. C-141s loaded with food and medical relief from the United States prepare to land. FSLN is suspicious. Pezzullo receives call from GN Colonel Smith. At dawn, the FI's Rolando Orozco mobile battalion begins attack on Granada. FI units takes Daria and Diriomo, south of Masaya. GN units evacuate Cerro Calvario overlooking Matagalpa after resuppled FNCF units attack their positions. FORL troops from León take La Paz Centro on the road to Managua. Luis Carrión leads the FORH column into Juigalpa, capital of Chontales.

July 18—Christopher calls Somoza in Miami; Somoza calls Urcuyo. Pezzullo holds last meeting with Urcuyo, phones Christopher, meets with press, and evacuates embassy with most of the remaining staff. O'Donnell meets with General Mejia, who says that he's now got Urcuyo under control. Junta members Robelo, Chamorro, and Ramírez fly to León, the "provisional capital." La Povora fortress in Granada surrenders to FI's mobile battalion. GN air force defects to Honduras. Guardsmen from the Southern Front flee the country via the port of San Juan del Sur, Rivas. GN units in Jinotepe surrender; GN abandons its positions in Chinandega. Urcuyo meets with commanders and flies to Guatemala. Internal Front units advance on Managua from Masaya. Southern Front units from Tola and Rio Ostayo liberate Rivas and advance on Nandaime. Northern Front units from Estelí reach Managua. Other Northern Front units from Matagalpa link up in Boaca with the Eastern Front column from Juigalpa. Somoza sails for the Bahamas. GN General Mejia flees, leaving Lieutenant Colonel Largaspada of the Traffic Police in charge of the GN.

July 20—The DNC and the junta are installed in Managua.

Notes

Chapter 1

1. Notes of Ambassador Lawrence Pezzullo.
2. Notes of Ambassador Lawrence Pezzullo and Anastasio Somoza, Jr., as told to Jack Cox, *Nicaragua Betrayed* (Boston: Western Islands, 1980), p. 333.
3. Notes of Ambassador Pezzullo; Somoza, *Nicaragua Betrayed,* p. 335.
4. Ibid., p. 333.
5. Notes of Ambassador Pezzullo.
6. Somoza, *Nicaragua Betrayed,* pp. 340–41.
7. Notes of Ambassador Pezzullo; Somoza, *Nicaragua Betrayed,* p. 341.
8. Ibid., p. 347.
9. Ibid., p. 343; notes of Ambassador Pezzullo.
10. Cable U.S. Embassy, Managua, to Secretary of State, 28 June 1979, 2857, "The First Visit."

Chapter 2

1. *Time,* November 15, 1948, p. 40.
2. Somoza, *Nicaragua Betrayed,* p. xi.
3. William Krehm, *Democracies and Tyrannies of the Caribbean* (Westport, Conn.: Lawrence Hill, 1984), p. 104.
4. Lester D. Langley, *The Banana Wars* (Lexington: University of Kentucky Press, 1983), p. 217.

5. *Time*, November 15, 1948, p 40.

6. Krehm, *Democracies and Tyrannies of the Caribbean*, p. 104.

7. Richard Millet, *Guardians of the Dynasty* (New York: Orbis Books, 1977) p. 55.

8. Gregorio Selser, *Sandino* (Monthly Review Press, 1981), p. 117.

9. Carleton Beals, "With Sandino in Nicaragua," *Nation*, March 28, 1929, p. 341.

10. Millet, *Guardians of the Dynasty*, p. 66.

11. Bernard Diederich, *Somoza and the Legacy of U.S. Involvement in Central America* (New York: Dutton, 1981), p.50.

12. Krehm, *Democracies and Tyrannies of the Caribbean*, p. 107.

13. *Time*, November 15, 1948, p. 40.

14. Krehm, *Democracies and Tyrannies of the Caribbean*, p. 110.

15. *Time*, November 15, 1948, p. 43.

16. Krehm, *Democracies and Tyrannies of the Caribbean*, p. 120.

17. *Time*, November 15, 1948, p. 39.

18. Ibid., p. 40.

19. Ibid., p. 39.

20. Ibid.

21. Ibid.

22. Ibid.

23. Ibid.

24. Diederich, *Somoza*, p. 16.

25. Krehm, *Democracies and Tyrannies of the Caribbean*, p. 121.

26. Diederich, *Somoza*, p. 40.

27. Patricia Taylor Edminster, *Nicaragua Divided: La Prensa and the Chamorro Legacy* (Pensacola: University of Florida Press, 1990), p. 21.

28. Diederich, *Somoza*, p. 48.

Chapter 3

1. R. S. Leiken and Barry Rubin, eds., *Central American Crisis Reader* (New York: Summit, 1987), p. 197.

2. Notes of Ambassador Lawrence Pezzullo.

3. Ibid.

4. Interview with Viron (Pete) Vaky, April 28, 1991, Baltimore, Maryland.

5. *Time*, January 23, 1978, p.19.

6. Diederich, *Somoza*, p. 155.

7. "World Beat," *Atlas World Press Review*, January 1978.

8. Claribel Alegria and D. J. Flakoll, *Nicaragua: La Revolución Sandinista—Una Crónica Política* (Mexico City: Seria Popular Era, 1982), p. 303.

9. Diederich, *Somoza*, p. 158.

10. Ibid., p. 160.

11. Ibid., p. 162.

12. Pilar Arias, ed., *Nicaragua: Revolución—Relatos de Combatientes del Frente Sandinista* (Mexico City: Siglo Veintiuno, 1980), p. 153.

13. Ibid.

14. Ibid., p. 154.

15. For more on Los Doce, see chapter 8.

16. Susan Meiselas, *Nicaragua, June 1978–July 1979* (New York: Pantheon, 1981), p. 83.

17. Phillip Zwerling and Connie Martin, *Nicaragua—A New Kind of Revolution* (Westport, Conn.: Lawrence Hill, 1982) p. 7.

18. Arias, ed., *Nicaragua: Revolución*, p. 162.

19. Zwerling and Martin, *Nicaragua—A New Kind of Revolution*, p. 7.

20. Ibid.

21. Interview with Luis Pallais, February 20, 1991, Miami, Florida.

22. Zwerling and Martin, *Nicaragua—A New Kind of Revolution*, pp. 7–8.

23. Diederich, *Somoza*, p. 179.

24. Somoza, *Nicaragua Betrayed*, p. 152.

25. Diederich, *Somoza*, p. 179.

26. Somoza, *Nicaragua Betrayed*, p. 153.

27. Zwerling and Martin, *Nicaragua—A New Kind of Revolution*, p. 9.

28. Robert A. Pastor, *Condemned to Repetition: The United States and Nicaragua* (Princeton, N.J.: Princeton University Press, 1987), p. 91.

29. Somoza, *Nicaragua Betrayed*, p. 316.

30. Pastor, *Condemned to Repetition*, p. 79.

31. Diederich, *Somoza*, p. 208.

32. Interview with Viron (Pete) Vaky, April 28, 1991, Baltimore, Maryland.

33. Pastor, *Condemned to Repetition*, p. 107.

34. Diederich, *Somoza*, p. 210.

35. *Washington Post*, November 21, 1978.

36. Somoza, *Nicaragua Betrayed*, p. 329.

37. Ibid., p. 330.

38. Ibid., p. 331.

39. Ibid., p. 328.

40. Interview with Luis Pallais, February 20, 1991, Miami, Florida.

41. Pastor, *Condemned to Repetition*, p. 114.

42. Ibid.

43. Shirley Christian, *Nicaragua: Revolution in the Family* (New York: Random House, 1985), pp. 86–87.

44. Diederich, *Somoza*, p. 231.

45. Ibid., p. 229.

46. Tomás Borge, Carlos Fonseca, Daniel Ortega, Humberto Ortega, and Jaime Wheelock, *Sandinistas Speak* (New York: Pathfinder Press, 1982), p. 68.

47. For more on the three tendencies of the Sandinista Front, see chap. 8.

48. Christian, *Nicaragua: Revolution in the Family*, p. 89.

49. Interview with Mario Rapaccoli, Managua, Nicaragua, February 18, 1991.

50. Alejandro Murguia, *Southern Front* (Tempe, Arizona: Bilingual Press, 1990), p. 22.

51. Ibid.

52. Pastor, *Condemned to Repetition*, p. 76.

53. Interview with Viron (Pete) Vaky, April 28, 1991, Baltimore, Maryland.

54. H. Ortega in *Sandinistas Speak*, p. 77.

55. Asembla Legislativa, San José, Costa Rica, Informe Sobre el Trafico de Armas, Primera Parte, Epe 8768, cited in Pastor, *Condemned to Repetition*, p. 125.

56. Pastor, *Condemned to Repetition*, p. 117.

57. Interview with Viron (Pete) Vaky.

58. Interview with Luis Pallais, February 20, 1991, Miami, Florida.

Chapter 4

1. Diederich, *Somoza*, p. 271

2. *Time*, January 1, 1973.

3. Doris Tijerino, as told to Margaret Randall, *Inside the Nicaraguan Revolution* (Vancouver: New Star Books, 1978), p. 127.

4. *Time*, January 15, 1973.

5. Notes of Ambassador Lawrence Pezzullo.

6. Ibid.

7. Ibid.

8. Patricia Taylor Edminsten, *Nicaragua Divided: La Prensa and the Chamorro Legacy* (Pensacola: University of Florida Press, 1990), p. 57.

9. Diederich, *Somoza*, p. 2.

10. Ibid.

11. Pedro Joaquín Chamorro Cardenal, *Estripe Sangrienta: Los Somozas* (Mexico City: Ediciones Patria y Libertad, 1957), p. 87.

12. Ibid., p. 89.

13. Ibid.. p. 232.

14. *Time*, May 5, 1958

15. "Crisis in Central America: Revolution in Nicaragua," Frontline (4/10/85), WGBH Transcripts, pp. 2–3.

16. Ibid., p. 4.

17. Somoza, *Nicaragua Betrayed*, p. 173.

18. Ibid.

19. Interview with Luis Pallais, February 20, 1991, Miami, Florida.

20. Leiken and Rubin, *Central American Crisis Reader,* pp. 141–42.
21. Ibid., pp. 145-46.
22. Diederich, *Somoza,* p. 102.

Chapter 5

1. Pastor, *Condemned to Repetition,* p. 133.
2. *Miami Herald,* June 23, 1979.
3. *State Department Bulletin,* August 1979, pp. 56–59.
4. Notes of Ambassador Lawrence Pezzullo.
5. Viron Vaky, letter to the authors, February 1992.
6. Pastor, *Condemned to Repetition,* p. 145.
7. Ibid., p. 148.
8. *Miami Herald,* June 23, 1979.

Chapter 6

1. Roger Mendieta Alfaro, *El Último Marine* (Managua: Editorial Union Cardoza, 1979), p. 30.
2. Ibid.
3. Edén Pastora, quoted in Christopher Dickey, *With the Contras: A Reporter in the Wilds of Nicaragua* (New York: Simon & Schuster, 1987), pp. 34–35.
4. Ibid.
5. Somoza, *Nicaragua Betrayed,* pp. 237–38.
6. Humberto Oretga, quoted in *Sandinistas Speak,* p. 75.
7. Ibid.
8. Humberto Oretga, quoted in *Nicaragua: Revolución,* ed. Arias, p. 183.
9. Ibid.
10. *Miami Herald,* June 4, 1979.
11. Ibid.
12. Interview with Virginia Sanchez, August 4, 1991, Washington, D.C.
13. Marc Zimmerman, ed., *Nicaragua in Reconstruction and at War* (Minneapolis: MEP Publishers, 1985), p. 104.
14. Sánchez, *Comandate El Sobrino Presente!!* (Managua: Editorial Union Cardoza, 1979), pp. 10–11.
15. Mendieta Alfaro, *El Último Marine,* pp. 30–33.
16. Sánchez, *Comandante El Sobrino Presente!!* pp. 11–12.
17. Ibid., pp. 11–15.
18. Ibid.
19. Interview with Virginia Sanchez.

20. *Miami Herald,* June 13, 1979.
21. Mendieta Alfaro, *El Último Marine,* p. 270.
22. *Miami Herald,* June 27, 1979.
23. Mendieta Alfaro, *El Último Marine,* p. 32.
24. Interview with Virginia Sanchez.
25. Ernesto Cardenal, from *Zero Hour and Other Poems,* ed. Donald Walsh (New York: New Directions, 1980).
26. Humberto Ortega, in *Nicaragua: Revolución,* ed. Arias, p. 170.
27. Murguía, *Southern Front,* p. 23.
28. Diederich, *Somoza,* p. 253.
29. Christian, *Nicaragua: Revolution in the Family,* p. 97.

Chapter 7

1. From *El Nicaragüense,* cited in Leiken and Rubin, *Central American Crisis Reader,* p. 46.
2. From "Tutecotzumi," in *Selected Poems of Rubén Dario,* trans. Lysander Kemp (Austin: University of Texas Press, 1965), p. 97.
3. Cited in Octavio Paz's prologue to *Selected Poems of Rubén Dario,* p. 13.
4. "Intermezzo Tropicale," from *Poema del Otoño y Otros Poemas* (Madrid: Biblioteca Ateneo, 1910).
5. Pedro Joaquín Chamorro, *La Patria de Pedro* (Managua: La Prensa, 1981), pp. 80–81.
6. Carleton Beals, *Banana Gold* (Philadelphia: Lippincott, 1932), p. 156.
7. From *Selected Poems of Rubén Dario.*
8. Henri Weber, *Nicaragua: The Sandinista Revolution* (London: Verso/NLB, 1981), p. 103.
9. Secret cable from U.S. Embassy, Managua, to Secretary of State, 28 June 1979, Managua 2870, "The Current Scene."
10. Secret cable, U.S. Embassy, Managua, to Secretary of State, 29 June 1979, Managua 2886, "Second Visit."
11. Somoza, *Nicaragua Betrayed,* p. 350.
12. Ibid.
13. Ibid.
14. Ibid., p. 355.
15. Ibid., p. 357.
16. Ibid., p. 355.
17. Ibid., p. 360.
18. Notes of Ambassador Lawrence Pezzullo.
19. Leiken and Rubin, *Central American Crisis Reader,* p. 125.
20. Diederich, *Somoza,* p. 60.

21. Cited in Zimmerman, *Nicaragua in Reconstruction and War,* p. 95.

22. Diederich, *Somoza,* pp. 125–26.

23. *La Prensa,* February 8, 1978.

24. Notes of Ambassador Lawrence Pezzullo.

25. Secret cable, U.S. Embassy, Managua, to Secretary of State, 28 June 1979, Managua 2876.

26. Notes of Ambassador Lawrence Pezzullo.

27. Ibid.

28. Ibid.

29. Secret cable, U.S. Embassy, Managua, to Secretary of State, 28 June 1979, Managua 2870, "The Current Scene."

Chapter 8

1. Tomás Borge, *Carlos, El Amanecer Ya No Es Una Tentación* (Havana: Ediciones Casa de las Américas, 1980), p. 20.

2. Carlos Fonseca, "A Nicaraguan in Moscow," *Bajo la Bandera del Sandinismo: Textos Políticos* (Managua: Editorial Nueva Nicaragua, 1981), p. 45.

3. Borge, *Carlos,* p. 24.

4. Ibid., p. 27.

5. Ibid., p. 37.

6. Daniel Waksman Schinca, interview in *El Día* (Mexico City), April 4, 1979.

7. Borge, *Carlos,* p. 42.

8. Omas Cabezas, *Fire From the Mountain* (New York: Crown, 1985), pp. 21–22.

9. Denis Lynn and Daly Heyck, *Life Stories of the Nicaraguan Revolution* (New York: Routledge, 1990), p. 65.

10. Henry Ruiz, "La Montaña era come in Crisol desde se forjaban los mejores cuadras," *Nicarauac,* no. 1 (May–June 1980), p. 18.

11. Cabezas, *Fire From the Mountain,* p. 28.

12. Heyck, *Life Stories,* p. 247.

13. Tina Rosenberg, *Children of Cain* (New York: William Morrow, 1991), p. 285.

14. Ibid.

15. David Nolan, *The Ideology of the Sandinistas and the Nicaraguan Revolution* (Miami: Univeristy of Miami Press, 1985), pp. 36–37.

16. Cabezas, *Fire From the Mountain,* p. 14.

17. Interview with Carolina C., Washington, D.C., August 3, 1991.

18. Heyck, *Life Stories,* p. 117.

19. Miguel Obando y Bravo, *Agonía en el Bunker* (Managua: Comisión de Promoción Social Arquidiocesana, 1990), p. 51.

20. Interview with Jaime Wheelock in *Latin American Perspectives* 6, no. 1 (Winter 1979), p. 122.

21. Borge, *Carlos,* p. 65.

22. Ibid.

23. Fonseca, *Bajo la Bandera del Sandinisimo,* pp. 308–09.

24. Borge, *Carlos,* p. 68.

25. *Miami Herald,* June 17, 1979.

26. Humberto Ortega Saavedra, *Cincuenta Años de Lucha Sandinista* (Mexico City: Editorial Diogenes, 1979), p. 150.

27. Interview with Daniel Ortega in *Latin American Perspectives* 6 (19), p. 115.

28. Interview with Humberto Ortega in *Granma* [Havana], August 21, 1979, p. 6.

29. Joaquín Cuadro Lacayo, quoted by Alan Riding, "National Mutiny in Nicaragua," *New York Times Magazine,* July 30, 1978, p. 47.

30. Interview with Arturo Cruz, August 3, 1991, Washington, D.C.

31. Obando y Bravo, *Agonía en el Bunker,* p. 81.

32. H. Ortega, in *Sandinistas Speak,* p. 68.

33. Obando y Bravo, *Agonía en el Bunker,* p. 142.

34. H. Ortega, in *Sandinistas Speak,* p. 66.

35. Interview with Jaime Wheelock in *Latin American Perspectives* 6, no. 1 (Winter 1979), pp. 124–25.

Chapter 9

1. Secret cable, U.S. Embassy, Managua, to Secretary of State, 30 June 1979, Managua 2911, "The Third Meeting."

2. Somoza, *Nicaragua Betrayed,* p. 362.

3. Interview with anonymous source, August 4, 1991, Washington, D.C.

4. Diederich, *Somoza,* p. 141.

5. Transcript of interview in Somoza, *Nicaragua Betrayed,* pp. 363–64.

6. Ibid., p. 365.

7. Ibid.

8. Ibid., p. 366.

9. Pastor, *Condemned to Repetition,* p. 176.

10. Secret cable, U.S. Embassy, Managua, to Secretary of State, 30 June 1979, Managua 2913, "Somoza Should Resign—The GN Could Maintain Cohesion."

11. Secret cable, U.S. Embassy, Managua, to Secretary of State, 30 June 1979, Managua 2928, "The Third Meeting—The Murphy Version."

12. Confidential cable, U.S. Embassy, Managua, to Secretary of State, 1 July 1979, Managua 2935, "Meeting with Jarquin: June 30."

13. Interview with Arturo Cruz, August 3, 1991, Washington, D.C.

14. Ibid.

15. "A Loyalty Test for the Guard," *Newsweek*, July 16, 1979, p. 45.

16. Elizabeth Reimann, *Los Tigres Vencidos* (Buenos Aires: Ediciones Reunir, 1988), pp. 86, 98.

17. Ibid., p. 88.

18. "A Loyalty Test for the Guard," p. 45.

19. Elizabeth Reimann, *La Historia de Moises: "Yo Fui Un Paladin de la Libertad"* (Lima, Peru: Editorial Horizonte, 1985), p. 13.

20. "A Loyalty Test for the Guard," p. 45.

21. Gabriel García Márquez, Gregorio Selser, et al., *La Batalla de Nicaragua* (Mexico City: Bruguera Mexicana, 1979), p. 79.

22. Interview with Arturo Cruz, Washington, D.C., August 3, 1991.

23. Interview with anonymous source, August 4, 1991, Washington, D.C.

24. "A Loyalty Test for the Guard," p. 45.

25. Reimann, *La Historia de Moises,* p. 57.

26. José Antonio Robleto Siles, *Yo Deserte de la Guardia Nacional de Nicaragua* (Costa Rica: Editorial Universitaria Centroamericana, 1979), pp. 69–70.

27. Ibid., p. 76.

28. Ibid.

29. Ibid., p. 77.

30. Ibid., p. 80.

31. OAS, Special Commission, *Report on the Status of Human Rights in Nicaragua,* November 1978, p. 33.

32. Ibid., p. 44.

33. Reimann, *Los Tigres Vencidos,* pp. 91, 100.

34. Ibid., p. 154.

35. Ibid., p. 230.

36. Ibid., p. 154.

37. Ibid., p. 230.

38. *El Infante* (Official Organ of the Basic Infantry Training School), January 1979.

39. Ibid.

40. *El Infante,* May 1979.

41. "A Loyalty Test for the Guard," p. 45.

42. Reimann, *La Historia de Moises,* p. 61.

43. Robleto Siles, *Yo Deserte de la Guardia Nacional de Nicaragua,* p. 171.

44. Ibid.

45. Ibid., p 172.

46. Ibid., p. 169.

Chapter 10

1. Interview with Humberto Ortega, Managua, Nicaragua, February 18, 1991.

2. Ibid.

3. Dianne W. Hart, *Thanks to God and the Revolution: An Oral History of a Nicaraguan Family* (Madison: University of Wisconsin Press, 1990), p. 95.

4. Ibid., p. 96.

5. Meiselas, *Nicaragua*, p. 94.

6. Interview with Manolo Gutiérrez, Managua, February 19–20, 1991.

7. *Miami Herald*, June 24, 1979.

8. Ibid.

9. Interview with Manolo Gutiérrez.

10. Carlos Nuñez, *Un Pueblo En Armas: Informe del Frente Interno* (Managua: Departamento de Propaganda y Educación Política del FSLN, 1980), p. 86.

11. César Sánchez, *Comandante El Sobrino Presente!!* p. 65.

12. Pablo Emilio Barreto, *El Repliegue de Managua a Masaya* (Mexico City: Editorial Cartago de México, 1980), p. 89.

13. Hart, *Thanks to God and the Revolution,* p. 97.

14. Nuñez, *Un Pueblo En Armas,* p. 98.

15. Barrreto, *El Repliegue de Managua a Masaya,* p. 85.

16. Alfaro Mendieta, *El Último Marine,* p. 246.

17. Barreto, *El Repliegue de Managua a Masaya,* p. 89.

18. Ibid., p. 94.

19. Alfaro Mendieta, *El Último Marine,* p. 248.

20. Barreto, *El Repliegue de Managua a Masaya,* p. 100.

21. Hart, *Thanks to God and the Revolution,* p. 97.

22. Alfaro Mendieta, *El Último Marine,* p. 250.

23. Sánchez, *Comandante El Sobrino Presente!!* pp. 70–71.

24. Ibid., p. 71.

25. Mendieta, *El Último Marine,* p. 255.

26. From "Los Muchachos," in *Zero Hour and Other Poems,* ed. Donald Walsh (New York: New Directions, 1980).

27. *Miami Herald,* June 13, 1979.

Chapter 11

1. Secret cable, Secretary of State to U.S. Embassy, Managua, 30 June 1979, State 167455.

2. *Washington Star,* June 16, 1979.

3. Notes of Ambassador Lawrence Pezzullo.

4. Ibid.

5. "Sandinista-backed Junta Pays a Visit to Panama," *Washington Post*, June 28, 1979.

6. Ibid.

7. Interview with Bill Bowdler, Virginia, July 13, 1979 and *New York Times*, June 30, 1979.

8. "Nicaraguan Rebels Reject U.S. Plan for Conservative Interim Regime," *New York Times*, June 30, 1979.

9. Ibid.

10. Pastor, *Condemned to Repetition*, p. 161.

11. Notes of Ambassador Lawrence Pezzullo.

12. Pastor, *Condemned to Repetition*, p. 162.

13. Ibid., pp. 163–64.

14. Christian, *Nicaragua: Revolution in the Family*, p. 107.

15. Ibid., p. 164.

16. Ibid.

17. Secret cable, U.S. Embassy, Managua, to Secretary of State, 30 June 1979, Managua 2914.

18. Secret cable, Secretary of State to U.S. Embassy, Managua, 29 June 1979, State 167435, "Discussion with G-12 member Arturo Cruz."

Chapter 12

1. Juan Velázquez, from "León, June 2, 1979," cited in Zimmerman, *Nicaragua in Reconstruction and War*, p. 104.

2. Interview with Lucía Gutiérrez, Arlington, Virginia, August 6, 1991.

3. Ibid.

4. *Miami Herald*, June 11, 1979.

5. Dickey, *With the Contras*, p. 52.

6. Somoza, *Nicaragua Betrayed*, p. 258.

7. Diederich, *Somoza*, pp. 259–60.

8. Somoza, *Nicaragua Betrayed*, p. 258.

9. Interview with Lucía Gutiérrez.

10. Somoza, *Nicaragua Betrayed*, pp. 258–59.

11. Murguía, *Southern Front*, p. 23.

12. Ibid.

13. Alfaro Mendieta, *El Último Marine*, p. 33.

14. Murguía, *Southern Front*, p. 25.

15. Christian, *Nicaragua: Revolution in the Family*, p. 105.

16. Interview with Manolo Gutiérrez, Managua, February 19–20, 1991.

17. Secret cable, U.S. Embassy, Managua, to Secretary of State, 25 June 1979, Managua 2503.

18. Interview with Manolo Gutiérrez.

19. Karen DeYoung, "Just Beyond the Terrace, the Country Is Dying," *Washington Post*, June 28, 1979.

20. Ibid.

21. Meiselas, *Nicaragua: June 1978–July 1979*, p. 94.

22. Alfaro Mendieta, *El Último Marine*, p. 270.

23. Argueles Morales, *Con El Corazón en El Disparador: Las Batallas del Frente Interno* (Managua: Vanguardia, 1986), p. 80.

24. Ibid., p. 82.

Chapter 13

1. Pastor, *Condemned to Repetition*, p. 167.

2. "U.S. Seeks Help in Latin America . . . ," *Washington Star*, July 6, 1979.

3. Diederich, *Somoza*, p. 291.

4. Secret cable, U.S. Embassy, Managua, to Secretary of State, 5 July 1979, Managua 2990, "The Fourth Meeting."

5. Ibid.

6. Ibid.

7. Ibid.

8. *New York Times*, July 14, 1979.

9. Pastor, *Condemned to Repetition*, p. 171.

10. Diederich, *Somoza*, p. 291.

11. "U.S. Presses Bid to Add Moderates to Sandinista Junta," *New York Times*, July 5, 1979.

12. Karen DeYoung, "Army Is Crucial Issue in Nicaragua," *Washington Post*, July 9, 1979.

13. Karen DeYoung, "U.S. Contacts Rebel Junta," *Washington Post*, July 11, 1979.

14. Ibid.

15. Cited in letter from Senator Edward M. Kennedy to President Carter, July 9, 1979.

16. Pastor, *Condemned to Repetition*, pp. 163, 169.

17. Somoza, *Nicaragua Betrayed*, pp. 273–74.

18. Secret cable, Secretary of State (drafted by Bob Pastor) to U.S. Embassy, Managua, 7 July 1979, State 17617, "Nicaragua: National Guard."

19. Alan Riding, "U.S. in Role of Key Nicaraguan Arbiter," *New York Times*, July 10, 1991.

20. Interview with Karen DeYoung, September, 1979, Managua, Nicaragua; Karen DeYoung, "Somoza Ready to Quit, Leaves Timing to the U.S.," *Washington Post*, July 7, 1979.

21. Ibid.

22. Diederich, *Somoza*, pp. 297–98.

23. Ibid.

24. Davis, *Where Is Nicaragua?* p. 36.

25. Secret cable, U.S. Embassy, Managua, to Secretary of State, 8 July 1979, Managua 3064, "U.S. Posture."

26. *New York Times*, June 30, 1979, p. 20.

27. "Mr. Murphy in Managua," *Washington Post*, July 6, 1979.

28. Karen DeYoung, "U.S. Contacts Rebel Junta," *Washington Post*, July 11, 1979.

29. Ibid.

30. Ibid.

Chapter 14

1. The following paragraphs are based on an interview with Virginia Sanchez, Washington, D.C., August 3, 1991.

2. The following paragraphs are based on an interview with Manolo Gutiérrez, Managua, February 19–20, 1991.

3. Interview with Lucia Gutiérrez, Arlington, Virginia, August 16, 1991.

4. "In Nicaragua's Second City, Sandinistas March to Different Economic Drummer," *New York Times*, July 29, 1979.

5. Ibid.

6. "Nicaragua's Rebels Plan for Economy," *New York Times*, July 10, 1979.

7. Interview with Tom O'Donnell, Arlington, Virginia, August 3, 1991.

8. Pastor, *Condemned to Repetition*, pp. 170–71.

9. Ibid., p. 172.

10. Diederich, *Somoza*, p. 302.

11. Secret cable, Secretary of State to U.S. Embassy, Managua, 12 July 1979, State 179651, "Nicaraguan Scenario."

12. Secret cable, U.S. Embassy, Managua, to Secretary of State, July 12, 1979, Managua 3123, "Meeting With Somoza July 12."

13. Ibid.

14. Somoza, *Nicaragua Betrayed*, p. 375.

15. Ibid., p. 376.

16. Ibid.

17. Ibid., p. 378.

18. Secret cable, U.S. Embassy, Managua, to Secretary of State, 12 July 1979, Managua 3135, "Meeting with Somoza—Further Details."

19. Somoza, *Nicaragua Betrayed*, p. 379.

20. Secret cable U.S. Embassy, Managua, to Secretary of State, 13 July 1979, Managua 3143, "The Urgency of Somoza Leaving Quickly."

21. Ibid.

22. Secret cable, Secretary of State to U.S. Embassy, Managua, 14 July 1979, State 183243, "Somoza's Departure."

23. *Washington Star,* July 9, 1979.

24. Notes of Ambassador Lawrence Pezzullo; Diederich, *Somoza,* p. 298.

25. Ibid.

26. Diederich, *Somoza*, p. 303.

27. Notes of Ambassador Lawrence Pezzullo.

28. Karen DeYoung, "Somoza Reported Meeting Latin Allies," *Washington Post,* July 14, 1979.

29. Pastor, *Condemned to Repetition*, p. 179.

30. Secret cable, U.S. Embassy, Managua, to Secretary of State, 14 July 1979, Managua 3178, "Meeting with Somoza—July 13."

31. *Washington Star,* July 13, 1979.

32. Pastor, *Condemned to Repetition*, p. 172.

33. Interview with Humberto Ortega, Managua, Nicaragua, February 18, 1991; H. Ortega, in *Sandinistas Speak*, p. 76.

34. Karen DeYoung, "Somoza Reported Meeting Latin Allies," *Washington Post,* July 14, 1979.

35. Ibid.

Chapter 15

1. Interview with Tom O'Donnell, Arlington, Virginia, August 3, 1991.

2. Secret cable, U.S. Embassy, Managua, to Secretary of State, 14 July 1979, Managua 3204, "New Guard Commander."

3. Notes of Deputy Chief of Mission Tom O'Donnell.

4. Interview with Tom O'Donnell.

5. Ibid.

6. Notes of Ambassador Lawrence Pezzullo.

7. Interview with Luis Pallais, Miami, Florida, February 20, 1991.

8. Interview with Tom O'Donnell.

9. Ibid.

10. Ibid.

11. "Nicaragua Rebels Say U.S. Is Ready to Back Regime Led by Them," *New York Times,* July 16, 1979.

12. Ibid.
13. Ibid.
14. Interview with Jaime Chamorro, Managua, Nicaragua, February 19, 1991.
15. Obando y Bravo, *Agonía en el Bunker*, p. 163.
16. Notes of Ambassador Lawrence Pezzullo.
17. Interview with Tom O'Donnell.
18. Alan Riding, "Somoza Retires 100 Senior Officers," *New York Times*, July 17, 1979.
19. Obando y Bravo, *Agonía en el Bunker*, p. 167.
20. Pastor, *Condemned to Repetition*, pp. 182–83.
21. *Washington Star*, July 17, 1979.
22. Viktor Morales Henríquez, *Los Últimos Momentos de la Dictadura Somozocista* (Managua, Nicaragua: Editorial Union, 1979), p. 57.
23. Ibid.
24. Diederich, *Somoza*, p. 314.
25. Notes of Ambassador Lawrence Pezzullo.
26. Ibid.
27. Ibid.
28. Ibid.

Chapter 16

1. Leiken and Rubin, *Central American Crisis Reader*, p. 199.
2. Francisco Urcuyo Maliano, *Solos: Las Últimas 43 Horas in el Bunker de Somoza* (Guatemala: EDITA, 1979), p. 117.
3. Notes of Ambassador Lawrence Pezzullo.
4. Ibid.; Urcuyo, *Solos*, pp. 117–19.
5. Somoza, *Nicaragua Betrayed*, p. 389.
6. Obando y Bravo, *Agonía en el Bunker*, p. 171.
7. Ibid., p. 172.
8. Murguía, *Southern Front*, p. 81.
9. Nuñez, *Un Pueblo en Armas*, p. 123.
10. Notes of Ambassador Lawrence Pezzullo.
11. Ibid.
12. Ibid.
13. Urcuyo, *Solos*, p. 120.
14. Notes of Ambassador Lawrence Pezzullo.
15. Urcuyo, *Solos*, p. 129.
16. Interview with Tom O'Donnell, Arlington, Virginia, August 3, 1991.
17. Notes of Ambassador Lawrence Pezzullo.
18. Urcuyo, *Solos*, pp. 123–25.

19. *Novedades,* July 17, 1979, p. 1.

20. Karen DeYoung, "Somoza's Successor Seeks to Hold Power," *Washington Post,* July 18, 1979.

21. Warren Hoge, "Rebel Junta, Its Sendoff Cancelled, Plans Trip to Nicaragua," *New York Times,* July 18, 1979.

22. Christian, *Nicaragua: Revolution in the Family,* p. 113.

23. Interview with A. Marenco, Washington, D.C, August 4, 1991.

24. Ibid.

25. "Florida Estate Is Somoza Refuge," *Washington Post,* July 18, 1979.

26. Notes of Ambassador Lawrence Pezzullo.

27. Urcuyo, *Solos,* p. 131.

28. Notes of Ambassador Lawrence Pezzullo.

29. Ibid.; Urcuyo, *Solos,* p. 131.

30. Notes of Ambassador Lawrence Pezzullo.

Chapter 17

1. Interview with Manolo Gutiérrez, Managua, February 19–20, 1991.

2. Notes of Ambassador Lawrence Pezzullo.

3. Ibid.

4. Urcuyo, *Solos,* p. 132.

5. Julio Sunol, *Insurrección en Nicaragua* (San José: Editorial Costa Rica, 1981), p. 67.

6. Warren Hoge, "3 in Sandinists' Junta Fly Home," *New York Times,* July 19, 1979.

7. Ibid.

8. *Washington Star,* July 18, 1979.

9. Ernesto Cardenal, from *Zero Hour and Other Poems,* ed. Donald C. Walsh (New York: New Directions. 1980)

10. Notes of Ambassador Lawrence Pezzullo.

11. *Washington Star,* July 18, 1979.

12. Ibid.

13. Ibid.

14. Don Oberdorfer, "U.S. Uses Hard Pressure in Nicaragua Changeover," *Washington Post,* July 19, 1979.

15. Interview with Luis Pallais, Miami, Florida, February 20, 1991.

16. Graham Hovey, "U.S., Exerting Pressure, Says Nicaragua Peace Plan Is Taking Hold," *New York Times,* July 19, 1979.

17. Urcuyo, *Solos,* pp. 132–33.

18. Notes of Ambassador Lawrence Pezzullo.

19. "Crisis in Central America: Revolution in Nicaragua," Frontline #313 (WGBH Transcripts, Boston), p. 13.

20. Notes of Ambassador Lawrence Pezzullo.
21. Ibid.
22. Interview with Tom O'Donnell, Arlington, Virginia, August 3, 1991.
23. Ibid.
24. Ibid.
25. Humberto Ortega Saavedra, *A Diez Años de la Rendición Total de la Guardia Somozocista* (Managua: EPS, Instituto de Historia de Nicaragua, 1989), p. 31.
26. Ibid., p. 38.
27. Ibid.
28. Ibid., p. 41.
29. Urcuyo, *Solos,* p. 140.
30. Diederich, *Somoza,* p. 321.
31. Guy Gugliotta, "Tropic Magazine," *Miami Herald,* September 13, 1979.
32. Morales, *Con el Corazón en el Disparador,* p. 32.
33. Reimann, *La Historia de Moises,* p. 65.
34. Ibid.
35. Alvin Levie, *Nicaragua: The People Speak* (South Hadley, Mass.: Bergin and Garvey, 1985), pp. 195–96.
36. Obando y Bravo, *Agonía en el Bunker,* p. 175.
37. Ibid., p. 180.
38. Ibid., p. 181.
39. Ibid., pp. 181–82.
40. Ibid., p. 183.
41. Ibid., p. 185.
42. Interview with Cardinal Obando y Bravo, Managua, Nicaragua, February 17, 1991.
43. Obando y Bravo, *Agonía en el Bunker,* pp. 187–88.
44. H. Ortega, *A Diez Años de la Rendición Total,* p. 48.
45. Ibid., p. 52.
46. Ibid., p. 71.

Chapter 18

1. Obando y Bravo, *Agonía en el Bunker,* p. 196.
2. Ibid., p. 197.
3. Ibid., pp 198–99.
4. Ibid., p. 200.
5. Ibid., p. 202.
6. Barreto, *El Repliegue de Managua a Masaya,* p. 134.
7. Arias, *Nicaragua: Revolución,* p. 202.
8. Dickey, *With the Contras,* p. 23.

9. Barreto, *El Repliegue de Managua a Masaya*, p. 141.

10. Nuñez, *Un Pueblo en Armas*, pp. 133–34.

11. *Miami Herald*, July 20, 1979.

12. Arias, *Nicaragua: Revolución*, pp. 202–03.

13. Meiselas, *Nicaragua: June 1978–July 1979*, p. 96.

14. The following narrative was related to me in an interview with Tom O'Donnell, Arlington, Virginia, August 3, 1991.

15. Arias, *Nicaragua: Revolución*, p. 203.

16. Arturo Cruz, Jr., *Memoirs of a Counterrevolutionary* (New York: Doubleday, 1989), p. 87.

17. Interview with Tom O'Donnell.

18. Ibid.

19. Nuñez, *Un Pueblo En Armas*, p. 139.

20. "Crisis in Central America: Revolution in Nicaragua," Frontline #313 [television broadcast] (WGBH Transcripts, Boston), p. 14.

21. Ibid.

22. Interview with Tom O'Donnell.

23. Notes of Deputy Chief of Mission Tom O'Donnell.

Chapter 19

1. Diederich, *Somoza*, p. 330.

2. Rolando Angulo Zeledon, *Los Últimos Minutos de Somoza* (San José, C. R.: Tico Texto, 1980), p. 26.

3. Stephen Kinzer, *Blood of Brothers* (New York: G. P. Putnam, 1991), p. 79.

4. Ibid., p. 378.

5. *Washington Post*, July 29, 1979.

Epilogue

1. Kinzer, *Blood of Brothers*, p. 73.

Index

Pitt Latin American Series
James M. Malloy, Editor

Argentina

Brazil

Cuban Studies, Vol. 22
Jorge I. Domínguez, Editor

Cuban Studies, Vol. 23
Jorge Peréz-López, Editor

The Economics of Cuban Sugar
Jorge F. Pérez-López

Intervention, Revolution, and Politics in Cuba, 1913–1921
Louis A. Pérez, Jr.

Lords of the Mountain: Social Banditry and Peasant Protest in Cuba, 1878–1918
Louis A. Pérez, Jr.

Mexico

The Expulsion of Mexico's Spaniards, 1821–1836
Harold Dana Sims

The Mexican Republic: The First Decade, 1823–1832
Stanley C. Green

Mexico Through Russian Eyes, 1806–1940
William Harrison Richardson

Oil and Mexican Foreign Policy
George W. Grayson

The Politics of Mexican Oil
George W. Grayson

Voices, Visions, and a New Reality: Mexican Fiction Since 1970
J. Ann Duncan

Peru

Domestic and Foreign Finance in Modern Peru, 1850–1950: Financing Visions of Development
Alfonso W. Quiroz

Economic Management and Economic Development in Peru and Colombia
Rosemary Thorp

The Origins of the Peruvian Labor Movement, 1883–1919
Peter Blanchard

Peru and the International Monetary Fund
Thomas Scheetz

Peru Under García: An Opportunity Lost
John Crabtree

Caribbean

The Last Cacique: Leadership and Politics in a Puerto Rican City
Jorge Heine

A Revolution Aborted: The Lessons of Grenada
Jorge Heine, Editor

To Hell with Paradise: A History of the Jamaican Tourist Industry
Frank Fonda Taylor

The Meaning of Freedom: Economics, Politics and Culture
After Slavery
Frank McGlynn and Seymour Drescher, Editors

Central America

At the Fall of Somoza
Lawrence Pezzullo and Ralph Pezzullo

Black Labor on a White Canal: Panama, 1904–1981
Michael L. Conniff

The Catholic Church and Politics in Nicaragua and Costa Rica
Philip J. Williams

Perspectives on the Agro-Export Economy in Central America
Wim Pelupessy, Editor

Other National Studies

The Overthrow of Allende and the Politics of Chile, 1964–1976
Paul E. Sigmund

Social Security

Ascent to Bankruptcy: Financing Social Security in Latin America
Carmelo Mesa-Lago

The Politics of Social Security in Brazil
James M. Malloy

Other Studies

Adventurers and Proletarians: The Story of Migrants in
Latin America
Magnus Mörner, with the collaboration of Harold Sims

Authoritarianism and Corporatism in Latin America
James M. Malloy, Editor

Authoritarians and Democrats: Regime Transition in
Latin America
James M. Malloy and Mitchell A. Seligson, Editors

The Catholic Church and Politics in Nicaragua and Costa Rica
Philip J. Williams

Chile: The Political Economy of Development and Democracy in
the 1990s
David E. Hojman

The Constitution of Tyranny: Regimes of Exception in
Spanish America
Brian Loveman

Female and Male in Latin America: Essays
Ann Pescatello, Editor

Latin American Debt and the Adjustment Crisis
Rosemary Thorp and Laurence Whitehead, Editors

Public Policy in Latin America: A Comparative Survey
John W. Sloan

Selected Latin American One-Act Plays
Francesca Colecchia and Julio Matas, Editors and Translators

The Social Documentary in Latin America
Julianne Burton, Editor

The State and Capital Accumulation in Latin America. Vol. 1: Brazil, Chile, Mexico. Vol. 2: Argentina, Bolivia, Colombia, Ecuador, Peru, Uruguay, Venezuela
Christian Anglade and Carlos Fortin, Editors

Transnational Corporations and the Latin American Automobile Industry
Rhys Jenkins